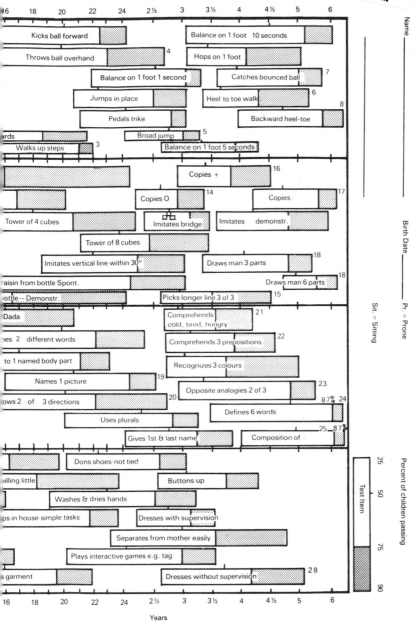

Denver Developmental Screening Test   (Revised)

Name _____

Birth Date _____   Pr. = Prone

Sit. = Sitting

Percent of children passing

Test Item

25   50   75   90

Years

16   18   20   22   24   2½   3   3½   4   4½   5   6

Kicks ball forward
Balance on 1 foot 10 seconds
Throws ball overhand   4
Hops on 1 foot
Balance on 1 foot 1 second
Catches bounced ball   7
Jumps in place
Heel to toe walk   6
Pedals trike
Backward heel-toe   8
rds
Broad jump   5
Walks up steps   3
Balance on 1 foot 5 seconds

Copies +   16
Copies O   14
Copies   17
Tower of 4 cubes
Imitates bridge
Imitates   demonstr.
Tower of 8 cubes
Imitates vertical line within 30°
Draws man 3 parts   18
raisin from bottle Spont.
Draws man 6 parts   18
ottle – Demonstr.
Picks longer line 3 of 3   15

Dada
Comprehends   21
cold, tired, hungry
nes 2   different words
Comprehends 3 prepositions   22
to 1 named body part
Recognizes 3 colours
Names 1 picture   19
Opposite analogies 2 of 3   23
ows 2   of   3 directions   20
87%   24
Uses plurals
Defines 6 words
Gives 1st & last name
25   87
Composition of –

Dons shoes-not tied
illing little
Buttons up
Washes & dries hands
ps in house-simple tasks
Dresses with supervision
Separates from mother easily
Plays interactive games e.g. tag
garment
Dresses without supervision   28

16   18   20   22   24   2½   3   3½   4   4½   5   6

Years

Library of General Practice

Editorial Board

General Editor
Cyril Hart MA DLitt FRCGP

Chairman
John Fry OBE MD FRCS FRCGP
James D. E. Knox MD FRCP FRCGP
M. Keith Thompson FRCGP DObst RCOG
John H. Walker MD FFCM FRCGP DPH
Ian M. Stanley MB ChB MRCP MRCGP

The First Year of Life

2

The First Year of Life

Graham Curtis Jenkins

MA MB BChir(Cantab) DRCOG MRCGP

General Practitioner, Paediatrician
Ashford, Middlesex

Richard C. F. Newton

MA MB BChir(Cantab) MRCP DCH DRCOG

Consultant Paediatrician
St Peter's Hospital, Chertsey & Ashford Hospital, Middlesex

CHURCHILL LIVINGSTONE
EDINBURGH LONDON MELBOURNE AND NEW YORK 1981

CHURCHILL LIVINGSTONE
Medical Division of Longman Group
Limited

Distributed in the United States of America by
Churchill Livingstone Inc., 19 West 44th
Street, New York, N.Y. 10036, and by
associated companies, branches and
representatives throughout the world.

First published 1981

ISBN 0 443 01717 4

**British Library Cataloguing in Publication
Data**
Curtis Jenkins, Graham
    The first year of life.—(Library of general
    practice; vol. 2).
    1. Infants—Diseases
    I. Title   II. Newton, Richard C F
    III. Series
    618.9'2   RJ45   80-40453

Printed in Hong Kong by
Wah Cheong Printing Press Ltd

To
Claudette, Lucy and Alexander
Marion, Louise, Clare and Thomas

Note

Our knowledge in clinical medicine and related biological sciences is constantly changing. As new information obtained from clinical experience and research becomes available, changes in treatment and in the use of drugs become necessary. The authors and the publisher of this volume have, as far as it is possible to do so, taken care to make certain that the doses of drugs and schedules of treatment are accurate and compatible with the standards generally accepted at the time of publication. The readers are advised, however, to consult carefully the instruction and information material included in the package insert of each drug or therapeutic agent that they plan to administer in order to make certain that there have been no changes in the recommended dose of the drug or in the indications or contraindications for its administration. This precaution is especially important when using new or infrequently used drugs.

Preface

We hope that our book will stimulate general practitioners to look at the ways in which they provide care to children, to start them thinking about their work styles and their communication with parents. The aim of the book is to promote understanding of the growing child within the context of the family and society. An understanding of organic disease and its management is a *sine qua non*. However, we hope by drawing on the knowledge gained by recent advances, to give a rounded picture of the child in the first year of life. What happens in this first year, lays the foundation for all that happens in the future.

This book contains an account of the interaction of child and environment in the first year, and provides a short introduction to the management of the disorders and dysfunctions that can arise. In a book of this size, it is impossible to cover the subject exhaustively. What is hoped is, that once stimulated, the general practitioner will seek to enlarge his knowledge by referring to the books listed in the Further Reading Lists at the end of the book. With the spread of postgraduate medical centres and the siting of a library service within many of them, it is no longer difficult to obtain many of the books listed. Some of the books are cheap enough to buy personally for constant reference. Having been convinced of the need for revolutionary change, the family doctor will then take the first steps along the path towards comprehensive child care. Maybe the words of Wilfred Sheldon in 1967 are prophetic: 'eventually the child health service will no longer be a distinct and separate entity, but will become part of a family health service provided by the family doctor in a family health centre'.

1981   G. C. J.
                                               R. C. F. N.

Contents

I.

Introduction

The survival and optimal development of the young child is dependent on the interplay of the socio-economic circumstances in which the child lives and the illnesses he develops or escapes.

Even today, acute illness remains a major problem. 'There is a large amount of acute illness; some is minor in the medical sense, but much is severe, life threatening or fatal' (Court, 1977a). More than half of all illness reported in children is respiratory. About 2000 children in England and Wales die

Table 1.1 Likely frequency of diseases in children, seen by a general practitioner in a 40 year professional life

Pyloric stenosis	11
Intussusception	2
Fibrocystic disease	1
Cot deaths	5
Diabetes, epilepsy	7 each
Congenital heart disease	8
Congenital dislocation of hip	1

from respiratory illness each year. Three-quarters of these deaths happen in the first year, half of them outside hospital. Many deaths and some of the morbidity are caused by relatively rare conditions, rare at least to the individual general practitioner who is likely to see a new case of cystic fibrosis once in his professional life-time and may never see an epiglottitis, so rare is the condition, yet potentially so fatal (Table 1.1).

Whilst British infant and post-neonatal mortality rates have fallen greatly over the past 50 years (Table 1.2) they can,

1

however, give little cause for satisfaction when compared with those of other EEC countries (Table 1.3).

The fall in rates has lagged further and further behind other European countries, and in 1974 the post-neonatal mortality in Glasgow's social class I and II children was double that of Finland. In Scotland in 1977, the infant

Table 1.2 Infant death rates. England and Wales*

| Period | Rates per 1000 live births | |
	Neonatal mortality (under 4 weeks)	Post-neonatal mortality (over 4 weeks and under 1 year
1926–1930	31·8	35·7
1946–1950	21·1	15·2
1974	11·0	5·3
1977	9·7	3·5

*From OPCS Registrar General's statistical reviews and vital statistics. S.D.52

Table 1.3 Infant mortality in selected countries (deaths in first year of life per thousand life births)*

	1960	1965	1970	1975
Denmark	21·5	18·7	14·2	10·3
Finland	21·0	17·6	13·2	11·0*
France	17·9	14·4	12·7	10·6
Switzerland	21·1	17·8	15·1	10·7
England, Wales	21·8	19·0	18·2	15·7
Scotland	26·4	23·0	19·6	17·2
N. Ireland	27·2	25·1	22·9	20·4
Sweden	16·6	13·3	11·1	8·6
Netherlands	17·9	14·4	12·7	10·7

*1974 (From various sources)

mortality rate actually rose from 14·8/1000 in 1976 to 16·1/1000. Even more striking is the wide variation in rates between regions in the United Kingdom which reveals clearly how affluence and poverty rather than medical care affect the life and death of the child (Table 1.4). In the U.K., 76 per cent of first day deaths and 58 per cent of all deaths in the first month occur in babies weighing 1·5 kg or less. The

Table 1.4 Infant deaths by region

| | Number and rates per 1000 legitimate live births | | | |
| | Perinatal mortality | | Infant mortality | |
	1973	1976	1973	1976
Wales	21·4	19·0	16·4	13·6
Northern R.U.A.	21·8	19·1	17·2	15·1
Yorkshire	22·9	18·4	19·9	15·0
Trent	21·0	19·2	16·1	14·7
E. Anglia	17·4	13·9	*13·7*	*11·6*
N.W. Thames	19·2	16·9	15·3	13·9
N.E. Thames	20·4	16·6	16·6	13·4
S.E. Thames	19·5	17·4	15·0	14·8
S.W. Thames	18·8	14·8	16·2	12·7
Wessex	20·6	15·1	14·6	12·7
Oxford	*17·0*	*13·8*	*13·7*	12·9
S. Western	19·0	16·1	15·0	12·9
West Midlands	23·6	**21·1**	19·1	**15·7**
Mersey	**24·6**	19·5	**20·0**	14·2
N. Western	23·4	18·7	19·2	**15·7**
italic type = lowest		bold type = highest		

survival rate of this group has improved in the last 10 years without, unfortunately, firm evidence of decrease of handicapping conditions caused by the initial smallness of the individual child, and the proportion of babies born with this weight has altered little. The fact is that small babies tend to be born to mothers living in the very poverty that is itself the cause (Neligan et al, 1976). In Scandinavian countries, the reduction in perinatal mortality seems to be associated with longer gestation, the better health of mothers, more dynamic management of pregnancy and delivery and the mothers' motivation to reduce alcohol and cigarette consumption. These effects stem from better education and higher standards of living (Wynn & Wynn, 1974). All have a considerable and lasting effect upon the child. In the U.K. the continuing improvement in the perinatal mortality rates achieved by better medical care during pregnancy and in particular delivery, is dissipated when the small baby returns to the poverty that caused the poor intra-uterine growth in the first place. The social environment therefore remains an important cause of mortality and morbidity (Neligan et al, 1976). Excess rates of squints, bed-wetting, language disorder, dental caries, fits, chest infections and gastro-enteritis are found in the lower social groups (Court, 1977b).

Schooling, job prospects and the inevitability of the repeating nature of upbringing experience from generation to generation cause the vicious circle of deprivation. The functioning of the medical inverse care law, as defined by Tudor Hart, is well shown in the clinic attendance of children at greatest risk from socially induced medical and developmental disorders. Zinkin and Cox (1976) have shown how radical the change may have to be to alter the present pattern.

The population of this country is now falling and the number of deaths per month has been greater than the

Table 1.5 Birthrates 1951–1976

	1951	1961	1971	1976
Live births per 1000* born to persons of all ages	15·7	17·8	16·1	11·9
Age specific birth rates				
Mothers: 15–19	21·0	37·0	51·0	33·0
20–24	126·0	173·0	155·0	111·0
25–29	135·0	178·0	155·0	120·0
30–34	91·0	104·0	78·0	58·0
35–39	47·0	49·0	33·0	19·0
40–44	14·0	14·0	8·0	4·0
Illegitimate births; as a percentage of all live births	4·9	5·8	8·4	9·2
Extra maritally conceived births as percentage of live births				
G.B.	11·5	13·0	17·0	15·5
England, Wales	11·5	13·3	17·0	15·3

From Social Trends No. 8 1977 H.M.S.O. London
* Crude figures

number of births for most of 1977 and 1978. Despite the forecasts of demographers, the trend seems likely to continue (Table 1.5).

The trends towards older parents, smaller families (families now average 1·8 children) and single parent families, all have effects on mortality and morbidity. For instance, it is well known that illegitimacy has a death-dealing affect on children. In one inner suburb of London 17 per cent of all births were illegitimate in 1976, and 30 per cent of the deaths in the first year of life occurred in this group (Graham, 1976).

Other factors such as family size also profoundly affect both mortality and morbidity. Although social class provides the best indicator of the risk factor in mortality, the relationship with morbidity is more complex (Wedge & Prosser, 1975). Osborn and Morris (1979), for instance, identified three such disadvantaged groups in a recent survey of nearly 1000 three and a half year old children. The first group were families in social classes IV and V; the second, poorly housed families; the third were large families in rented accommodation with shared hot water supply. The second group contained many 'problem families' but only one third of these were in the social class IV and V categories. The mother's actual care of her baby is certainly dependent not only on her social class but also on her own upbringing experience, which creates the greatest differences in care.

Abortion law reform and investment of money and manpower in family planning have both contributed to the drop in birth rate. This, in turn, has led to less pressure on maternity services, allowing an ever higher hospital delivery rate and an increasing awareness by hospital obstetricians of the needs of mother and child. It has also contributed to the increasing amount of time that nursing staff can spend with mothers, for example, guiding and supporting them through the early days of the puerperium. The sudden and unexplained rapid fall in 1977 of the perinatal mortality rate in England and Wales may well be due to the synergistic effects of these apparently unrelated trends. They may also account for the recent rise in breast feeding rates at three months, from 18 per cent to 28 per cent, reported by a baby food manufacturer who regularly samples over 1300 mothers with babies up to 12 months of age.

Although in 1977 a dramatic reduction occurred in perinatal mortality rates, the virtual standstill in post-neonatal mortality rates over the past 15 years should be causing disquiet to all in the child care services (Court, 1977c). It must, I* believe, be in part a reflection of the ineffective way in which health care is actually organised and *used* by the consumer, as well as being an indicator of the slow rise in the standard of living (Zinkin & Cox, 1976).

Three separate services exist to give care to the young

*Dr G. Curtis Jenkins.

child; the hospital services, the community health and social services, and the primary care (general practitioner, midwife and health visitor) services. With the re-organisation of the N.H.S. there has been a coming-together of these services in many parts of the country. Benefits have been seen to occur with improved communication and liaison between the hospital and district community health services. The general practitioner services have not been drawn so successfully into the *menage-à-trois* but in those places where general practitioners are running efficient surveillance services, as well as offering illness care, there has been a big improvement in their effectiveness (Starte, 1974, 1976; Bain, 1974; Stark et al, 1975).

The hospital provides two distinct services, for acute illness and for the follow-up and supervision of children with suspected chronic disorder. The pattern of acute illness care is altering. Fewer children stay in for shorter periods and many more infants and toddlers than older children are admitted acutely ill. Accidents are an increasingly important cause of admission, although the actual accident rate is falling (but not fast enough). Special care units for neonates have become common, often attached to maternity departments, and much closer co-operation between obstetricians and paediatricians has played an important part in reducing perinatal mortality. The supervision and long term follow-up of children is an important task, carried out with the greatest difficulty in those areas where close follow-up is needed most—in inner cities and areas of poverty and unemployment. Regional centres have also been created for rare diseases in which treatment is sometimes still experimental and often costly; kidney and oncology units are two such examples. Effective supervision depends on the provision of support in the form of physiotherapy, psychology services, social services and other units of specialised care, and recent funding cut-backs cause major problems out of all proportion to the sums involved.

In some large cities the hospitals have been forced to provide a third service, the provision of primary paediatric care through accident and emergency departments. Where one in seven children is not registered with a doctor and one in three of the population moves house annually, it is not surprising that what strictly constitutes general practice paediatric care tends to be given instead by the hospital.

There is a pathetic trust in the doctor 'down the hospital' and the quality of paediatric service provided by untrained casualty officers in accident and emergency units has caused alarm. As a result, 24-hour paediatric dispensary services are being organised to answer the needs of inner cities. In the short term this will help. In the long term however, only a drastic re-organisation of primary care services generally will solve the problem in these areas (Komrower, 1977).

At present, the general practitioner is responsible for the bulk of illness care of children. He will have anything between 30 and 300 children under the age of five registered on his list. In some areas with low birth rates and an ageing population (e.g., the South Coast), 30 or 40 children under the age of five years will make small demands upon the individual doctor's time. In other areas such as new towns with perhaps 45 per cent of the population under 15 years old, the majority of the general practitioner's time may be occupied with child care. Even worse, the hospital and community services are likely to be inadequate, as the lesson remains unlearned of the need to match prospectively, not retrospectively, the health service requirements of new towns with rapidly expanding populations.

Inner city areas have a different set of problems. Urban blight and decay, and the colonisation of such housing accommodation as is left by mobile and often migrant populations, is often accompanied by the breakdown in all sorts of services, from transport to housing. Inevitably, social and medical services are fighting a losing battle. The problems for the child unlucky enough to be growing up in these surroundings, and for those responsible for keeping services functioning, are well documented (Court, 1976d). It is estimated that about one-sixth of the child population lives in an environment where at least some of the stresses mentioned are working to reduce the individual child's life chance. It is in just those areas that the improvement of medical services is a long way down the list of priorities.

The problems needing solution before efficient general practice-based services can be provided in these areas are manifold. The existing general practitioner population is often predominantly single-handed and elderly (Lowenberg & Nee, 1978). The relative absence of group practices is caused both by the inability of inner city area health authorities to provide health centre accommodation (because of the exorbitant cost of land), and by the relatively small incomes of the general practitioners, which prevent them from being able to fund and service borrowed money with which to build or convert existing accommodation. Health visitor attachment to general practice, now virtually universal, has not improved the lot of the parent and child in the inner city. Often one health visitor is attached to as many as six or seven general practitioners. The trend away from practice attachment back to geographical or parish responsibilities, although a retrograde one for those general practitioners who have learned to work with a health visitor in a dynamic way, is nevertheless probably going to benefit those that she now does not reach. This is of great importance for the one in seven children not registered with a general practitioner in some inner city areas.

Apart from the inner cities where the problems of general practice itself are acute and the actual service given is worsening, the general practitioner has a pivotal role to play in giving care to children. At the moment, the lack of any vocational training programme which incorporates realistic paediatric teaching to fit the young trainee for general practice, has an adverse effect. The existing work force is also relatively untrained when one looks for evidence of fitness to practise. Less than five per cent of general practitioners possess the D.C.H. The requirement of a six months' paediatric resident post before being able to sit the exam ensures that very few general practitioners will take it once in practice. More worrying, the two to four per cent paediatric content of current post-graduate training programmes in, for instance, the London area, makes it difficult for the general practitioner to further his education even if he wants to. How to maintain medical skills, refresh memory and maintain a high index of suspicion to cover the serious and sometimes life-threatening conditions which occur with so little warning and so rarely, is a great challenge to those responsible for the continuing education of the doctor. With fewer than 600 consultant paediatricians and over 20 000 general practitioners, the question of who teaches what still remains unanswered. Unless the community paediatric services accept some responsibility for teaching paediatrics and monitor the effectiveness of the teaching and the taught, it would appear that little progress is likely in the immediate future. Yet, at the moment, the medical care of children is entrusted predominantly to general practitioners with widely varying skills.

The Court Report's proposals for general practitioner paediatricians and the rejection of them by the profession is now history. Many general practitioners have already become what the Court Report proposed. They have extended their role into health care and surveillance. Individual general practitioners, Hooper who has published a succession of papers on nutrition of children, and Starte, working on communication in children, have shown the way (Hooper, 1965, 1971; Starte, 1974, 1975, 1976). Starte's developmental profile system for the examination of small children has been expanded and modified by a group of general practitioners for use as a surveillance tool and encouraging results are already being produced which are discussed in Chapters 3 to 5 (Curtis Jenkins et al, 1978). The theme running through all these papers has been clear. Children deserve good quality medical care and general practice is the place where they must obtain it.

Since long before the War the Community Health Services have offered developmental and surveillance services for children under five. Seven thousand wholetime equivalent medical officers have staffed child health clinics offering a wide range of preventive services, developmental guidance and assessment, routine examinations, immunisation and counselling.

In addition, some general practitioners have run child health clinics for many years, offering counselling, treatment and immunisation. It is in the last seven or eight years, with the attachment of health visitors to general practice nationwide, that many more general practitioners have been running child health clinics. I estimate that nearly 20 per cent are now doing so. It is also plain that the health visitors sometimes do most of the work.

The disadvantages are, firstly, that there are no training requirements for the general practitioner, leading to widely varying quality and secondly, that usually only children on the doctor's list are seen (Bain, 1977) (Table 1.6).

The advantages of a well-run general practice child care clinic however, with committed, trained medical and paramedical staff, are obvious (Curtis Jenkins et al, 1978) (Table 1.7).

Near 100 per cent attendance rates (achieved ONLY when

Table 1.6 Tests performed by general practitioners at routine surveillance examinations

5–8 weeks	87% of children had head circumference measured
	93% of children had hips examined
	73% of children had light response elicited
	58% of children had sound response elicited
7–10 months	93% of children had hips examined
	89% of children had head circumference measured
	64% of children had hearing test
	39% of children had tests for squint
	60% of children had test for visual acuity
2 year olds	28% of children had test for hearing
	24% of children had test for squint
	32% of children had test for visual acuity
	22% of children had test for speech
4 year olds	71% of children had test for hearing
	30% of children had test for squint
	67% of children had test for visual acuity
	76% of children had test for speech

From: Bain, D. J. B., 1977. Methods used by general practitioners in developmental screening of preschool children. British Medical Journal 2:363–365

the doctor himself does all the examinations), a lower illness consultation rate and a much lower out-patient paediatric referral rate have been achieved (Curtis Jenkins, 1977). The rates to other referral agencies, of course, may rise significantly, as vision, hearing and language disorders are detected with greater frequency, Table 1.8.

The referral or secondary services are often under extreme pressure due to lack of money and the inability to attract staff to some areas. Speech therapists are a rarity in some areas of Northern England; elsewhere their distribution is very patchy. Orthoptists work almost exclusively in hospital ophthalmology services, yet experiments have shown that a small number in a mobile clinic can cover the vision screening needs of thousands of preschool children, picking up squint and myopia long before amblyopia has established a sufficient foothold to do permanent harm (Cameron, 1977). The school eye clinic service is under fire from all who see its imperfections. Some say that it is the place to go to ensure that you don't need to wear glasses. Others point to the 25 per cent of children in other areas who see better without their glasses

Table 1.7 Detection rate of suspected disorders April 1975–April 1977

Disorder detected	Boys	referred	Girls	referred
7 month examination: 384 performed on 201 boys and 183 girls				
Strabismus	7	7	6	6
Myopia	2	2	–	–
Suspected hearing loss	4	4	2	2
Developmental delay	1	–	–	–
Maternal deprivation	1	–	–	–
12 month examination: 410 performed on 194 boys and 216 girls				
Strabismus	4	4	4	4
Myopia	1	1	2	2
Suspected hearing loss	–	–	1	1
Cerebral palsy	3	3	1	1
Depression	1	–	–	–
Battered baby	1	1	–	–
Maternal deprivation	1	1	–	–
28–30 month examination: 369 performed on 177 boys and 192 girls				
Strabismus	4	4	3	3
Myopia	1	1	2	2
Suspected hearing loss	8	8	6	6
Speech delay	13	6	7	1
Language delay	1	1	–	–
Developmental delay	2	1	1	–
Behaviour disturbance	–	–	1	–
Depression	3	–	–	–
3 year examination: 167 performed on 104 boys and 63 girls				
Strabismus	–	–	3	3
Myopia	–	–	2	2
Suspected hearing loss	1	1	1	1
Speech delay	20	20	9	9
Language delay	1	1	–	–
Development delay	4	4	–	–
Behaviour disturbance	–	–	2	–
Depression	1	–	–	–
$4\frac{1}{2}$ year examination: 445 performed on 229 boys and 216 girls				
Strabismus	1	1	2	2
Myopia	8	8	7	7
Suspected hearing loss	3	3	1	1
Speech delay	10	10	8	8
Cerebral palsy	–	–	1	1
Developmental delay	1	1	–	–
Behaviour disturbance	1	–	2	–
Depression	3	–	–	–

From Curtis Jenkins et al, 1978. British Medical Journal 1:1537–1540

Table 1.8 Referral rates from the under five year old population of a general practice offering developmental surveillance (excluding referrals made outside routine examination)

	Numbers	% child pop./annum
Ophthalmology	59	3·0
Audiology	27	1·5
Speech therapy	54	2·7
General surgery	8	0·4
Developmental paediatric	15	0·7
General paediatric	3	0·15
Orthopaedic services	3	0·15
Social services	1	0·01

From Curtis Jenkins et al, 1978. British Medical Journal 1:1537–1540

than with them (Gardiner, 1977). A physiotherapy service directed at children's needs exists only in a few places. Family aids or home-makers, paid for by some more progressive social service departments, are a vital requirement in precisely those places where there are least of them. Audiologists depend on the quality of referral to them to diagnose children with hearing loss.

As the Court Report highlighted, and as Zinkin and Cox (1976) have confirmed, the take-up of preventive services, developmental surveillance and immunisation in many parts of the country is lamentably low and what there is appears disorganised. There is overlap of services; one in eight mothers consult their general practitioner and the clinic doctor for the same problem. Only 28 per cent of children aged between two and four years attend a child care clinic. In many parts of the country, part-time medical officers who can work where and when they please are employed often in two health districts, not infrequently in two separate health authority areas. This trend is most marked around the great conurbations where continuity is most required. All this attests to the ineffectiveness of much of the present organisation.

Even when a highly efficient and well motivated Community Health Service is running a research programme aimed at providing help, support and a diagnostic service, it is still very difficult to persuade those mothers who need support and help most to attend. There is a tradition of attendance at clinic for the social class IV and V mother with a young baby, but the consumers, the mother and her child, may well be trying to say something about the quality of the product, the developmental surveillance service, by not keeping up a high rate of attendance in subsequent years. Perhaps the low priority given to ancillary referral services, speech therapy, audiology and child guidance, and the long waiting lists, makes the mother feel that the service provided is not worth bothering with. It is instructive that where general practitioners have offered a developmental surveillance service, properly organised and staffed, and where efficient ancillary referral services are available, very high take-up rates are reported. Despite Barber's views (1977) that the size of the practice is the critical factor affecting attendance, it can be argued that the real reasons for high take-up of services are efficient organisation of the community services, proper motivation of the staff, and no delegation of the actual examinations to the health visitors. Health visitors are not trained developmental paediatricians; their skills are of a different order and their time much better spent doing other things, especially when a general practitioner makes himself available and is motivated to run such a programme and accepts the appropriate training.

The Seebohm re-organisation of social services in 1970 has not hastened progress in child care. The former children's officers with their years of experience were often swallowed up in the revolution it caused and were forced, often against their will, to become 'generic' social workers. The generic idea is becoming discredited and attempts are now being made to recognise individual skill and inclination in the social worker. Alas, many of the erstwhile child care officers have now retired, and lost with them are the skills and experience of years on the job. Luckily, in many cases, the adoption services have managed to survive with their expertise unimpaired as the various voluntary adoption agencies have continued to provide their own social workers skilled in adoption work. Even social service departments have been forced to recognise the special expertise this requires, by giving the responsibility for this work to individual social workers. Private social service agencies have also sprung up and encourage, quite rightly, specialisation in social work skills.

Various Acts of Parliament, the Children's Act 1948 for example, established children's committees which were meant to look after children in care. Early realisation that children living in their own homes were sometimes just as much at risk, led, in part, to the Children's and Young Persons Act of 1963. Greatly extended responsibilities for provision of advice and assistance, so preventing children appearing before the Courts as being in need of care, together with the setting up of family advice centres, rehabilitation services and day centres, were all designed to improve quality of care. Many of the provisions of this Act were never implemented. A second Act in 1969 was meant to extend the range of services controlled by the social service departments, but prevailing attitudes and progressive ideas ostensibly designed to guard the rights of children have negated the Act's intentions and hidden much of the good that could well have stemmed from it. It was predicted in 1970 that the Local Authority Social Services Acts, following the Seebohm Report, would strengthen the concept of a family service by bringing yet more services including day nurseries under the social services umbrella. In 1974, a further commitment to provide social work support for the National Health Service was undertaken.

The reality is very different. Successive financial crises, pay freezes and strikes, together with the inheritance of further responsibilities in other fields (probation and court work) have combined to hamstring efforts even to maintain the social services for children, let alone improve them. Crisis intervention has seemed to many in the service the only work carried out (Table 1.9).

Other services have gone, in many cases by default—usually in just those areas needing them most—from inner city areas with blight and decay and with large immigrant populations. It is certainly economic sense to concentrate attention and resources on families who appear to have *social* at-risk factors. However, the problems raised by such an exercise in cities, like Manchester, Newcastle or Glasgow, would denude their more affluent suburbs of social workers, health visitors and family aids and concentrate them into areas where virtually every family would qualify for extra surveillance and help. Political considerations apart, the exercise would be complex and difficult to organise and to maintain effectively. For instance, in this country as elsewhere, 'clinics' maybe identified as hostile places by just those families who, it is felt, need to use their facilities most (Wilson, 1973).

Table 1.9 Priorities in social work

1. An immediate social work initiative will be provided to those clients who are suffering serious harm and for whom the Department has a primary responsibility

2. Social work action will be taken to assist clients likely to find themselves in situations as described in Priority 1, unless the Department takes prompt action

3. Social work help will be offered to clients potentially able to achieve a more personally or socially acceptable level of functioning with the assistance available, thereby avoiding the possibility of deterioration to the point of Priorities 1 and 2

4. Where resources permit, social work help will be provided to clients who are already being maintained at a reasonably acceptable level of functioning but where it is considered that their general wellbeing could be further enhanced if the Department were to become involved

Within this framework, the Department will, of course, make every endeavour to take account of individual circumstances and to fulfil any statutory requirements that may arise in relation to particular clients.

From Surrey Area Health Authority Guidelines to general practitioners using social services, 1975.

At this point, it is worth considering what steps could be taken to prevent illness and death in young children.

Nearly three-quarters of all deaths from birth to fifteen occur in the first year of life and social factors contribute largely to this figure. An attack on this problem is an obvious first choice but the techniques required are perhaps at first sight outside the remit of this book. However, it is useful to consider how to set about lowering specifically the perinatal mortality rate. Perhaps the rate could be lowered by reducing the number of stillbirths and the number of preterm live births, or by salvaging more members of this preterm group (Gordon, 1977). Recent evidence suggests that an attack on reducing the number of preterm live births is probably the most effective method. Yet social factors seem to be the most important single cause of spontaneous preterm births, as the condition occurs with greater frequency in social classes IV and V. Perhaps the experience of other countries will provide the answer. Certainly, on the mainland of Europe, lessons must have been learned and the experience put to practical use, producing profound changes in the pattern of morbidity and death.

In France a complete restructuring of social benefits, dependent on attendance at antenatal clinics and surveillance examinations for the baby after birth, has produced a shift downwards in perinatal mortality rates that cannot be explained other than by the effects of social and financial legislation. The French experience shows, moreover, that the biggest financial or economic returns that can be earned by a National Health Service, derive from the prevention of long-term morbidity and handicap (Wynn, 1977).

In Finland, as already mentioned, the overall national post-neonatal mortality rates are half those of Glasgow's social classes I and II population. This success demonstrates the enormous importance of the *character* of the health care system, as well as the socio-economic factors in society. Ninety per cent of all Finnish children are registered at child health centres by the end of the first month and 98 per cent of all children are being seen at child health centres by the end of the first year of life; moreover, the number of contacts totals ten in the first year. Compare these figures with those from Glasgow, which show that in 1972 just 60 per cent of all children attended child health clinics in the first year of life, and only 30 per cent of 146 infants that died from no known predisposing organic disease (Richards & McIntosh, 1972). An even more telling statistic shows that, of the 146 who died, only 28 per cent had received any inoculations at all. This must point to the gross under-use of facilities provided to prevent such problems. Systematic *home* visiting providing support and help seems to be in part the key to success. In Finland, each child receives, on average, between three and four visits annually in the home from the paediatric nurse—in this country, the rate is three times less (Wynn, 1976). Of course, there are three times more qualified nurses employed in Finland; yet at the moment there are proposals in this country to reduce even further the home visiting carried out by health visitors (Cartwright et al, 1975). Unless the full implication of these findings can be appreciated by *all* who are responsible for the child care services, there is little hope of any significant downward shift in rates in those regions where poverty and social class are the greatest contributors to the high mortality and morbidity.

The lessons that are to be learned from experience both in this country and abroad are very simple. For a further example, let us consider cot deaths. According to the Court Report, more than one-quarter of all cot deaths are preventable. In a recent study, more than *two-thirds* were due to factors labelled social or parental failure (Oakley, 1978). In one-fifth of the avoidable causes, blame could be attributed to the general practitioner—although it should be said that this included an element of communication failure between parent and doctor. More work reported in the same study shows that in Sheffield it was possible to construct a simple check list at about the time of the baby's birth to predict which children would die.

Recently, a paper from this same group pointed to totally unexpected side effects of the research study. The health visitors, who frequently visited those high-risk families were, by merely making *contact*, substantially reducing the cot death rate and actually caused the 'failure' of the research project. This occurred despite difficulties in interpreting what was the actual causes of deaths. It is apparent that the most effective way to reduce cot deaths is to adopt measures identical with those required for the improvement of the quality of child health generally, namely, to improve the accessibility of health services for young children, to train doctors and nurses better, and above all to ensure regular contact between the consumer and the services available.

The inevitable conclusion is that the general practitioner and his colleagues, the providers of primary care, must ensure that they are accessible, available and, above all, sympathetic to the needs of their patients. It is not difficult to see why so many general practitioners, who have sensed what is required and have, by organisation and effort, achieved greater contact with the families and the children on their list, are now running a *comprehensive* service incorporating illness care and surveillance. At-risk registers at practice level are relatively easy to maintain. Local knowledge of the area, provision of services generally and personal knowledge of each family can guide the team of health visitor, nurse and doctor towards greater awareness and effectiveness.

REFERENCES

Bain B J G 1974 Results of developmental and screening in general practice. Health Bulletin 32:189

Bain D J G 1977 Methods employed by general practitioners in developmental screening of preschool children. British Medical Journal 2:363–365

Barber H 1977 Primary paediatric care. In: Mitchell R (ed) Child health in the community. Churchill Livingstone, Edinburgh, ch 11

Cameron H 1977 Vision screening in preschool children. British Medical Journal 2:701

Cartwright K, Down J, Snaith A M, Tricker A J 1975 In: McLachlan G (ed) Bridging in health. Reports of studies on health services for children. p 161–200. Nuffield Provincial Hospital Trust. Oxford University Press, London

Court D 1977a Fit for the future. The report of the committee on child health services. Command 6684 HMSO, London p 40

Court D 1977b Fit for the future. HMSO, London p 50

Court D 1977c Fit for the future. HMSO, London p 48

Court D 1977d Fit for the future. HMSO, London pp 4, 6, 30–32, 37–38, 48–54

Curtis Jenkins G H 1977 Recent trends in child care. In: Hart C J (ed) Child care in general practice. Churchill Livingstone, Edinburgh, ch 2

Curtis Jenkins G H, Collins C, Andrew S 1978 Surveillance in general practice. British Medical Journal 1:1537–1540

Gardiner P A 1977 Children's eye clinics. British Medical Journal 2:1083

Gordon R 1977 Neonatal and perinatal mortality rates by birthweight. British Medical Journal 2:1202–1204

Graham R 1977 Personal communication

Hooper P D 1965 Infant feeding and its relationship to weight gain and illness. Practitioner 194:391–395

Hooper P D, Alexander E L 1971 Infant mortality and obesity. Practitioner 207:371–376

Komrower G M 1977 The role of the hospital in primary care for the child in the community. British Medical Journal 2:787–789

Lowenberg P, Nee P 1978 Health care in Thornhill. A case for inner city deprivation—a report from the Thornhill Neighbourhood Project

Neligan G, Kolvin I, Scott D McL, Garside R F, 1976. Born too soon or born too small. Clinics in Development Medicine, no 61, Heinemann Medical, London

Oakley J R 1978 Identifying children at risk from unexpected death in infancy. Archives of Disease in Childhood 53:88

Osborn A, Maurice T 1979 Rationale for composite index of social class and its evaluation. British Journal of Sociology 30: no 1

Richards I D G, McIntosh H T 1972 Confidential enquiry into 226 consecutive infant deaths. Archives of Disease in Childhood 47:697–706

Sheldon W 1967 Report of a sub-committee of the Standing Medical Advisory Committee in child welfare centres. Central Health Services Council (Chairman W Sheldon) HMSO, London

Stark G S, Basset J J, Bain D J G, Stewart F I 1975 Paediatrics in Livingstone new town. British Medical Journal 4:387–390

Starte G D 1974 The developmental assessment of the young child in general practice. Practitioner 213:823–828

Starte G D 1975 The poor communicating 2 year old and his family. Journal of the Royal College of General Practitioners 25:880

Starte G D 1976 Results from a developmental screening clinic in general practice. Practitioner 216:311

Wedge R, Prosser P 1975 Born to fail? Arrow, London

Wilson H 1973 Child development study, Birmingham 1968–71. A study of inadequate families. Centre for Child Study, University of Birmingham

Wynn M, Wynn A 1974 The protection of maternity and infancy. A study of the services for pregnant women and young children in Finland. Council for Children's Welfare, London

Wynn A 1976 Health care systems for preschool children. Proceedings of the Royal Society of Medicine 69·5, 340–343

Zinkin P M, Cox C A 1976 Child health clinics and inverse care laws. British Medical Journal 2:411–413

Part I

Care throughout the year

2.

From conception to the first hour

The delivery of a baby is not, in the majority of births, associated with ill health either for the mother or infant. Why, then, does this process have to take place in hospital? Many parents ask this question and some, resentfully. Most potential problems may be predicted during the antenatal period, but some cannot. It is certainly safer, particularly for the child, for the birth to take place in an environment where immediate medical attention is available. In the modern maternity unit there should be paediatric advice and practical care close at hand and it has become the mode that the majority of births take place in hospital. Arrangements vary: some maternity units share care between the general practitioner and obstetric consultant; in others, there are general practitioner units near the hospital unit.

So today, healthy mothers with uncomplicated pregnancies have normal babies away from their home and family. Though many parents will understand and wish to go along with these arrangements, some will not; some will find the experience confusing and even frightening. It is, therefore, of paramount importance that the atmosphere surrounding the birth of a child and the subsequent stay in hospital should be such that attention is given towards developing the new relationship between the child and its parents along secure lines.

The professional staff, doctors and nurses should understand the problems and potential problems that may arise from this type of management. It is important that the hospital communicates closely with those involved in primary home care and vice versa. It is also necessary that those involved in primary home care have some knowledge of the problems that may arise in the immediate newborn period; knowledge also of the techniques used so that unnecessary confusion and anxiety do not persist in the parents' minds. One says 'persist', as however carefully the pattern and treatment of illness are explained to anxious parents, there will often be a discrepancy between what one thinks has been communicated to the parents and the actual understanding that has occurred. Parents often go straight to the library and read up information they have directly or indirectly received. This may give rise to longstanding worry unless an opportunity is given to them for discussing these early aspects of the care of their newborn child.

The postnatal medical and social problems are not the only factors influencing the welfare and development of children. Disorders and difficulties affecting infants so often originate solely or partly in the experience and circumstances of the parents' upbringing. For example, the mode of discipline experienced by the parents frequently affects the way they handle their own children. There is a need to assess the factors which have led to the decision, or lack of it, to have a child and to supervise the antenatal period to ensure confidence for the future parents which will contribute to the well-being of the potential offspring. The level of success in supervision which is achieved should be reflected in the well-being of future generations. Commonsense dictates that the maximum attention should be extended to the antenatal and perinatal periods. However, if more evidence is needed it may be found (Emery, 1976).

It is worthwhile to emphasise here the importance of education and preventive medicine, so that children reach adolescence with an understanding and knowledge which enables them to do the best for their own children. Many future parents will obtain beneficial experience and advice from a secure family environment of their own. A substantial proportion will not, and it is amongst this group that many problems of child health arise. The school will have a part to play in this preparation but it is primarily the responsibility of the family. It is here that the family practitioner working with health visitors in the primary care team can give his guidance and exert his influence.

Particular attention needs to be directed towards the problems associated with unmarried mothers, single parent families and broken marriages. The number of divorces has increased markedly in the last ten years. There is also an increase in the number of mothers returning to work. These factors have a profound effect on the first years of a child's life and anticipation of the ensuing problems may help to make their management easier.

The care of the pregnant mother and her preparation for parenthood is the concern of the general practitioner, midwife, health visitor and, usually, hospital obstetric and paediatric departments. At present, overall in the U.K., about 98 per cent of deliveries occur in hospital. Arrangements for antenatal care will vary in different parts of the country depending on local needs and facilities. Broadly, there are three patterns of care. Firstly, those patients whose antenatal visits are shared between the general practitioner and the district obstetric department, the delivery in this arrangement being the responsibility of the consultant obstetrician. Secondly, those whose pregnancies and deliveries are supervised entirely by the general practitioner, the delivery usually taking place in a GP obstetric unit, situated ideally adjacent to the consultant unit so that help is at hand should complications arise. Thirdly, there is the group of patients entirely under the supervision of the consultant obstetric unit. This type of care should be confined to the small group of women with major obstetric problems. Every effort should be made to integrate care (Zander et al, 1978). Usually, the shared care system involves a booking visit to the consultant's antenatal clinic at 12 weeks; the general practitioner then continues supervision until 28 weeks, referring back to the hospital clinic as indicated. Between 28 and 36 weeks, visits alternate between the general practitioner and hospital clinic, and the last month involves weekly visits to the hospital clinic. Postnatal care is the responsibility of the consultant unit until the mother is discharged home, which may be within 48 hours.

Management of delivery in the general practitioner unit will vary with the practitioner's experience and wishes. Close proximity of the obstetric and paediatric departments will allow immediate cover for unexpected complications. Postnatal management is the responsibility of the general practitioner; here again, how much the paediatric department is involved will vary with local arrangements.

If staffing allows, at least one routine examination of the newborn infant should be carried out by the paediatric unit.

This will not be feasible for those mothers only staying a few hours.

The roles of the midwife and health visitor are not perhaps within the brief of this book, but the general practitioner is in a position to help co-ordinate those involved with the family at this time. The midwife's responsibility continues until the 10th or, in some cases, 28th postnatal day. The health visitor may know the family from involvement with previous children, but even during the first pregnancy, there may be factors which will be important to the child's future well-being in the early months or years of life. It is vital that the midwife and health visitor should understand each other's role and work closely together during the antenatal and postnatal period. It seems that this does not always take place. For example, the midwife may call until day 10, then on day 11 the health visitor, perhaps a substitute for the usual health visitor who is on leave, takes over. This continuity of care may, at times, be discontinuity of information—each well-qualified and well-meaning professional putting over a different point of view. When the primary care team is a working reality, this sort of problem should not arise.

The aim of antenatal care should be more than just supervision of the pregnancy, focusing on maternal and fetal well-being. The opportunity should be taken to guide and prepare both parents, for the art of child care is not necessarily a heaven sent instinctive talent. Antenatal classes are an important part of management and ideally should include both mother and father. The more highly motivated father will attend, but often those who would obtain the greatest benefit are too inhibited to take part or find it too difficult to be 'free' at the appropriate time. Whether the classes are held at the hospital or in the local health clinic, it is essential that integration between primary based care and hospital care should be fully effective. If delivery is to take place in hospital, a prior visit by the mother to the maternity unit to meet some of the staff is essential. One has at this time a captive audience of future parents and it would seem an ideal opportunity to discuss the psychological and emotional needs of infants as well as the practical side of child care. If this is combined with further advice and discussion during the postnatal months and at intervals during the preschool period, then many problems seen later in the general practitioner's surgery or hospital out-patient department, can be avoided. Mothers and fathers may feel ashamed that they need advice, little knowing that their feelings are shared by many. When a nurse, midwife or doctor herself becomes a mother, problems arising from such attitudes are often highlighted. Everyone assumes that their knowledge of child care is complete, or perhaps the professionals around them are too inhibited to offer advice, whereas often their need for guidance is just as great as that of the lay public.

The antenatal period is not the immediate brief of this book, but there are certain aspects which have direct repercussions on the first year of life. The aims of antenatal care need to be explained so that mothers understand the relevance of regular measurements of blood pressure, weight and fetal growth assessment. General education via the media, comparison of experience between mothers, and not least, the mother's own acute observation of the manner and reaction of the doctor or midwife, all enhance the need for time to be spent in discussion. Mothers very often have anxieties, as do the professional staff caring for them. Unexpressed anxieties are usually greater than those discussed; the fear of what might be, is usually worse than the reality. The mother's emotional well-being during the pregnancy and labour can have a profound effect on the first and subsequent years of the child's life.

Clinical assessment of the pregnant mother, particularly with regard to drugs, smoking and nutrition, is the mainstay of management. There are other measures which may be used to elucidate further the normal or abnormal progress of the developing fetus.

Antenatal diagnosis

The advent of techniques to diagnose abnormality in the fetus has opened a new field of preventive medicine bringing with it medical, ethical and religious problems. It is now possible to diagnose chromosomal abnormalities, an increasing number of metabolic inborn errors and some congenital malformations. In view of the ability to sex the fetus, the risk in sex-linked conditions can now be defined. Table 2.1 lists the commoner disorders.

A full family history has great significance in modern obstetric management. With some conditions one need no longer wait for the first affected child to arrive in the family.

Table 2.1 Diseases that are detectable prenatally

Chromosomal	—abnormal genotype
	    e.g., Trisomy 21 (Down's syndrome)
	    can be used for identifying male fetus
	    in sex-linked diseases
	    e.g., Duchenne muscular dystrophy
	    e.g., Haemophilia

Neural tube abnormality	—Anencephaly —Myelomeningocoele

Metabolic disorders	—Mucopolysaccharidoses
	    e.g., Hunter's syndrome
	—Lipidoses
	    e.g., Tay Sach's disease
	—Amino-acid disorders
	    e.g., Galactosaemia

Haemoglobinopathies	—Sickle-cell disease —Thalassaemia

For example, if it is known that a mother has a balanced translocation for chromosome 21, and therefore a risk of one in three for any child to have trisomy 21 (Down's syndrome), amniocentesis carried out at about 14 weeks will make it possible to exclude chromosomal anomaly in the fetus. Obviously, it is not feasible to monitor every pregnancy for a chromosomal anomaly because of the cost. However, the usual cause of trisomy 21 is a mutation and the risk of this rises with increasing maternal age. The overall U.K. incidence of regular trisomy 21 is about one in 600 births. When the maternal age is less than 30 years, then the risk is one in 2000, but at 40 years, the risk rises to one in 100 and over the age of 45 years to one in 40 (Penrose & Smith, 1966). About 50 per cent of mongol children are born to mothers aged 35 years or more (Smith & Berg, 1976). The practicability of antenatal diagnosis is therefore of importance to those parents who have a significantly increased risk of having a mongol child, on the basis of maternal age. The age of conception at which this diagnostic service can be offered at present varies according to the availability of genetic services in the particular district. It certainly should be available to mothers aged 37 or more, and to mothers who have already had a mongol child whatever the maternal age. It is vital that the parents understand exactly what abnormality is being screened and the limitations of the procedure in diagnosing other possible abnormalities. No test can be a guarantee of a normal baby.

There is an increased risk of central nervous system malformation in mothers who themselves have midline spinal abnormalities and in those mothers whose first degree relations have spina bifida. Measurement of α-feto-protein in the liquor makes it possible to diagnose anencephaly or open spinal column defect. This investigation becomes even more important if a mother has already given birth to a child with a midline neural tube abnormality. As this chapter is being written, screening of all mothers by analysis of the α-feto-protein in the maternal serum at booking is becoming a reality. High levels of maternal α-feto-protein require investigation by amniocentesis, but it is likely to be an exercise without undue false positives if the cut-off level is made at the 95 centile of serum values (Ferguson-Smith et al, 1978).

Amniocentesis carries very little risk in experienced hands. The recent multi-centre trial has suggested a slightly increased incidence of abortion, also the possibility of neonatal respiratory and orthopaedic problems (MRC report 1978, 1979). However, the techniques in the centres involved in the trial and during the trial were not uniform, perhaps the most significant fact being that ultrasound was not always available; and if amniocentesis is carried out with synchronous ultrasound control, then the procedure is safer (Crandon & Peel, 1979).

The decision to abort an abnormal fetus is difficult and the ethical issue is of tremendous importance, not least to those responsible for the termination of the pregnancy. It is not possible to discuss this in further detail but however one views scientific knowledge, once acquired, its use and application should not be the prerogative of any single individual without informed discussion with all those most closely involved. The new techniques of antenatal diagnosis can help in preventing the birth of handicapped children and the ensuing suffering of the children and their families.

Fetal growth and development

A number of factors can be specifically analysed to monitor fetal growth. There are various types of placental function tests and also ultrasonic techniques which measure the

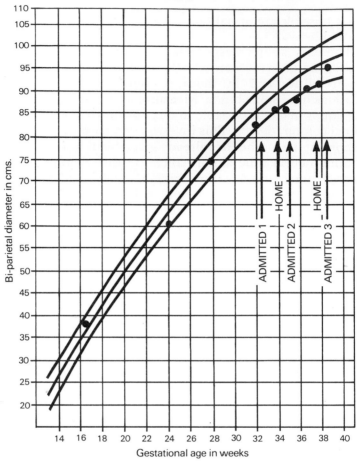

Fig 2.1   Fetal growth assessed by biparietal ultrasound measurement. (With acknowledgement to Mr T. Spencer for permission to report this patient and Dr R. Stevenson, Ultrasound Department, Maternity Unit, St Peter's Hospital, Chertsey, Surrey.)

growth of the fetal skull and abdominal circumference. The value of these investigations has been challenged in the past but it is now clear that they have an important part to play in the identification of the fetus at risk, so allowing early and appropriate action to be taken. Figure 2.1 represents fetal growth assessed by bi-parietal ultrasound measurement. This was the fourth pregnancy of a mother with a history of two pregnancies ending with intra-uterine deaths and a third pregnancy producing a low birth weight preterm living child. It can be seen that the early scan at $16\frac{1}{2}$ weeks allowed correlation to be made with the clinical gestational age. This early measurement is very important, enhancing the value of subsequent observations. Fetal growth had slowed when the fetus was scanned at 32 weeks, the oestriol levels were low and the mother was admitted to hospital for two weeks rest. After being allowed home, there was further evidence of poor fetal growth and she was re-admitted. Growth improved over the next three weeks and this was associated with a rising oestriol level. Labour was induced at 39 weeks; close monitoring of this labour, where the fetus was already known to be in jeopardy, showed fetal bradycardia and therefore delivery was expedited by caesarean section. The male infant weighed 2·54 kg and was in good condition at birth; Apgar score, eight at one minute.

Ultrasound techniques may also be used to detect fetal abnormality by direct screening using the high definition grey scale equipment.

Labour

Antenatal care will pick out some of those pregnancies at particular risk and the full benefit of monitoring labour in hospital is now available. There are, of course, some pregnancies which are straightforward and some in which antenatal care is not sought where problems during labour may arise unexpectedly. It is for this reason that the aim should be for labour and delivery to take place under full supervision of mother and baby and this is likely to be in hospital, rather than at home.

The standard clinical care of labour will pick up many problems, but not all. More detailed monitoring of labour will pick up problems earlier and is likely to miss fewer of them. The fetus may be in an environment which is compatible with survival prior to labour but which becomes increasingly hazardous once labour has started. By monitoring the fetal heart rate and relating this to the onset and length of uterine contractions, and by obtaining blood samples from the fetal scalp for acid-base estimation, a fuller picture of the intra-uterine environment is obtained. Warning signs are picked up early and intervention can be planned and undertaken without undue haste. Prolonged fetal hypoxia associated with acidosis makes delivery more hazardous and resuscitation more difficult. To monitor this, of course, involves machines but such techniques need not exclude humanity. The general practitioner and primary care professionals by their own full understanding of the techniques being used in the maternity department will be able to counsel their patients and remove their unjustified fears.

Drugs during pregnancy

It would seem that notwithstanding the thalidomide tragedy, unnecessary medication is still prescribed during pregnancy. Prescribing for the potential child-bearing female should be reduced to essential medication only. This is not to suggest that one never prescribes for this group of patients, but medication must be considered in the context of possible teratogenicity and also the effect the drug may have on the developing fetus, after embryogenesis is complete.

Drugs undergo extensive testing prior to release. Such tests include attempts at assessing teratogenic effects, but these relate necessarily to species other than man. It is therefore essential to maintain accurate records of drug use and dosage and to report side effects promptly to the Committee on the Safety of Medicines.

Drugs may damage the fetus in four ways. The most well-recognised is that caused by direct toxicity to the embryo, as occurred with thalidomide. Drugs may affect the feto-placental unit directly or *via* the mother or father. It should be remembered that untoward effects may occur after many years delay. The longer the delay, the more difficult it is to determine cause and effect. An example of this delayed effect can be seen in the development of vaginal neoplasia in children and adolescents in association with diethylstilbo-estrol treatment for the mother during pregnancy (Dewhurst, 1974).

Induction of labour

There are indications both maternal and fetal for inducing labour preterm. The balance of risk must be carefully assessed (Howie, 1977). It is important, particularly if it is the fetus at risk, that one does not exchange a likely intra-uterine death for a perinatal death. One of the greatest hazards of preterm delivery is immaturity of the lungs leading to respiratory distress syndrome (RDS) of the newborn. This condition arises from the lack of production of surfactant by the alveolar cells. It is possible to assess the surfactant 'maturity' by analysis of the amniotic fluid. Amniocentesis has to be carried out prior to induction of labour and the lecithin/sphingomyelin ratio in the fluid biochemically analysed. If the ratio of lecithin to sphingomyelin is $1 \cdot 8 : 1 \cdot 0$ or greater, the lungs are likely to be mature. If the ratio is less there is a high chance of RDS and, if possible, induction of labour should be postponed and the test repeated as indicated by circumstances. There is good experimental and some clinical evidence that the production of surfactant can be enhanced by giving steroid, usually in the form of betamethasone, to the mother for 48 hours prior to delivery. The steroid probably works by inducing the enzyme system necessary for surfactant formation (Liggins & Howie, 1972).

Delivery

This is the most critical time in the infant's life. Ideally, someone capable of resuscitating the child should always be present. In practice, this may be impossible in every case but it is mandatory when problems are anticipated, for example, in preterm deliveries, operative deliveries (particularly if there have been problems during labour) and where there is a history of a previous handicapped child.

Control of delivery of the head is important in preventing intracranial damage. The preterm infant with its softer skull bones is particularly at risk and the routine use of forceps will reduce the hazard. The infant presenting by the breech is also vulnerable and in the case of the preterm infant, markedly so. This latter presentation, for the child's future well-being, is probably best managed by caesarean section (Ingemarsson et al, 1978).

Resuscitation

The majority of newborn infants establish regular respirations without any difficulty usually within 60 seconds. The first gasp should occur within 30 seconds; many babies give their first cry as they are being delivered. The stimulus to the respiratory centre is probably related to changes occurring in the arterial Po_2 and Pco_2 during the separation of the placenta, and the external stimuli which occur as the infant is born.

The most important manoeuvre to aid the onset of respirations is clearance of the airway. The nose and mouth should be wiped free from liquor as the head is being delivered. The nose and oropharynx should be gently aspirated using a soft catheter, care being taken not to push the catheter into the larynx and thereby induce laryngeal spasm. Once respirations are established, it is a useful procedure to pass gently a suction catheter into the stomach and aspirate any liquor and mucus which may have been swallowed. An added bonus from this procedure may be the early diagnosis of tracheo-oesophageal atresia.

During the first 10 to 20 minutes there may be short episodes of slight grunting or slight sternal recession. These symptoms should quickly settle. Close attention should be given to the baby's airway, particularly during these early minutes. Mucous plugs may be obstructing the airway and if they are not cleared promptly, more acute hypoxia may follow.

Assessment of the newborn infant's status is important in deciding whether or not more active resuscitation is required. The observations are best summarised by the Apgar score, see Table 2.2.

This measurement can be carried out at one, three and five minutes depending on circumstances. Those infants whose Apgar score is below 7 need particularly close observation.

The heart rate is the most important of the signs. At birth, the rate is normally 120–160/min.

When fetal distress occurs during birth, with or without warning, the baby needs more active resuscitation. If the Apgar score is below 5 at one minute, or more specifically, if the heart rate is below 100/min at birth and then slows, preparation for intubation and intermittent positive pressure respiration should be made.

Endotracheal intubation should be carried out only by those trained in the technique and also those regularly involved in the care of the newborn. An infant laryngoscope must be employed. The first step is to visualise the larynx, as direct vision may identify airway obstruction by a mucous plug. The pharynx is aspirated and the endotracheal tube passed. If a Warne's tube with a shoulder is used, care must be taken not to push the tube too far as it is possible to

Table 2.2 The Apgar score

Sign	Score		
	0	1	2
Heart rate	Absent	Less than 100/min	More than 100/min
Respiratory effort	Absent	Slow Irregular	Good Cry
Colour	Blue Pale	Body pink Extremities blue	Completely pink
Muscle tone	Limp	Some flexion of extremities	Active
Response to catheter in pharynx	Nil	Grimace	Cry

Modified from Apgar V 1953 Current Researches in Anesthesia and Analgesia 32: 260–267

introduce the shoulder through the larynx. Oxygen is usually delivered from a system which automatically prevents pressure greater than 30 to 35 mm of water being used. A water manometer, allowing the excess pressure to escape, is the usual system. The first and second inflations are held for two to three seconds. If there is considerable fluid in the lungs, it may be necessary to aspirate down the endotracheal tube but excess suction must be avoided as this will tend to collapse the lung. It is vitally important to prevent meconium from reaching the lungs but the liquor will be cleared by the usual mechanism once the lungs are inflated and given positive airway pressure.

If the necessary skills for intubation are not immediately available, adequate ventilation can be achieved by use of the Cardiff mask and bag. The airway is first cleared, an oral airway of the correct size is inserted into the baby's mouth and then the mask applied over the face. The bag is squeezed with controlled pressure about 30 times/min and the chest observed to ensure the thorax is moving adequately and equally. During resuscitation, oxygen via a face mask should be held over the baby's face so that any gasps result in the intake of oxygen-enriched air.

Babies who have had considerable intra-uterine hypoxia may be acidotic and if regular respirations are not established after 5 to 10 minutes, administration of sodium bicarbonate via the umbilical vein should be considered.

If no heart beat is present at birth, then external cardiac massage and immediate intubation will be required.

During resuscitation of the baby, it is essential to maintain body temperature. A wet baby loosely wrapped in a wet towel in a draught rapidly loses heat. Hypoxia, hypothermia and acidosis soon lead to hypoglycaemia. The combination is not only potentially lethal but greatly increases the likelihood of morbidity in the form of neurological handicap. Ideally, the baby is dried, then placed in a warmed dry towel and any resuscitative measures, other than naso-pharyngeal suction and oxygen from a face mask, should take place under a radiant heat supply.

The use of other drugs should be limited to a specific morphine/pethidine antagonist. There is no place for general respiratory stimulants. Nalorphine was the first narcotic antagonist to be developed and has been very useful but its main disadvantage is that the drug itself can cause respiratory depression. It should no longer be used, it has been replaced by naloxone hydrochloride (Narcan) which does not have this drawback. There is a neonatal preparation which contains 0·02 mg naloxone per ml. The initial dose is 0·01 mg/kg body weight. The affect may wear off quite quickly and so the respiratory effort needs to be observed carefully and a repeat dose given as required.

Examination of the newborn

The initial examination of the newborn is directed towards observing the satisfactory establishment of regular respirations and detection of problems related to maturity, birth trauma or congenital malformations. The congenital malformations noted at the time will be those leading to immediate problems, or those readily visible.

The general observations will include colour, posture, and response to stimulation. The normal newborn infant is usually alert immediately following delivery. The hands and feet may be cyanosed but once regular respirations are established, the tongue and body should be pink. Start at the top of the infant observing carefully the head and facies.

There may be a considerable degree of moulding, a caput succedaneum or trauma from the delivery; these should be assessed and explained to the parents. Minor blemishes, which the staff know will soon fade, may cause considerable anxiety to the mother. As the trunk and limbs are examined, always check the clavicle as this can be injured in a difficult delivery of the shoulders.

The chest is next inspected to assess movement and any evidence of respiratory difficulty which shows as intercostal or sternal recession. Auscultation of the chest is helpful in assessing satisfactory expansion of the lungs, but it is of limited value because of the small area of an infant's chest, and may occasionally be misleading. The heart rate is an important indicator but a murmur immediately after birth, although worth noting, may commonly not be significant. The abdomen may be difficult to assess, but it should be observed for undue distension. Malformation of the renal tract may present with enlarged kidneys at birth. The liver edge is normally palpable in the infant. It is also worth counting the vessels in the cord; a single artery is associated with a slightly increased incidence of congenital malformation.

The genitalia should be inspected; the testicles should be in the scrotum in the normal full term male. Ambiguous genitalia are a rare but important malformation. Hypospadias may be associated with renal tract anomalies.

It is important to feel for the femoral arteries, but better to defer routine examination of the hip joints until the end of the first week. The limbs and extremities should be inspected; one of the first things parents do is to look closely at the hands and feet. It is important to remember to inspect the back for dimples, hair tufts, etc. Maturity may be determined by external features or neurological examination. The latter has to be interpreted with regard to the infant's general state and degree of alertness. A well tried and useful regime is that designed by Dubowitz (see Appendix I below). If a decision needs to be made about where the infant is to be actually nursed then a gestational assessment will be valuable. It is also of practical importance to relate the infant's birth weight to the expected weight for the gestational age (see Appendix II). The other problem with regard to the immediate care of the newborn may be the development of respiratory symptoms. These also may be assessed and scored

(Silverman & Anderson, 1956; Gomez et al, 1969). These measures will make anticipation of neonatal problems more likely and thereby optimum management for the baby possible (see Ch. 3).

REFERENCES

Crandon A J, Peel K R 1979 Amniocentesis with and without ultrasound guidance. British Journal of Obstetrics and Gynaecology 86: 1–3

Dewhurst C J 1974 Vaginal adenocarcinoma in adolescence. Editorial. Clinics in Obstetrics and Gynaecology 1, no 3: 678

Dubowitz L M S, Dubowitz V, Goldberg C 1970 Clinical assessment of gestational age in the newborn infant. Journal of Pediatrics 77: 1–10

Emery J L 1976 Unexpected death in infancy. In: Hull D (ed) Recent advances in paediatrics no 5. Churchill Livingstone, Edinburgh, ch 8, pp 203–220

Ferguson-Smith M A, Rawlinson H A, May H M, Tait H A, Vince J D, Gibson A A M, Robinson H P, Ratcliffe J G 1978 Avoidance of anencephalic and spina bifida births by maternal serum-alphafetoprotein screening. Lancet 1: 1330–1333

Gomez P C W, Noakes M, Barrie H 1969 A prognostic score for use in the respiratory-distress syndrome. Lancet 1: 808–810

Howie P W 1977 Induction of labour. Benefits and hazards of the new obstetrics. Spastics International Medical Publications. Heinemann, London, ch 6

Ingemarsson I, Westgren M, Svenningsen N W 1978 Long-term follow up of preterm infants in breech presentation delivered by caesarean section. Lancet 2: 172–175

Liggins G C, Howie R N 1972 A controlled trial of antepartum glucocorticoid treatment for prevention of the respiratory-distress syndrome in premature infants. Pediatrics 50: 515–525

MRC Report 1978 An assessment of the hazards of amniocentesis. British Journal of Obstetrics and Gynaecology 85: Suppl. No. 2. 1–41

Penrose L S, Smith G H 1966 Down's Anomaly. J and A Churchill, London

Silverman W A, Andersen D H 1956 A controlled clinical trial of effects of water mist on obstructive respiratory signs death rate and necropsy findings among premature infants. Pediatrics 17: 1–10

Smith G F, Berg J M 1976 Down's Anomaly 2nd edn. Churchill Livingstone, Edinburgh, p 247

U.K. Collaborative Study 1977 Maternal serum-alphafetoprotein measurement in antenatal screening for anencephaly and spina bifida in early pregnancy. Lancet 1: 1323–1332

U.K. Collaborative Study 2nd report 1979 Amniotic-fluid alpha-fetoprotein measurement in antenatal diagnosis of anencephaly and open spina bifida in early pregnancy. Lancet 2: 651–662

Zander L I, Watson M, Taylor R W, Morrell D C 1978 Integration of general practitioner and specialist antenatal care. Journal of the Royal College of General Practitioners 28:455–458

Appendices

Dubowitz Assessment:

The assessment should be carried out within the first twenty-four hours of birth.

There are two parts of the assessment, the external (superficial) criteria, and the neurological criteria. Each criterion is scored as indicated on the charts. The individual scores are added and the total score is then related to the gestational age on the graph (reproduced with permission).

SOME NOTES ON TECHNIQUES OF ASSESSMENT OF NEUROLOGICAL CRITERIA

Posture

Observed with infant quiet and in supine position. Score 0: Arms and legs extended; 1: beginning of flexion of hips and knees, arms extended; 2: stronger flexion of legs, arms extended; 3: arms slightly flexed, legs flexed and abducted; 4: full flexion of arms and legs.

Square window

The hand is flexed on the forearm between the thumb and index finger of the examiner. Enough pressure is applied to get as full a flexion as possible, and the angle between the hypothenar eminence and the ventral aspect of the forearm is measured and graded according to diagram. (Care is taken not to rotate the infant's wrist while doing this manoeuvre.)

Ankle dorsiflexion

The foot is dorsiflexed onto the anterior aspect of the leg, with the examiner's thumb on the sole of the foot and other fingers behind the leg. Enough pressure is applied to get as full flexion as possible, and the angle between the dorsum of the foot and the anterior aspect of the leg is measured.

Arm recoil

With the infant in the supine position the forearms are first flexed for 5 seconds, then fully extended by pulling on the hands, and then released. The sign is fully positive if the arms return briskly to full flexion (Score 2). If the arms return to incomplete flexion or the response is sluggish it is graded as Score 1. If they remain extended or are only followed by random movements the score is 0.

Leg recoil

With the infant supine, the hips and knees are fully flexed for 5 seconds, then extended by traction on the feet, and released. A maximal response is one of full flexion of the hips and knees (Score 2). A partial flexion scores 1, and minimal or no movement scores 0.

Popliteal angle

With the infant supine and his pelvis flat on the examining couch, the thigh is held in the knee-chest position by the examiner's left index finger and thumb supporting the knee. The leg is then extended by gentle pressure from the examiner's right index finger behind the ankle and the popliteal angle is measured.

Heel to ear manoeuvre

With the baby supine, draw the baby's foot as near to the head as it will go without forcing it. Observe the distance between the foot and the head as well as the degree of extension at the knee. Grade according to diagram. Note that the knee is left free and may draw down alongside the abdomen.

Scarf sign

With the baby supine, take the infant's hand and try to put it around the neck and as far posteriorly as possible around the opposite shoulder. Assist this manoeuvre by lifting the elbow across the body. See how far the elbow will go across and grade according to illustrations. Score 0: Elbow reaches opposite axillary line; 1: Elbow between midline and opposite axillary line; 2: Elbow reaches midline; 3: Elbow will not reach midline.

Head lag

With the baby lying supine, grasp the hands (or the arms if a very small infant) and pull him slowly towards the sitting position. Observe the position of the head in relation to the trunk and grade accordingly. In a small infant the head may initially be supported by one hand. Score 0: Complete lag; 1: Partial head control; 2: Able to maintain head in line with body; 3: Brings head anterior to body.

Ventral suspension

The infant is suspended in the prone position, with examiner's hand under the infant's chest (one hand in a small infant, two in a large infant). Observe the degree of extension of the back and the amount of flexion of the arms and legs. Also note the relation of the head to the trunk. Grade according to diagrams.

If the score for an individual criterion differs on the two sides of the baby, take the mean. For further details see Dubowitz et al 1970 J. Pediat. 77:1.

1. EXTERNAL (SUPERFICIAL) CRITERIA

EXTERNAL SIGN	SCORE 0	1	2	3	4
OEDEMA	Obvious oedema hands and feet; pitting over tibia	No obvious oedema hands and feet; pitting over tibia	No oedema		
SKIN TEXTURE	Very thin, gelatinous	Thin and smooth	Smooth; medium thickness. Rash or superficial peeling	Slight thickening. Superficial cracking and peeling esp. hands and feet	Thick and parchment-like; superficial or deep cracking
SKIN COLOUR (Infant not crying)	Dark red	Uniformly pink	Pale pink: variable over body	Pale. Only pink over ears, lips, palms or soles	
SKIN OPACITY (trunk)	Numerous veins and venules clearly seen, especially over abdomen	Veins and tributaries seen	A few large vessels clearly seen over abdomen	A few large vessels seen indistinctly over abdomen	No blood vessels seen
LANUGO (over back)	No lanugo	Abundant; long and thick over whole back	Hair thinning especially over lower back	Small amount of lanugo and bald areas	At least half of back devoid of lanugo
PLANTAR CREASES	No skin creases	Faint red marks over anterior half of sole	Definitie red marks over more than anterior half; indentations over less than anterior thirds	Indentations over more than anterior third	Definite deep indentations over more than anterior third
NIPPLE FORMATION	Nipple barely visible; no areola	Nipple well defined; areola smooth and flat diameter <0·75 cm	Areola stippled, edge not raised; diameter <0·75 cm	Areola stippled, edge raised diameter >0·75 cm	
BREAST SIZE	No breast tissue palpable	Breast tissue on one or both sides 0·5 cm diameter	Breast tissue both sides; one or both 0·5–1·0 cm	Breast tissue both sides; one or both >1 cm	
EAR FORM	Pinna flat and shapeless, little or no incurving of edge	Incurving of part of edge of pinna	Partial incurving whole of upper pinna	Well-defined incurving whole of upper pinna	
EAR FIRMNESS	Pinna soft, easily folded, no recoil	Pinna soft, easily folded, slow recoil	Cartilage to edge of pinna, but soft in places, ready recoil	Pinna firm, cartilage to edge, instant recoil	
GENITALIA MALE	Neither testis in scrotum	At least one testis high in scrotum	At least one testis right down		
FEMALES (With hips half abducted)	Labia majora widely separated, labia minora protruding	Labia majora almost cover labia minora	Labia majora completely cover labia minora		

(Adapted from Farr et al. Develop. Med. Child Neurol. 1966. **8**, 507)

2. NEUROLOGICAL CRITERIA

NEUROLOGICAL SIGN	SCORE					
	0	1	2	3	4	5
POSTURE						
SQUARE WINDOW	90°	60°	45°	30°	0°	
ANKLE DORSIFLEXION	90°	75°	45°	20°	0°	
ARM RECOIL	180°	90–180°	<90°			
LEG RECOIL	180°	90–180°	<90°			
POPLITEAL ANGLE	180	160°	130°	110°	90°	<90°
HEEL TO EAR						
SCARF SIGN						
HEAD LAG						
VENTRAL SUSPENSION						

GRAPH FOR READING GESTATIONAL AGE
FROM TOTAL SCORE

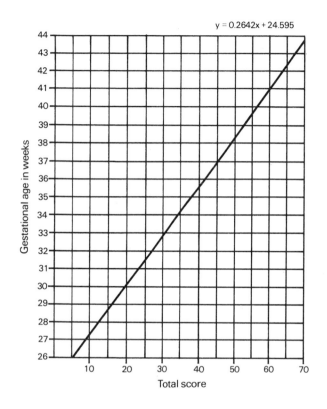

APPENDIX II

WEIGHT CHARTS FOR NEWBORN BABIES 10TH, 50TH AND 90TH CENTILES

[After Thomson et al 1968 J. Obstet. Gynaec. Brit. Cwlth. 75:903–916 (Table XI b+c) and Babson et al 1970, Pediatrics 45:937–944 (28–31 weeks)]

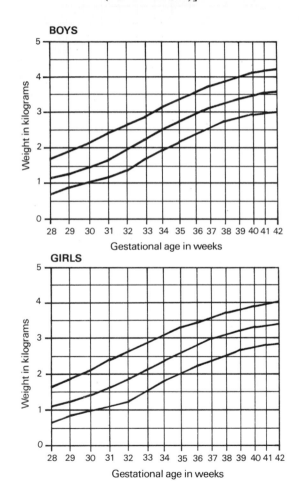

3.

The first ten days

Physiology

Two major physiological changes occurring at birth are those affecting the lungs and circulation. The pulmonary vascular resistance in the fetus is high due to the lungs being filled with fluid and the relative low arterial Po_2 to which the pulmonary arterioles are exposed. The pulmonary artery pressure is thereby marginally higher than the aortic pressure. There are two levels of a right-to-left shunt in the fetus, via the foramen ovale and the ductus arteriosus. At birth, the fluid is cleared from the lungs, some mechanically squeezed out as the infant passes through the birth canal. The more important clearance occurs as the lungs are expanded and the fluid drained *via* the lymphatics of the lung. As the lungs expand, the pulmonary vascular resistance starts to fall and the shunts at atrial and ductus level close physiologically. Anatomical closure follows after a variable interval, thus there is a potentiality for a left-to-right shunt in the newborn child. The fall in the pulmonary vascular resistance in the normal baby occurs during the first two to three weeks of life, the major part of the change occurring soon after birth. These changes are important as they influence the clinical presentation of problems in the neonatal period.

The ability of the lungs to remain partially inflated during the expiratory phase of the respiratory cycle is of vital importance, this being made possible by production of a lipoprotein from the alveolar cells—surfactant.

Temperature control is of great importance for the survival of all warm blooded species; it is particularly so for small naked infants. The control of skin blood flow is well developed in infants but the ability to conserve heat is only 50 per cent or less of that of the adult (Hey, Katz & O'Connell, 1970). Newborn infants do not shiver. Heat production in response to cold is achieved by metabolism of brown fat, a specialised type of adipose tissue situated around the great vessels and mediastinum (Hull, 1966). The ability of the infant to sweat is also limited, particularly in the preterm infant. There is, therefore, also a risk from hyperthermia. This system of heat production requires the fuel of metabolism, oxygen and glucose. Close attention needs to be paid to the environmental temperature to improve the survival of the neonate (Hey, 1971).

Other physiological variations which are important to the well-being of the neonate are those involving the kidneys, the enzyme systems, particularly of the liver, and the immunological system. The neonate is poor at concentrating urine and dealing with a solute load. Glucuronyl transferase, the enzyme necessary for conjugation of bilirubin, may be immature, particularly in the preterm child. The immunological status of the infant is also immature. Some protection may be obtained from the mother but the preterm infant is particularly vulnerable.

The normal infant

The initial resuscitation and examination of the neonate has been discussed in Chapter 2. Once the initial assessment has been made, the infant should be handled by the parents. There is evidence for a particularly sensitive period occurring soon after birth during which attachment between mother and child may be enhanced (see below). Immediately after birth the infant is likely to be alert and have the eyes open. Eye contact between parent and child is one of the more important aspects of this early relationship. After an hour or so the newborn child is likely to sleep and be less responsive; the degree of alertness during the first week will vary. It is important to ensure that the mother is aware that her newborn infant can see, hear and smell. Since this early period is so vital any event which upsets or causes anxiety to the mother may cause difficulties in building up the relationship between mother and child. Attention to this aspect is particularly pertinent if the baby is of low birth weight or has symptoms or congenital anomalies requiring immediate specific treatment, resulting in separation of mother and child. Every effort should be made for the mother to see and handle the baby, prior to any transfer, and information on progress and future contact with the child must be arranged as regularly and frequently as possible.

There are two important advantages in allowing the infant to suckle at the breast immediately after delivery, in addition to the mother-infant interaction. The stimulus of suckling results in the release of oxytocin which causes contraction of the uterus. The infant also has the chance to become colonised by the bacteria on the mother's skin which are probably non-pathogenic. It is likely that this discourages the growth of pathogenic strains.

There are a few general points relating to the routine care of the neonate. The ligation of the umbilical cord and subsequent care of the stump needs close attention to detail. The ligature must be one that does not slacken as the cord dries. Plastic clips are effective. If neonatal problems are anticipated, the cord stump should be left 5 to 10 cm longer than the usual 5 cm for the purpose of catheterisation. The cord dries and usually separates after 7 to 10 days. Daily application of powder will help keep the site dry and prevent infection.

There is no particular urgency to bathe the newborn infant, nor is there need for daily baths. Maintenance of body temperature is far more important. The ideal way is by keeping the baby clothed in a cot in a warm and thermally stable environment (Smales & Kime, 1978).

Apart from the initial examination, the child should be seen at least daily by an experienced person and a further full examination given at 8 to 10 days. This should be timed so that the infant is alert (about two to three hours after a feed); neurological assessment may then be made. This will include observation of response to stimulation, ability to fix and follow, tone, posture and the neonatal responses (see below). At this examination, there should also be routine testing for congenital dislocation of the hips.

Feeding

There has been and probably will continue to be controversy concerning breast feeding versus artificial feeding. There is little doubt that for the normal full term infant the mother's breast milk is best physiologically (this is further discussed in

Chapter 4). However, science is not the sole guide line and emotional aspects need to be considered. Mothers should be encouraged to discuss the feeding of their infant during the antenatal period; this is the best time to prepare for successful breast feeding. Practical attention is given to the breasts and nipples, and the ideas and wishes of the mother are considered and discussed. Whatever the antenatal decision reached, this must be flexible so that the mother may change her mind in the postnatal period. Excessive pressure and encouragement for breast feeding may cause mothers who are unable or do not want to breast feed their babies, to feel that they are failing as mothers.

Most of the artificial milks have vitamin supplements. Breast milk gives a poor supply of vitamin D and iron; it may also predispose to vitamin K deficiency. This latter deficiency is a particular hazard if the infant is prescribed antibiotics, which may alter the natural production of vitamin K by the intestinal flora.

Factors affecting choice of feeding

The overall nutrition and electrolyte load of the artificial milks have been modified so that they are now comparable to breast milk. However, the quality of the protein differs and there is evidence that absorption of foreign protein from the intestine in the early months may lead to problems in later life. Atopic symptoms, notably eczema and asthma, may be related to early feeding with cows' milk. There is some evidence that avoidance of cows' milk during the early months by genetically susceptible atopic infants may prevent symptoms developing (Matthew et al, 1977).

Infection

Gastrointestinal infections are very rare in the fully breast fed infant. Respiratory infections are also less common, as is the sudden infant death syndrome (cot death). Breast milk protects the infant by providing immunoglobulin, particularly IgA, which occurs in large amounts in colostrum. Breast feeding also exerts a beneficial effect on the pH of the baby's intestinal contents. The prevalence of the lactobacilli is enhanced and pathogenic strains of *Escherichia coli* are discouraged. Breast milk contains lactoferrin in high concentrations compared with cows' milk and this particularly protects against these strains too.

Emotional

There are strong emotional reasons for mothers wishing to breast feed. There is no doubt this gives pleasure and satisfaction. It must be remembered that a close attachment still occurs during bottle feeding and each mother has to be advised as an individual. The establishment of breast feeding may take time and some of the initial difficulties may be overcome by knowledgeable and sympathetic handling (Gunther, 1973). A common anxiety is that of not knowing how much the infant has taken. This can be enhanced by rigid criteria laid down for fluid requirements and weight gain in infancy. These feeding criteria must be considered only as a guide and it is important to remember that each child is unique. The basic fluid requirement during the first six months, from one week of age, is 150 ml/kg/24 hours. For the normal full term infant, a four-hourly feeding regime is usually satisfactory, though it is best for this to be varied by demand of the baby particularly in the early days. It has been shown that in a maternity hospital, demand feeding may result in a wide variation of feeding intervals initially (less than two-hourly to six- to eight-hourly) but by 10 days the majority of babies have settled to four-hourly feeds (Cruse et al, 1978). It is also worth mentioning that 10 minutes suckling on each breast can be only a rough guide; some babies will be satisfied with less and some may need longer. At times, of course, suckling provides comfort rather than nutrition (non-nutritive suckling).

Drugs

The effect on breast feeding of maternal ingestion of drugs is a complicated problem. At present, there is not sufficient knowledge concerning the concentration of drugs in breast milk and their effect on the infant. Most drugs pass into the milk and hence, to some degree, reach the child. Lewis has suggested, on present knowledge, which drugs are safe and which dangerous: (see Tables 3.1, 3.2 and 3.3).

The normal full term infant loses up to 10 per cent of the birth weight during the first four to five days, but this is

Table 3.1 Drugs which are not safe for nursing women

Amantadine	Indomethacin
Antineoplastic drugs	Iodine
Anthroquinone	Isoniazid
Carbimazole	Kanamycin
Cascara	Lithium
Chloramphenicol	Phenindione
Cortisone	Potassium iodide
Diazepam	Sulphonamides
Ergotamine	Tetracycline
	Thiouracil

Table 3.2 Drugs which are probably safe for nursing women—no deleterious effects reported

Alcohol	Iron
Ampicillin	Lincomycin
Antihistamines	Mefenamic acid
Caffeine	Morphine
Carbenicillin	Nitrofurantoin
Cephaloridine	Para-amino salicylic acid
Chloral	Penicillin
Chlordiazepoxide	Pentazocine
Chloroquine	Pethidine
Chlorpromazine	Phenothiazines
Codeine	Phenylbutazone
Desipramine	Propanthelene
Dichloralphenazone	Quinine
Digoxin	Salicylates
Folic acid	Sodium fucidate
Frusemide	Thyroxine
Guanethidine	Tolbutamide
Heroin	Warfarin
Imipramine	

Table 3.3 Drugs about which there is too little information, but doubt remains as to their safety for use by nursing mothers

Barbiturates	Oral contraceptives
Erythromycin	Propranolol
Methyldopa	Reserpine
Metronidazole	Streptomycin
Novobiocin	Thiazide diuretics

Tables 3.1, 3.2 and 3.3 were reproduced from Lewis P 1978 Journal of Maternal and Child Health 3:128, with kind permission

regained by 10 days. It is wise not to be too rigid in approach to weight changes over short periods of time. The fact that a baby is feeding well and is alert, is more relevant to short term progress than minor fluctuations or slow weight gain. It is also important to relate weight to the other criteria of growth, length and head circumference.

PROBLEMS OF THE FIRST TEN DAYS

Problems relating particularly to the first 10 days of life will now be considered. Reference to the appropriate section in Chapter 8 may be found useful.

Neonatal problems are often divided into minor and major. It is essential that the frequency with which 'minor' problems are encountered does not lead to a lack of understanding by those involved in the care of mother and child. It must be remembered that what may be minor and commonplace with regard to the infant may be unfamiliar and a major anxiety to the parents.

Trauma

Moulding of the skull and *caput succedaneum* (oedema of the scalp) resolve over the first 48 to 72 hours. *Cephalohaematoma* is haemorrhage beneath the periosteum of the outer table, usually becoming obvious after 24 hours. Commonly, it occurs over the parietal bone and the swelling is limited by the periosteum at the suture lines. It is often bilateral. A hard ridge may become palpable giving the impression of a fracture or skull defect. The swelling will take about six weeks to resolve. It may calcify, in which case a bony prominence will be produced which will gradually be incorporated into the skull contour. *Subconjunctival haemorrhage* produces easily seen red patches over the sclera. These are relatively common and worth pointing out to mothers who may be unnecessarily concerned that the vision of the eye is affected. *Petechial* haemorrhage may be apparent in the skin of the face and neck. This may be associated with general discoloration of the face, making differential diagnosis from cyanosis difficult. The clue is the normal pink colour of the rest of the child. The cause is often the cord having been tightly round the neck, or less commonly, constriction by the cervix during delivery. More severe problems resulting from trauma include damage to the brachial plexus, the commonest form being *Erb's palsy* following damage to the lower roots; less commonly one encounters *Klumpke's palsy*. An infant who is shocked following delivery may have signs of respiratory distress, or be unduly irritable or pale; these signs will require close observation and paediatric referral.

The skin

Blemishes of the skin cause great concern to parents. *Erythema toxicum* is a self-limiting rash which may be mild or profuse and often fluctuating in degree during the first week. There are erythmatous areas, 5 to 10 mm in diameter with pin-point creamish yellow raised centres. *Milia* are tiny white papules usually over the face particularly around the nose. Erythema toxicum and milia are very common, harmless and not related to infection. *Fat necrosis* is an area of subcutaneous induration usually over a bony prominence and may be related to forceps application. It is seldom a problem and resolves spontaneously. It is important to identify areas of superficial infection of the skin. The staphylococcus is the usual organism but herpes infections may occur and also monilia, particularly of the oral mucosa, tongue and napkin area. Careful attention should be given to the umbilical area and the nails inspected for paronychia. Local treatment may be adequate for minor umbilical or skin infections. Bathing with Phisomed (3 per cent hexachlorophane) may be undertaken with care in full term infants; the preparation must be rinsed from the skin. Any evidence of spread, such as an extending red flare around the umbilicus and all but very minor paronychia, should be treated after bacteriological investigation with systemic antibiotics, flucloxacillin being the most appropriate until cultures are available. Monilia can be treated by local nystatin ointment or drops.

Enlargement of the breasts is common in neonates due to maternal hormones crossing the placental barrier. Though termed neonatal mastitis, it is not an infection and usually resolves spontaneously. Unnecessary handling of the swellings should be avoided. Occasionally, infection occurs in which case the lump will become red and tender. Early treatment with an antibiotic will often suffice but sometimes an abscess forms, and this will require surgical drainage.

Conjunctivitis

The eyes are a common site of infection in the newborn infant. Minor degrees of discharge occur in the first few days and this very often clears after bathing the eye with sterile water or saline. More profuse purulent discharge with swelling of the eye-lids requires local antibiotic treatment after taking bacteriological swabs; 0·5 per cent chloramphenicol or 10 per cent sulphacetamide drops may be used. It is important to instil the drops frequently, initially hourly or two-hourly during the first 12 to 24 hours, and then continue for four days three- to four-hourly, or for 48 hours after the disappearance of infection. This regime is the ideal which can be achieved in the maternity ward but more difficult for the single-handed mother at home. Profuse discharge occurring soon after birth raises the possibility of gonococcal infection. Bacteriological confirmation requires special attention as the gonococcus survives poorly on a swab or in the ordinary transport medium. It is occasionally necessary to use systemic antibiotics in the more severe infections.

Chlamydia trachomatis causes a mucopurulent conjunctivitis presenting towards the end of the first week and sometimes leading to conjunctival follicles. Identification of the organism requires scrapings from the conjunctiva as it does not survive outside cells. Treatment is usually satisfactorily achieved with 1 per cent chlortetracycline eye ointment, but systemic erythromycin may be required.

Vomiting

Many babies will have an occasional vomit as feeding is established during the first week. Most of these episodes will not be related to any specific cause, yet they must be considered seriously for two reasons. Firstly, vomiting is a common presentation of a variety of problems in the neonate and if symptomatic, the infant may become acutely ill in a matter of hours. Vomiting may be the first sign of otitis media, upper respiratory tract infection, renal infection, meningitis, septicaemia or disorder of the alimentary system. Secondly, assessment of the baby may allay parents' anxiety. There is need to be aware of other pointers that help in deciding the significance of the vomiting. Warning signs of ill-health include a change in the baby's behaviour, lethargy, irritability and reluctance to take feeds. Other signs suggesting intra-abdominal disease include bile-staining of the vomit, abdominal distension and abrupt change in stool frequency or quality. Signs and symptoms suggesting intestinal obstruction, though relatively uncommon, require urgent investigation. Prompt treatment has every chance of success, whereas delay rapidly leads to ischaemic changes in the bowel, severely compromising survival.

Haemorrhage

The commonest site of blood loss is that from the anal mucosa due to mucosal excoriation or a small fissure. Blood in the stool may be fresh or associated with diarrhoea and may indicate an enterocolitis. Melaena may occur due to prothrombin deficiency (see later). Purpura may also be a symptom of infection and requires urgent investigation and treatment.

Haemorrhagic disease of the newborn

This condition arises from a deficiency of vitamin K leading to decreased prothrombin activity.

The usual presentation is bleeding from the gastro-intestinal tract, causing haematemesis or melaena during the first week of life. It is unusual for the haemorrhage to be severe, but a more serious situation with tachycardia and shock may develop. The problem is more likely to arise in breast fed infants since breast milk contains only 1·5 mg vitamin K per 100 ml compared with 6 mg in cows' milk.

The diagnosis is confirmed by estimating the prothrombin time. Other haemorrhagic disorders need to be excluded such as thrombocytopoenia and disseminated intravascular coagulation, these both tending to be associated with petechiae and, on investigation, a low platelet count. Haemophilia has to be considered in a male infant, particularly with haemorrhage from the cord or following circumcision.

Treatment will involve transfusion if bleeding is severe but this situation is not common. Usually, there is a quick response to vitamin K, 1 mg konakion intravenously, returning the prothrombin time towards normal in four to six hours. It is important to consider the problem of intra-vascular coagulation associated with severe neonatal infection. It is also of importance to remember that the total blood

volume of a 3000 g baby is only 240 ml and so careful observation of a baby with a haemorrhagic tendency is essential.

Prophylaxis. Many paediatric units give prophylactic
intramuscular vitamin K (1 mg) to all newborn infants or
selectively to those following operative delivery. It should be
given to all neonates undergoing surgery, including circumcision. Vitamin K should be considered as additional treatment
for a breast fed infant receiving oral antibiotic.

Jaundice

This is one of the commonest problems of the newborn
period. A number of babies, otherwise well, become
jaundiced about the second or third day, this reaches a
maximum during the first week and then quickly fades. This
is termed *physiological jaundice*, an unsatisfactory label as not
all babies are affected, but it is a harmless occurrence.
Important causes of jaundice need to be differentiated.
Haemolytic disease of the newborn has to be considered
urgently if jaundice appears within the first 24 hours. Rhesus
incompatibility, now largely controlled by the administration
of anti-D serum to the mother post-partum, used to be the
major cause of haemolytic anaemia in this age group. Other
causes are now relatively more important and need to be
considered—ABO or rarer blood group (e.g., Kell, Duffy)
incompatibility, hereditary spherocytosis and red cell
enzyme deficiencies, such as glucose-6-phosphate dehydrogenase deficiency. Immediate investigation of suspected haemolytic anaemia is always necessary. Management
is easiest when the condition has been anticipated and cord
blood obtained for haemoglobin, blood film, Coomb's test,
blood group and bilirubin estimation. The bilirubin at birth
is relatively low as it has been cleared via the placenta, but it
may rise abruptly after delivery. Close monitoring is
necessary clinically and biochemically, until the rate of rise
has been established. A serum bilirubin level rising above 340
mmol per litre (20 mg per cent) carries a high risk of causing
irreversible brain damage (kernicterus). Treatment depends
on the severity of the disease, but an early onset of jaundice is
more safely managed in hospital where phototherapy and
exchange transfusion may be carried out promptly as
indicated by the course of the condition.

Differentiation of the other causes of jaundice depends on

observation and investigation. A sudden deepening of the jaundice, particularly if associated with a change in feeding or activity of the baby, should alert one to the possibility of infection. The spleen may become enlarged or a purpuric rash appear. The site of infection may be specific or septicaemic a particularly important cause to be excluded being a urinary tract infection. Infection in the neonatal period may be fulminating. It requires urgent assessment and investigation and should always be managed in hospital where close nursing supervision is available.

There are other less common but important causes of jaundice which need to be considered. Jaundice persisting into the second week, particularly if deepening, may be due to neonatal hepatitis or abnormality of the biliary system. The latter may be associated particularly with pale stools; this situation will need hospital investigation. Prolonged jaundice persisting into the third week may be an early sign of hypothyroidism and since prompt diagnosis carries an improved outlook with treatment an estimation of the thyroxine level should be made. Galactosaemia may present as persistent jaundice; this can be investigated simply by testing the urine for reducing sugar.

Finally, discussed last not due to its rarity but because of difficulty in diagnosis, is the jaundice which persists in the breast fed infant. This fades if the infant is taken off breast milk but this is an unsatisfactory and unnecessary manoeuvre to carry out in what is a harmless condition. Dispute continues as to the precise cause but a factor in breast milk has been shown to inhibit liver enzyme systems *in vitro*. The degree of jaundice is not severe (110 to 200 mmol per litre) and tends to fluctuate from day to day, continuing up to four to six weeks.

Respiratory distress

This is an important symptom of disease in the newborn. It is defined by the presence of two or more of the following criteria:

(i) a respiratory rate greater than 60/minute

(ii) sternal and/or intercostal recession

(iii) grunting respiration (a noise of variable intensity produced on expiration)

(iv) cyanosis

Table 3.4 Causes of respiratory distress in the neonate

a. *Respiratory*
   Airway obstruction, e.g. mucous plug.
   Pneumothorax. Pneumomediastinum.
   Transient tachypnoea of the newborn.
   Respiratory distress syndrome (hyaline membrane disease).
   Tracheo-oesophageal atresia or fistula.
   Diaphragmatic hernia.
   Pneumonia.

b. *Congenital heart disease*

c. *Cerebral irritation caused by*
   traumatic delivery
   intracranial haemorrhage
   drugs

d. *Hypoglycaemia*

Respiratory distress may arise from respiratory, cardiac or cerebral problems, see Table 3.4. It may be difficult to elucidate the cause and close supervision and investigation is necessary. The infant is best observed in an incubator; this may be possible in the maternity ward, but often the baby with these symptoms will need to be transferred to a special care baby unit.

The most frequent cause of respiratory distress is airway obstruction and this has been considered in Chapter 2. Its management depends on the degree of distress and cause of the signs. Observations of the chest wall to assess the pattern of respiration and degree of sternal and intercostal recession will show the degree of respiratory embarrassment. If the symptoms are mild and the baby pink and breathing air, one can afford to observe progress without active intervention. If the signs persist without improvement or if the baby's condition shows signs of deterioration, then further action and investigation is needed.

The infant who fails to establish regular respiration at birth or does not become pink, requires a chest X-ray to exclude abnormalities needing immediate attention, such as a pneumothorax, diaphragmatic hernia and major abnormalities of heart or lungs. It may be impossible to aspirate the stomach or the child may have persistent problems with upper airway secretions; this combination of difficulties should suggest oesophageal atresia. Prompt diagnosis and prevention of aspiration of secretions enhance the results of treatment. For more specific details of these problems, the reader is referred to paediatric texts. From the general practitioner's viewpoint, a quick decision is required. Survival of these babies without permanent brain damage from anoxia depends on the speed with which special care, with full facilities, is instituted. If the baby needs to be transferred, then close attention to *body temperature, blood sugar* level, and *respiratory effort and ventilation* is essential. Transfer to hospital of infants born at home who develop this complication should be by incubator; this needs to be mentioned when ordering the ambulance.

Congenital heart disease

Congenital heart disease may present in the immediate neonatal period, during the first week of life or later in the first year. The earlier the infant develops symptoms from congenital heart defects, the more likely is the lesion to be complicated. Though some problems still carry a high mortality, continuous advances in paediatric surgery have increased both survival and quality of life in some of these conditions. Cyanotic heart disease requires urgent referral for assessment to a specialised centre. Some problems, though rare, such as severe pulmonary stenosis present early with cyanosis, and untreated, may soon be lethal. Prompt recognition and treatment gives the child a good chance of a normal life. Progress in techniques has also led to an improved survival and quality of life for the commonest cause of cyanotic heart disease in the neonatal period, that of transposition of the great arteries. It will though rarely be encountered by an individual practitioner, the incidence being about one in 4500 births. The most important point to make is that the earlier these babies are referred to a cardiac centre, the better the chance of survival. The abnormal circulation leads to cyanosis, the hypoxia of the tissues to an acidosis, the combination of which is soon toxic to the myocardium.

Acyanotic heart disease may present during the first 10 days of life, either as a murmur which may be heard on routine examination, or by the onset of heart failure. The symptoms will be similar to those described under the appropriate section in Chapter 6. A particular clue in the newborn period may be in the weight chart; there may be a lack of the usual initial weight drop or a sudden unusual increase in weight due to fluid retention.

Low birth weight infants

It is essential that all infants of low birth weight and born preterm should be delivered where there are adequate facilities for resuscitation and subsequent care of infants. This can only be in hospital. Forty per cent of all childhood deaths occur in the first week of life, 25 per cent of all childhood deaths occur in the first 24 hours of life and nearly three-quarters of all neonatal deaths (deaths 0 to 28 days) occur amongst low birth weight infants.

The early definition (International Committee, Geneva 1937) of small babies based on birth weight alone does not adequately distinguish between two important groups of babies; those who have grown adequately during intra-uterine life, and those who have achieved poor growth. The latest terminology aims to differentiate the infants who are born too soon from those born too small. The term *low birth weight* corresponds to the earlier definition of premature, that is, a baby weighing 2·5 kg or less at birth. It is then necessary to relate the birth weight to the length of gestation. Gestation is defined as *preterm* (less than 37 weeks from the last menstrual period), *term* (37 to 42 weeks) and *post-term*. Intra-uterine growth charts are available so that one can assess whether a baby is of normal weight for the gestational age. Infants whose birth weights are below the 10th centile for their gestational age can thus be identified. These are 'too small', described as *small-for-dates* or *dysmature*. A dysmature infant may be born pre- or post-term or at term. This definition of dysmaturity will, however, include some normal babies, those that make up the lower 10 per cent of normal growth variation. It is also important to relate growth standards to the baby's particular ethnic group.

Preterm and low birth weight babies will, at times, need to be nursed at least during the early neonatal period in a special care baby unit. Unnecessary separation of mother and child should be avoided and it is important to ensure that the need for *general* care does not lead unnecessarily to transfer of the baby to a special unit. Where separation of the baby from the mother has to occur, it is vital to minimise its effects. The mother must be given details of progress particularly as she may less easily be able to visit her child immediately. It is also during the period following the separation that those caring for the family need to be able to understand and answer the queries which may arise concerning the child's management.

At birth, the preterm infant can usually be identified by external signs. Neurological assessment of gestational age immediately after birth can be used when necessary in the well baby to aid identification. The Dubowitz assessment scoring system is a practical and useful method of establishing maturity (see Ch. 2).

The normal low birth weight baby

Newborn babies have a large surface area compared with their body weight and all are therefore prone to hypothermia. The preterm infant is at greatest risk. A warm environment is required at birth and this must be readily available. Observation is most easily accomplished by nursing the child in an incubator. The normal preterm infant has an irregular pattern of respiration and may have short episodes of apnoea. These spells may be self-limiting but if longer than 20 to 30 seconds, may lead to secondary problems. If they are noted early, external stimulation of the baby usually results in the re-establishment of respiration. Use of an apnoea mattress, with an alarm system enables respiratory arrest to be detected promptly.

Feeding

This plays a very important part in the management and survival of preterm infants. If the sucking reflex is absent or the infant ill, then tube feeding will be required. This requires specifically trained nurses. In addition to immaturity of sucking, there may be incoordination of swallowing and poorly developed pharyngeal reflexes, leading to increased risk of aspiration of gastric contents. Initially, attention is needed to avoid hypoglycaemia and dextrose feeds may be tolerated more easily at the start. However, full nutrition is important to ensure optimum brain growth. Milk feeds, though less perfectly adapted to physiological needs than nutrition obtained via the placenta, are adequate and well tolerated in the majority of preterm infants. Parenteral nutrition only becomes vital in the very low birth weight infant (<1000 g) and is as yet available only in specialist centres as there are considerable technical and biological problems associated with the technique. If the mother aims to breast feed then she is encouraged to express her milk until the baby is mature enough to take from the breast. Her milk may be then given to the infant via a nasogastric tube. The volume of feed is gradually increased over the first two weeks of life when the infant should be receiving about 200 ml/kg/day.

PROBLEMS ARISING IN THE LOW BIRTH WEIGHT INFANT

The most frequent problem is respiratory distress which is the leading cause of death in this age group; the differential diagnosis has already been discussed (p 58).

Respiratory distress syndrome

This is still the single most important cause of death in preterm infants. The post mortem appearance of the lungs gives rise to the synonym *hyaline membrane disease*. The condition. is due to lack of surfactant, a phospho-lipid produced by alveolar cells which is a prerequisite for the normal functioning of the lungs. Lungs lacking surfactant do not remain partially inflated at the end of expiration; this leads to *decreased* compliance of the lung and the need for an *increased* respiratory effort by the infant which gives rise to the clinical picture.

The onset of symptoms—raised respiratory rates, grunting and recession of the chest wall—occurs within 12 hours of birth. The natural history of the illness is one of gradual increasing severity; in those recovering, the illness reaches a plateau during the first 48 to 72 hours and then the symptoms gradually improve. Treatment consists of attention to hydration, nutrition, warmth and respiratory effort. The infants often require intravenous feeding; in the short term, this is dextrose. They also require continuous monitoring of blood gases and acid-base balance. This may involve catheterisation of the umbilical vessels, though the use of peripheral vessels may be possible. The baby may need to be nursed in an increased concentration of oxygen, which is likely to involve the use of a perspex head box within the incubator and facilities to monitor the oxygen concentration. The more severely affected baby may require continuous positive airway pressure. There are various techniques used, the original method via a special head box (Gregory et al, 1971) has generally been replaced by the use of a special face mask or nasal speculae. The picture for the parents is complicated and frightening. Explanation of the disease and treatment should be discussed with them, but ability to grasp what is being said is likely to be limited, because of their anxiety. As the lungs recover, the support needed by the baby is gradually withdrawn and by the end of the first week, the baby is usually recovering and starting to tolerate oral feeding. The lungs, once the disease is over, are *normal* and this needs to be stressed to the parents. Complications of the condition are not discussed here; this, and more detailed descriptions, can be found by reading further texts (Davies, 1976).

Much can be done to prevent mortality and morbidity from this condition by attention to the immediate newborn period in those infants at risk. Delivery of the preterm infant in hospital where monitoring of labour is available and prompt resuscitation of the child obtainable with avoidance of the hazards of hypothermia, hypoxia and hypoglycaemia is of paramount importance. Antenatal precautions are also of value. Measurement of the lecithin-sphingomyelin ratio (see Ch. 2) will help in preventing the delivery of a child with immature lungs. The giving of betamethazone to the mother from 48 hours prior to delivery is probably also of benefit. The rationale of this treatment (which is still under assessment) is that steroids induce activity of the enzyme system in the alveolar cells responsible for surfactant production. The current impression is that administration of betamethazone in suitable cases *does* reduce the incidence of the respiratory distress syndrome.

Intracranial haemorrhage

The low birth weight infant has an increased risk of subdural, intraventricular and intracerebral haemorrhage. The easily malleable skull bones need protection at birth and the control of delivery of the head is even more important in this group of infants than the full term child and the habitual prophylactic use of forceps is wise. There is also evidence that the preterm breech when delivered by caesarean section has improved survival and decreased morbidity (Ingemarsson et al, 1978). Intracranial haemorrhage may also complicate other neonatal problems, particularly the respiratory distress syndrome.

Infection

Immaturity of the immune system leads to an increased susceptibility of the preterm infant to infection. Care must be taken to prevent cross infection and this may be more easily achieved in special care units. However, it is evident that absolute isolation of the preterm infant is neither necessary on a routine basis nor is the least desirable. It is important for parents and siblings to be able to visit and be involved as closely as possible with the care of the preterm child. Attention to the general code of hygiene and scrupulous attention to hand washing is important to minimise cross infection.

The diagnosis of infection depends on a high index of suspicion and alertness. There is an absence of localising signs and the progression of the illness may be rapid. Prompt investigation will include blood culture, lumbar puncture and examination of the urine. Treatment may require to be started before results of investigations are known. Warning signs include a change in the activity of the baby, lethargy, listlessness, irritability, poor feeding, pallor, suddenly increasing jaundice, apnoea episodes and convulsions. Urgent action is always required when these signs appear.

Hypoglycaemia

This is a hazard of all small and ill babies. It is the major hazard of the dysmature infant and one of the main reasons for identifying this group from the point of view of management. The other group at risk of developing hypoglycaemia are babies of diabetic mothers. In view of the mother's problem these will certainly be born in hospital. Management is essentially a specialised undertaking but a general practitioner should be aware of the principles, if only to assist his support of the parents. The raised maternal blood sugar leads to hypertrophy of the baby's islets of Langerhans and excess insulin secretion. Affected infants may become severely hypoglycaemic within an hour of birth. The signs of hypoglycaemia are lethargy, apnoeic episodes, jitteriness and convulsions. Preventive care is important. This susceptible group of babies must be observed closely and the blood sugar regularly monitored using dextrostix test strips. Feeding should be started within an hour of birth. The first feed may be dextrose but as soon as possible the infant should be given milk. If the blood sugar falls below the normal range, which in the neonate is 1·15 mmol per litre (20 mg per cent) extra sugar in the form of one to two grams of 25 per cent dextrose should be given as an addition to the next feed and the blood sugar again checked. Occasionally, it is necessary to give an intravenous infusion of dextrose. If the baby develops symptoms, then treatment is more urgent and intravenous glucose will be needed. It is important not to give an excessive load of glucose as this induces reactive hypoglycaemia and makes subsequent management more difficult. This must always be kept in mind even with oral feeding.

The small-for-dates, dysmature infant may also develop hypoglycaemia soon after birth, and the liability to do so remains for the first 72 hours of life. Monitoring these babies should therefore continue throughout this period but if progress is normal and there are no abnormal signs, the dextrostix estimation need only be carried out six to eight hourly after the first 12 hours. Initially, hourly or two-hourly monitoring should be the routine. Hypothermia makes the development of hypoglycaemia more likely, so regulation of the baby's environmental temperature is essential. Brain function is dependent on an adequate supply of glucose and so the prevention of hypoglycaemia can be a major factor in preventing neurological handicap.

The dysmature infant (small-for-dates)

The causes of dysmaturity and problems of intra-uterine growth are not fully understood. It is likely that placental dysfunction plays a part and this can be monitored to a degree during pregnancy as can the rate of fetal growth (see Ch. 2).

These infants are particularly vulnerable during labour. The placental function may adequately support the fetus until uterine contractions and finally placental separation occur when the metabolic reserves of the infant may become insufficient. The availability of paediatric support may then be vital; these are the babies which may be born normally but require resuscitation. They will also need to be recognised immediately so that particular observation is made of their progress with special attention to the hazard of hypoglycaemia. It may, of course, be much less easy to anticipate the birth of this group of babies—the problem occurring unexpectedly as it is not associated with any particular gestational age but often arises with the term or post-term infant.

The problems that arise in this group of infants overlap those already discussed. Hypothermia and hypoglycaemia are the most important hazards of the dysmature infant.

Prognosis of low birth weight infants

Increased attention to the above factors has led to an increased survival of low birth weight babies over the past two decades (Stewart, 1977). Both the chance of survival and the quality of survival depend on maintaining and striving to improve on the present standards of care. The required advances may be particularly related to that of nutrition outside the uterus, especially for the very low birth weight baby. The improvements in prognosis for these smaller babies (less than 1500 g) may be less clear cut at present (Jones et al, 1979).

There is an increased liability of handicap in these infants overall and good primary care follow-up is important to detect problems early and once identified, to ensure the appropriate help is given to the child and parents. This vigilance continues long past the first year of life. The more obvious handicap may very well be identified, but the less obvious sequelae, particularly those affecting learning and co-ordination, will only be identified by continued surveillance not only during infancy but right through to the school years.

Parent-infant relationships

Already, mention has been made of the parent-infant relationship and of the importance of minimising the effect of separation of the mother from her new born infant.

It is only in the last 15 years that attention has been focused on these early hours and days of attachment of the baby to its mother and, equally important, the mother to her child. In

1965 the first reports were published about the long term effects of disruption of early social relationships in animals. Many experiments have since been carried out which have shown what happens if the mammal concerned (usually a rhesus monkey) is removed from its parent at birth (Harlow et al, 1965, 1969).

There is an almost universal failure to 'mother' when these deprived monkeys themselves become mothers, as well as aberrant and disordered behaviour in their infancy. Although these particular experiments were dramatic in their results, it would be foolish to extrapolate directly research carried out on other mammalian species to human beings.

Nevertheless, although one cannot ask monkeys, for instance, how they feel, it is apparent that in terms of observed behaviour they enjoy watching their babies moving (Hinde & Simpson, 1973). Therefore, it is probably valid to argue that the disruption in the mother and infant monkey's relationship in the early days, does have a lasting effect. It now appears that a disruption like early separation has an effect on human parent-infant interaction too (Kennell et al, 1975).

Many reports of the ill effects of separation (for what are often sound medical reasons) are now available. Disproportionate rates of rejection and non-accidental injury have been found in those babies whose early days are characterised by enforced separation. The very premature baby nursed for many weeks in an incubator whom the mother and father can view only through the transparent sides, and only then if both parents are wearing masks, is often rejected. Supreme efforts of nursing and medical staff are set at nought by the attitudes of what seem to be ungrateful parents.

The experience at one hospital where 160 babies of less than 1500 g birth weight, who survived after perinatal intensive care, and who have been followed for many years, has shown the benefits of attempting to minimise maternal separation (Blake et al, 1975). Continuous improvement in management of the unit over several years, which allowed greater maternal (and paternal) contact, has reduced markedly the rejection rate of these babies. Lynch (1975) showed that 40 per cent of an abused group of children had been reared in special care baby units not practising such techniques. Blake and his co-workers have also shown clearly the evolving pattern of maternal behaviour when these very small babies are first discharged from such a unit. The 'honeymoon phase' of euphoria which lasts for the first one to three weeks, with only minor apprehensions about ability to cope, is followed by a 'phase of exhaustion'. The mother finds it increasingly difficult to cope. She rings the unit frequently for help and often runs into feeding difficulties, reverting for instance, to three-hourly feeding day and night, so exhausting herself, and in turn becoming increasingly inefficient. Suddenly, when the baby's gestational age is sufficiently advanced for social smiling to begin, troubles vanish and the mother, often for the first time, can talk about the harrowing experience she has endured, often becoming very tearful and emotional (Kaplan & Mason, 1960).

It is now established, therefore, that the frightening experience of giving birth to a very small preterm baby can cause such a grave disturbance in the mother that only a carefully planned and executed programme of support to the developing parent-infant axis can prevent rejection. It is not difficult to see the relevance of this work to the baby normally delivered in the average maternity unit in this country. So often, good intentions are overcome by understaffing which can provoke midwives to take the line of least resistance and seize control just when a mother and baby are beginning to establish a relationship. The mother is thus subjected to overwhelming and sometimes frighteningly strong emotions, so reassurance and sedation is offered. Breast feeding *is* more work, so sometimes discouraged by the staff; allowing the mother to keep her baby alongside her bed sometimes does wake other mothers, so the baby is moved out at night into nurseries. Picking up, the universal urge of all mothers, is countered with 'Don't, you'll spoil him'. A mother's obvious delight in her new baby's social smile is rudely destroyed when the smiles are deemed 'wind' by the world at large. It is not unknown for the mother who wants to put her baby to the breast immediately after birth to be considered an oddity by inexperienced helpers.

Yet simple steps can be taken to reorganise a unit to encourage the effective bonding of baby to mother. Allowing a mother to handle her baby immediately after delivery and to put the baby to the breast is a very positive distraction as the perineum is being sutured.

The alert neonate with wide open eyes can be allowed to see

its mother's face clearly if mother is told that her baby will focus clearly on her face from 20–30 cm away, and will be seen to respond. At the simplest level, the mother so obviously *enjoys* her new born baby more if she knows he sees, hears and smiles, and it is hard to believe that what is so obviously *mutual* enjoyment does not materially and permanently affect the quality of the infant-mother relationship. Long term studies of mothers and their babies who have been allowed specially extended time with each other immediately after delivery demonstrate the lasting effect of this experience.

Having made these points, it is important that the idea of human bonding in this sensitive period is not overplayed for there are certainly many babies, mothers and fathers who can withstand, unscathed, considerable lengths of separation neonatally (Kennell et al, 1975).

Nevertheless, it is an important consideration, and to a large extent separation *is* preventable in terms of maternity unit management. Furthermore it would be unwise in the extreme not to be aware of the much greater risk of rejection that exists where separation is unpreventable. Whatever the potential problems are, it is incumbent on those caring for the mother and her new born baby (midwife, health visitor, general practitioner, obstetrician and paediatrician), to pay the fullest attention to this aspect of a new born child's life.

Until the necessary changes have been made in the management of maternity units to take account of the needs of the baby and its mother, intervention by the general practitioner, health visitor and midwife is only possible when the pair are discharged from hospital. The mother returning home with her new baby, if a 48-hour or 'early' discharge policy is practised by the hospital, is normally routinely visited by the midwife until the tenth day when the health visitor visits for the first time.

The mother's vulnerability is extreme. She has to cope with feeding problems, a sore perineum and a dramatically altered sleep pattern. She may worry unduly. In many cases the household will not yet have recovered from antenatal nestbuilding activities. The dust, the lack of comfort, and absent hot water supply resulting from do-it-yourself husbands (and wives) not finishing home improvements in time, also causes stresses usually unappreciated by the general practitioner if he does not routinely visit all mothers and babies discharged from hospital. A survey carried out by one of the authors in 1972 showed that one mother and baby in eight returned to a home with unfinished building activity going on, causing severe disruption.

The midwife, already involved with her specific aims and objectives, visits to ensure that the mother's postnatal condition evolves normally and that feeding, whether breast or bottle, is monitored efficiently. In addition, she will have heard a little about the mother's hospital experience and will probably have been drawn into explanations of what went on, but what happens when the doctor calls for the first time to 'examine' the baby can either be a flat clinically oriented examination of the new born baby, confirming normality, or an experience that will lastingly alter the mother's perceptions of her doctor and his interest in her and her baby.

We have found that even with an efficient antenatal education programme and informed and interested health visitors, only 10 per cent of mothers believe that their 7 to 10 day old babies see, hear and smile at them. The effect of not knowing must be important. All too often, these mothers have experienced similar ignorance in their own upbringing, which preconditions their attitudes to their babies. When seen for the first time in the home, young mothers with this unfortunate background are already tending to show greater anxiety than other mothers.

The first full neonatal examination at home

A carefully carried out examination of the baby *in front* of the mother is the best way to alleviate so many of her anxieties. (A substantial minority of mothers do not see a doctor in hospital examine their babies before discharge, for a variety of reasons.)

Only practice can enable the doctor to carry out a relatively noise-free examination of a 7 to 10 day old baby. It all looks so simple at first, particularly when watching an expert. It is worth trying hard to keep the baby at a wide-awake, alert level of arousal. Any shift of arousal towards tears needs to be quickly checked and when the examination is successfully concluded, it should attest to 'the touch of the expert'. Agreed that there is a touch of the showman in some of the paediatric tyros at work today, the mother *is* very sensitive to the skill of a doctor examining her baby, rating gentleness and appreciation of *her* baby first on her list of priorities.

It is impossible to be definitive about how to examine a small baby of this age. There are many manuals and descriptions available, only Brazelton's (1973) however, stresses the effect such an examination has on the *mother*. With a well performed examination, the doctor has a friend for life. No examination or one performed with little explanation and on a crying baby, leaves the mother anxious and unimpressed.

Case history

A primigravid mother was discharged on the seventh day from a hospital in another part of the country. Before discharge, she was told by a doctor that her baby 'might have a congenital disease of the lungs' (cystic fibrosis) 'as a result of a test' (meconium). She did not see the doctor examine her baby but was merely told 'be careful'. On return home she was terrified. The health visitor called once but the mother couldn't bring herself to discuss the problem. Not knowing of the hospital's provisional diagnosis, the health visitor didn't mention the subject either. The family doctor did not call. The mother only handled her baby to feed and change it and left the baby quite alone, allowing no-one near it 'for fear of giving it an infection'. A return visit to the hospital a month later for a further test was unfortunate because the 'salt' test gave an equivocal result, so she was again sent home 'to be careful'.

Not until the third visit after three months did the 'salt' test successfully establish the absence of cystic fibrosis. The mother was told '*everything is all right, there is now no need to be careful*'.

When the baby was 14 months old he was registered, with the rest of the family, on my list. Eleven consultations in as many weeks had already persuaded me to label the mother as anxiety prone and it was only when I said to the mother 'Tell me, why do you worry so much about your son?' that I extracted the truth. By this time, however, the baby was quite disturbed. He avoided eye contact, had extreme separation anxiety, not allowing his mother out of his sight for more than a few seconds, and slept little. Developmental delay, although mild, was manifest. The mother was patently over-protective and defensive. A long discussion of the whole lamentable episode with a lot of tears shed has gone a long way to heal the mother, and her son is improving too. The creation of anxiety by inadequate explanation and lack of awareness nearly permanently spoilt this mother's enjoyment of her child and had nearly as disastrous an effect on the baby.

The first principles of successful examination depend on the establishment of a set routine of examination, so that nothing is missed. The patient's home may not, at first sight, be the best place to conduct an examination, but a changing mattress on the kitchen table or even on the sofa in the living room usually provides a warm well-lit environment. It is best to bring babies down from bedrooms, as a cot makes examination impossible, as does an impossibly soft double bed taking up nearly all the space in a crowded bedroom. The temperature of the kitchen is usually a lot higher than a bedroom on a cold winter's day. Warmth, in fact, is the key to success, the doctor's hands and the room temperature making all the difference between success and failure.

The following is an account of how the author* demonstrates to every mother in his practice, her baby's abilities to see, hear and (usually) smile. There are many differing techniques to how to do this and this method is not suggested as definitive. It nevertheless works.

If necessary, fan heaters, gas or paraffin heaters, can be turned up to provide more warmth. With the changing mattress on a flat surface covered by a towel or nappy, the actual examination can begin. Ensure that the mother is sitting down and able to see what you are doing. Whilst talking, begin by picking up the baby and assessing its wakefulness. A deeply asleep baby will need to be progressively undressed to be wakened, whilst a wide-awake one can be left fully dressed at this stage. Start by asking how the mother is getting on with her new baby. 'What sort of person is he?' (sleepy, irritable, cries all the time, good, got a temper); then ask the mother if she thinks her baby can see, hear or smile. Ten per cent of primiparous mothers in my practice believe babies can see, hear and smile ('I know it's not wind, doctor'). Fifty per cent believe their babies can see and hear but deny the smile. Thirty per cent believe that they see or hear, and 10 per cent deny all three. When mother has answered, proceed to demonstrate that the baby can see, hear and smile in response to a 'talking head'.

It is important to hold the baby upright and even the most deeply asleep rarely fails to open his eyes and express interest in a 'talking head' 8 to 10 inches from his face. Talk in a calm conversational voice looking straight at the baby.. The fleeting changes of expression, raised eyebrows, wrinkled forehead, never fail to convince the mother that her baby sees *and* hears even if she previously believed the contrary (see Fig. 3.1).

Once attention is held, it is surprising how long the baby sustains it. The on-off-on eye movements are very noticeable

* Dr G. Curtis Jenkins.

Fig. 3.1   Five-day-old baby smiling *en face*

as the baby scans the whole presented face, looking intently at the face, then looking away. The rhythm continues and not infrequently the baby smiles and actually vocalises, occasionally becoming overwhelmed by the stimulation, and crying. Calming, by holding the baby's face close to one's own and talking in a softer and softer voice almost always will stop the crying, as it always does in the physical part of the examination which follows.

A further, even more impressive, demonstration of the baby's abilities can also be made to the mother. Gaze avoidance (violation), the phenomenon whereby babies cry if interaction ceases between them and an observer *en face* has been well described in older babies (Brazelton et al, 1975).

However, new born babies usually demonstrate the phenomenon clearly and mothers are quick to draw the correct conclusions. From tape recording: (Doctor *en face* with baby, see Figure 3.2).

> *Doctor*: Look, he's really looking at me and enjoying what's going on; as long as I go on talking, he'll go on looking. Are you convinced now he sees and hears?

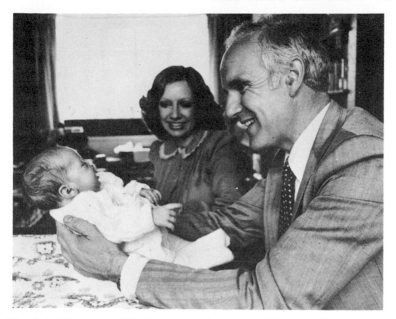

Fig. 3.2   Five-day-old baby copying 'open mouth' of examiner

Mother: Oh yes. Yes, it's marvellous, look at him, look at
him.
Doctor: I want to show you something else now. While I
talk to him he's content to look at me, pull faces and
so on, but watch what happens if I stop talking.
When I stop, don't say anything yourself—just
watch to see what happens.
(Doctor stops talking and waits)

The baby at first quietens and on-off rhythm ceases. The
baby then moves hands and head and often wrinkles his brow
and the on-off rhythm restarts. The baby becomes disturbed
by the silence. Some babies even give a nervous smile. After
about 60–90 seconds, the baby after longer and longer periods
of looking away, turns his head away from the *en face* observer
and stays immovable. This is *violation* (see Figs 3.3, 3.4).

Attempts to attract the baby to face forward by talking
usually fail and only by presenting a 'talking head' directly *en
face* to the baby can attention be regained.

The mother is usually profoundly impressed by this
demonstration and appreciates the implications, namely that

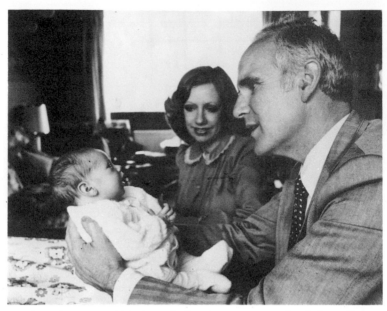

Fig. 3.3   Five-day-old baby quiet but intent on examiner's face after examiner has stopped talking

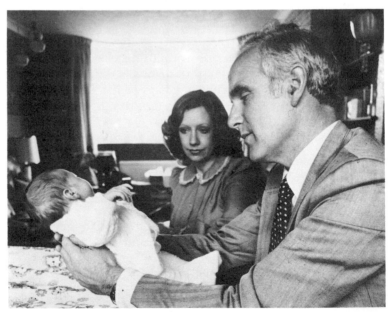

Fig. 3.4   Five-day-old baby after 60 seconds of silence; turns away from examiner's face, arches back and stays quiet and immovable demonstrating gaze avoidance

talking is of great importance when handling a new born baby and that the baby has skills and abilities she never realised existed.

Once this initial part of the examination has been completed, it is important to carry out a complete physical examination, see Chapter 2.

It may seem to be unnecessary but this re-examination often reveals information that allows the doctor to both reassure the mother of her baby's normality, and occasionally to detect abnormality.

Already a good impression will have been gained of the baby's general state. Is he calm and relaxed, self quietening when startled, or is he fractious, irritable and difficult to quieten. Is the muscle tone strong or is the baby floppy when held. All these variations and others can help the doctor advise the mother on management. A particularly fractious, miserable baby needs a different technique from the calm, relaxed baby and it is worth noting these differences as they materially affect the way the mother copes.

It is my custom to write, as suggested by Brazelton (1973) a brief account of the baby in general terms: 'a descriptive paragraph'.

Seven day old boy seen at home. 10.5.78

A well built and proportioned active, responsive boy. Alerted quickly *en face* and smiled and vocalised within a few seconds. He self quietened by sucking on his hand when overstimulated. His moro reflex had already changed to 'hands up'.

Violation was almost impossible to achieve as he still attempted to coax a response from me after two and a half minutes. Turned quickly to the spoken voice. This baby is developmentally mature. The mother comments 'He's so easy to manage, he quietens the moment I pick him up'.

Once the examination is complete, I collect the baby's medical registration card and remind the mother to attend her own doctor for her postnatal examination. I also arrange my next meeting with the mother and baby at my paediatric clinic. Seventy per cent per annum do not need to be seen routinely until seven months. Thirty per cent need a greater frequency of surveillance, dependent on environment or problems associated with mother or child.

REFERENCES

Blake A, Stewart A, Turcan D 1975 Parents of babies of very low birth weights. In: Parent infant interaction. CIBA Foundation Symposium 33 (New Series) Elsevier, Amsterdam

Brazelton T B 1973 Neonatal behavioural assessment scale. Clinics in developmental medicine 50. Heinneman, London

Brazelton T B, Tronik E, Adamson L, Als H, Wise S 1975 Early mother-infant reciprocity. In: Parent infant interaction. CIBA Symposium 33 (New Series) Elsevier, Amsterdam

Cruse P, Yudkin P, Baum J D 1978 Establishing demand feeding in hospital. Archives of Disease in Childhood 53:76–78

Davies P A 1976 Infants of very low birth weight. In: Hull D (ed) Recent advances in paediatrics, no 5. Churchill Livingstone, Edinburgh, ch 4

Gregory G A, Kitterman J A, Phibbs R H, Tooley W H, Hamilton W K 1971 Treatment of the idiopathic respiratory distress syndrome with continuous positive airway pressure. New England Journal of Medicine 284:1333–1340

Gunther M (1973) Infant feeding. Penguin Books, Harmondsworth.

Harlow H F, Harlow M K 1965 The affectional systems in behaviour of non-human primates. Schrier A M, Harlow H F, Stollnitz F (ed) Academic Press, London, vol 2

Harlow H F, Harlow M K 1969 Effects of various mother/infant relationships on Rhesus monkey behaviour. In: Determinants of infant behaviour. Foss B M (ed). Methuen, London, vol 4

Hey E N, Katz G, O'Connell B 1970 The total thermal insulation of the newborn baby. Journal of Physiology 207:683–698

Hey E N 1971 The care of babies in incubators. In: Gairdner D, Hull D (eds) Recent advances in paediatrics, 4th edn. Churchill Livingstone, Edinburgh, ch 6

Hinde R A, Simpson M J A 1973 Qualities of mother infant relationships in monkeys. In: Parent infant interaction. CIBA Foundation Symposium 33 (New Series) Elsevier, Amsterdam

Hull D 1966 The structure and function of brown adipose tissue. British Medical Bulletin 22:92–96

Ingemarsson I, Westgren M, Svenningsen N W 1978 Long-term follow up of preterm infants in breech presentation delivered by caesarean section. Lancet 2:172–175

Jones R A K, Cummins M, Davies P A 1979 Infants of very low birth weight. A 15 year analysis. Lancet 2:1332–1335

Kaplan D M, Mason E A 1960 Maternal reactions to premature birth viewed as an acute emotional disorder. American Journal of Orthopsychiatry 30: 539–552

Kennell J H, Trause M A, Klaus M H 1975 Evidence for a sensitive period in the human mother. In: Parent infant interaction. CIBA Foundation Symposium 33 (New Series) Elsevier, Amsterdam

Lewis P 1978 Drugs in breast milk. Journal of Maternal and Child Health 3:128–132

Lynch M A 1975 Ill health and child abuse. Lancet 2:317–319

Matthew D J, Taylor B, Norman A P, Turner M W, Soothill J F 1977
  Prevention of eczema. Lancet 1:321–324
Smales O R C, Kime R 1978 Thermoregulation in babies immediately
  after birth. Archives of Disease in Childhood 53:58–61
Stewart A L 1977 The survival of low birth weight infants. British
  Journal of Hospital Medicine 18:182–190

4.

The first seven months

From the tenth day to the seventh month

By the tenth day most babies are home and mother and child are well on the way to establishing the bond that usually binds child to mother for life. The formal responsibilities of the midwife have normally ended although occasionally she will continue to visit to supervise a slowly healing perineum, cracked nipples or delayed involution of the uterus.

The health visitor should have received notification from the Community Health Services of the mother and child's discharge from hospital, and on or about the tenth day, will make her first visit. Normally, she will have already met the mother at the general practitioner's antenatal clinic and at mothercraft and relaxation classes she often runs, so she will be welcomed by the mother as an old friend. When hospital obstetric departments insist on attendance at their antenatal clinics throughout pregnancy, and when they run relaxation and mothercraft classes without involving the patient's own health visitor, they inhibit the growth of this relationship. Zander et al (1978) have shown that even in inner city areas with high mobility and social classes IV and V families, general practitioners, working closely with health visitors and midwives, can run effective antenatal surveillance programmes with high attendance rates and at the same time, inevitably greatly enhance the quality of the health visitor's relationship in the postnatal period with the mother and baby.

The attachment of health visitors to general practice is, of course, a recent phenomenon. Formally declared national policy in 1968, the rapid spread of attachment has nearly covered the country; over 90 per cent of all health visitors are now formally attached. Alas, as with every policy decision, it is not a uniformly satisfactory arrangement. In some parts of the country, attachment to general practice has led to a marked decline in the health visitor's effectiveness—usually in those areas where her services are most required. As has already been mentioned the attachment of one health visitor to sometimes as many as six or seven elderly, single-handed, general practitioners in run-down inner city areas, ensures the almost inevitable inefficiency and ineffectiveness of her role in attempting to care for the families with young babies on each doctor's list. The one in seven children not registered with a doctor are not even touched (Graham, 1977). It is not surprising that in these areas, health visitors are clamouring to be given back their geographical 'parish' responsibilities, working from the Community Health Service's child health clinics. Because of the problem of multiple attachment and because the time spent with families and children by the average health visitor has fallen from 90 per cent of her total work time in 1963 to less than 60 per cent in 1972, many feel that her role needs to be redefined and her workstyle redesigned to make her more effective (Court, 1976). The D.H.S.S. guidelines for the future of child care services make specific recommendations to allow this to happen (D.H.S.S., 1978). However, where she is working as part of a primary care team in a group practice, closely co-operating with general practitioners and practice midwives, her job is a great deal easier and her work is almost certain to be more effective.

The first visit on the tenth day is an important one. The mother will want to discuss a whole range of topics—what happened in hospital, what her labour was like, what the doctor in hospital said about her and her baby. She will seek interpretation of the occasionally conflicting advice given by the hospital medical and nursing staff about feeding and management. A long period of discussion may be required before the mother is fully satisfied. By the way this first meeting goes, the health visitor decides on how much further support the mother is going to require. She will know already the family's financial situation, and the likely role of father in helping in these early days. She will have a shrewd idea already of the mother's ability to cope (often more realistic than the doctor's) and will plan her visiting accordingly.

It is important she makes herself available at all times (at least in the daytime, five days weekly) so that the mother knows she can reach her with those so-called panic calls about blue hands, vomiting, feeds and inconsolable crying that so trouble mothers and their attendants. I believe that in large practices, where there are three or four health visitors, a 24-hour on call rota like that run by practice nurses should be organised. This would certainly fill a need and allow mothers to seek advice from professionals without the fear of 'worrying the doctor' that so often inhibits their seeking of help. In some practices, health visitors have already discarded the tenth day custom and with sensible co-operation from the midwife, have visited on the mother's first or second day home. This, I believe, is a good practice especially where hospital obstetric units have a routine 48-hour discharge policy.

Some general practitioners who make it their business to visit mothers and babies when first discharged, tend to focus their attention on the mother and her uterus rather than on the carefully wrapped up baby in the crib at the foot of the bed. Yet, if done well, a carefully performed examination of the baby combined with a demonstration of the baby's abilities will show the mother the doctor's interest in her and her baby, confirm his expertise, and demonstrate his confidence in handling a small and seemingly fragile baby (Ch. 3).

By effective co-operation and co-ordination, the health visitor and general practitioner can really enhance each other's role *vis-a-vis* the family. Common policies on advice about feeding, what to put on baby's bottom and how to manage small babies generally, demonstrate to the mother the team's worth and encourage her to draw on its expertise and to ask for help and advice sensibly and intelligently, and before worries have become problems (which are usually less easy to cope with). Fractious, non-sleeping, colicky, vomiting babies can try the patience of the most capable mother, and support which includes practical help and sound advice is essential. Sometimes, where there is little contact between health visitor and doctor, conflicting and therefore damaging advice tends to be given; even worse, a collusion of anonymity can occur, with each thinking the other is dealing with the problem (Balint, 1973). Adequate and continuing communication, daily is not too often, can prevent situations like this occurring.

Depression, a frequent problem in mothers with young babies, tends to be seen by the health visitor as a natural occurrence needing little more than support until it lifts. The doctor, on the other hand, may see it as a medical problem requiring drugs to help it go away. Yet Dalton (1971) has shown that a good pregnancy with mid-trimester euphoria and previously reported pill intolerance are strong pointers to the likelihood of its occurrence. When these are already noted *both* doctor and health visitor need to ensure they are ready for its emergence, so that both the medical and social components of the condition are adequately treated.

It is equally important to realise that depressed mothers reject their babies and fail to make eye contact, talk to them and cuddle them (Brazelton et al, 1974). Encouraging the mother to do these things helps to 'switch on' the bonding process and the baby responds by being more contented. This can often prevent the otherwise likely end result of a miserable, crying and rejected baby contributing to the continuation of the mother's anxiousness long after the depression, the original cause, has disappeared (Klaus & Kennell, 1976).

The growing baby is programmed to ensure survival (Dunn, 1977). Crying brings succour and help. Soon the mother finds she can recognise cry quality, not just her own baby's individual cry but the specific cries accompanying a dirty nappy, the need for food and drink, or attention and warmth (Bell et al, 1972). The onset of the recognised social smile is especially important. By smiling, the infant can ensure that adults and other children will respond. All adults respond to a baby's smile, but the *mother's* attitude to her baby is greatly changed once the mother appreciates social smiling. Until this time, she will believe that talking to her baby, calling him by name and treating him personally is important because other people say so. Once she realises the baby is smiling at her, the intellectual response ceases and instinctive behaviour takes over.

Once mother is 'turned on' by the smiles of her baby, the communication between the two becomes much more intense. The dance, as Brazelton et al (1975) call it, when mother and child are interacting, is exciting even to the observers. Slow motion film has demonstrated how the baby's generalised movements coincide with the voice rhythms of the mother. A sustained pitch of excitement can be maintained for minutes at a time. This intensity of interaction is not appreciated except by those who have themselves experienced it. Some mothers actually feel foolish and slightly guilty about the almost ecstatic exhilaration it produces and it is important to tell mothers (and fathers) that it is normal and above all natural to feel like this. This interaction continues to strengthen the bonds between mother and baby throughout the first year of life; the visible manifestations of the process are there for all to see. Dunn (1977) in *Distress and Comfort* reviews the recent research in this field in an easily readable and understandable way, and this book is essential reading for all the health visitors and doctors involved in child care.

Recently, some of the myths of the extended family, its beneficial effects on child upbringing, and its recent decline with reported ill effects on the family, have been effectively exploded (Illick, 1976). In reality, for hundreds of years in urban Europe and before that in rural Europe, the extended family has been the exception. Large families were broken as soon as the children were old enough to be sent away to earn their own living. The appalling maternal mortality rates ensured that only a minority of children knew their natural mother throughout childhood. It is therefore sensible to be aware of the sometimes pernicious influence that an older relative can have in a household when a new baby is born. Advice flows freely—'don't pick him up or you'll spoil him', 'that's not a smile, that's wind'—and sometimes there is gross interference in the actual process of care, giving cause to considerable anxiety and tension. Outmoded and wrong advice about feeding, rigidity of time schedules and ideas about the dangers of 'over stimulation' of the new baby can even cause members of a family to come to blows. At the first examination of the baby in the home, an open discussion of some of these ideas with the husband or relative present can do much to defuse a potentially serious situation.

In some households, such considerations are of marginal importance; here the glaring inadequacies of people and environment are the major hazards to the child. Recently, the social 'at risk' concept has displaced that of the more conventional idea of medical risk factors as the inconsistencies and inadequacies of the latter have been exposed. Kempe et al (1962) described the syndrome of child abuse (non-accidental injury) and stressed the importance of identifying these children at risk. More recently, it has been shown that the battering of older children and wives is merely an extension of the spectrum of violence within the family (see Ch. 19). The parallel fields of risk and emotional deprivation are in sheer numbers of infinitely greater importance. Neligan (1974) has shown that as survival continues beyond the immediate postnatal period, obstetric and biological factors, birth weight and sex, become progressively less important than socially determined ones in establishing prognostic significance.

What are the indicators of risk? Children in large families in poor housing with low incomes are obvious to all. One parent families, children already suffering from mental and physical handicap, and somewhat paradoxically, those children in care, are all at increased risk. The non-accidental injury rate is thought to be about six per 1000 children in Great Britain. The emotionally deprived are estimated by Pringle (1974) to be a group as large as 160 per 1000. The primary care team must have a policy to deal with this. Since the medical 'Inverse Care Law' operates most balefully in those areas most needing help from social and medical services, it is vital that special efforts are made in these areas, to ensure that the team offers increased surveillance of the single parent families in the practice. The risk, of course, varies. A young unmarried mother and her baby living at home with her parents is much less at risk than a woman with many previous pregnancies, other children in care, living with her current consort in inadequate housing. The work-shy, the mentally ill, the alcoholic, and often the violent, are numbered highly amongst these women and their men. The team *can* do something. Rehousing, when possible, stabilising rent and rates problems, ensuring the claiming and proper application of ligitimate welfare benefits, contraceptive advice and practice, and making the team available for repeated cries for help, as the lives of these patients lurch from crisis to crisis, are all contributions an effective team can make. The social services must be invited, encouraged, and occasionally bullied into playing their part in care.

Identification of the individual mother at risk is not difficult. Frommer (1973) has shown the way. When British born married primigravida attending St Thomas's Hospital antenatal clinics were asked whether they could remember any period of separation in their own childhood before the age of 11 years that affected them emotionally, 116 gave a positive reply. They were matched with a control group who had no such memories. Significant differences appeared between the two groups. The 'separated' mothers reported more problems in behaviour both in themselves and their babies. The babies cried more often and sleep was more broken. The mothers were tired, irritable and anxious, the marriages often showed extra stress.

The author* has observed a close correlation between the mother's own separation experience and her attitude to her new born baby. A mother with a deprived, or 'separated' upbringing, who has been orphaned or fostered, denies her baby's abilities of seeing, hearing and smiling more frequently than mothers with no such experience. Le Chateau (1977) has described how the mother with a deprived or 'separated' history tends to hold her baby differently, nursing her baby on the right arm, not the left as is the case with mothers with no such experience. This effect is not dependent on the cerebral dominance of the mother and is not demonstrable in fathers.

MacCarthy and Booth (1974) have described the stunting of growth that occurs in emotionally deprived children. Those who have suffered rejection from an early age or from birth eventually show physical signs of this syndrome. Their noses, cheeks, hands and feet have a curious red or purplish tint and the extremities feel cold. The combination of inertia caused by lack of stimulation, inadequate clothing and malnutrition, their inability to play and the depression so often manifest, are all parts of the syndrome. Pica, the scavenging of food, the paradoxical gorging followed by vomiting, are less common signs of the condition. Another striking finding is the virtual absence of separation anxiety when these babies enter hospital (see Ch. 19). The dramatic disappearance of all these signs without any treatment, apart from the giving of love, food, warmth and attention by specially trained nurses in hospital, is usually confirmation of this condition, as is their rapid reappearance once the child is discharged from hospital. Although these children often take in optimal amounts of food once in hospital, usually weight gain does not occur until eye contact has been established by the nurses.

*Dr Curtis Jenkins.

The primary care team is ideally placed to identify such families where all these situations are likely to occur. The early contact by home visiting by midwife, health visitor and doctor, the easy access to all members of the team by the parents, the recognition of the early signs of stress and the transmission of the information to other members of the team when appropriate, are the ways the possibilities are translated into action. The cries for help, the avoidance of eye contact by mother and child, the extreme expressions of anxiety 'I'm desperately worried about him', 'I'm frightened I'll harm him', 'I can't go on' should never be disregarded. Urgent defusing of the situation is required. A sympathetic ear and a cup of tea *sometimes* are all that are needed. However, a much more positive approach is often necessary.

Social services, if they can be persuaded of the urgency of the situation and have staff available, should be approached for help. All too often their ability to act is limited except in crisis intervention (see Introduction) and then recourse to voluntary organisation is a possible alternative. Sometimes, volunteers are available to push a pram, do shopping or even clean a flat. The spread of the volunteer bureau movement in the U.K. has raised hopes of starting such a service. Small, locally run, 'parents anonymous' groups are springing up in all parts of the country. The one extra chore is often the dividing line between coping and not coping. Family aids, or home-makers, are just beginning to make their appearance, employed by social service departments. There are few of them, jealously guarded by the departments who employ them. They can help young mothers by showing them how to cook how to run a budget, how to clean and how to cope with a young baby, and by working with them help them to succeed. Health visitors and doctors are taught that they must not do anything otherwise 'the mothers may become dependent'. There are perhaps good reasons for this attitude, but in the absence of home-makers, who else can show the way? The employment of family aids is perhaps the best investment that a social service department can make to cope with these situations.

Problems of management

It is impossible to cover, in a book of this size, all the problems of management that can occur in the first seven months of life. Excellent texts cover the field in great detail. Illingworth's *The Normal Child* and Jolly's *The Book of Baby Care* are two such books that should be on every general practitioner's bookshelves. The fact that the second was written for parents detracts in no way from its invaluable information and advice, and any doctor who works in child care will profit from reading it.

Therefore, only the more important subjects, such as feeding, and its associated problems, colic and wind, and the more important myths and non-diseases that cause the vast bulk of anxiety to mothers and their doctors will be discussed. Their perpetuation attests to the power of cultural myths and the resistance of myth to scientific explanation, alas not a feature of child care only.

Feeding

Most authorities on child care believe that for the full term normal infant 'breast is best'. Despite current trends, it is obvious that a lot of mothers remain unconvinced of the benefits (see Ch. 3).

At its simplest level, breast feeding is the most natural and primitive contact between mother and child, ensuring as it does, the virtual certainty that they develop a close relationship. The mutual enjoyment usually so manifest is, of course, a powerful influence. Eye contact is inevitable at feeding time. The nipple to nose distance of about 25–35 cm is the distance at which a baby's eye can focus easily on the mother's face. The economic benefits are difficult to calculate. Cow's milk now costs about the same as powdered milk. When the additional costs of bottles, teats, sterilising tablets and water heating are included, and the risks of inadequate sterilisation, dirty utensils and wrongly made-up milk are taken into account, the balance must come down on the side of breast milk (see Ch. 3 and Table 4.1).

Problems do not end once breast feeding is established. Breast feeding is never easy. It is often tiring and time consuming. A substantial minority of mothers have to concentrate a lot of effort to ensure success. Rest, however brief, is a powerful stimulator of breast milk. As it is the one factor that is least likely to operate at this generally most exhausting time in a mother's life, her own health is of paramount importance. Adequate nutrition, the maintenance

Table 4.1 Advantages of breast milk

(a) Protection against infection:
1. Iron binding protein (lactoferrin) + IgA, IgM and IgG (the milk immunoglobulins) + bicarbonate inhibit multiplication of enteropathic strains of *E Coli*.
2. Lyzozyme, polymorphs, lymphocytes and macrophages, all present, protect against viral infection of the gut.
3. IgA, IgM, IgG absorbed via the gut from colostrum and milk probably protect the respiratory tract from infection.
4. The acid stools of breast fed babies contain more sugars than bottle fed babies. This also inhibits bacterial growth in the gut.
5. Hygiene is guaranteed.

(b) Protection against allergy:
Breast feeding and the avoidance of cow's milk in the first months of life prevents the onset of the atopic trait in susceptible babies.

(c) Protection against cot death:
Hardly any of the 3000 deaths per annum from this condition occur in breast fed babies.

(d) Solute concentration:
Concentrations of salt and protein are much lower in breast milk than powdered milks. The possibility of hypernatraemic dehydration in the unlikely event of gastro-enteritis in the breast fed baby is almost impossible. Its dangers in bottle fed babies are well documented and convulsions, coma and even permanent brain damage are not unknown.

(e) Nutrition:
Various intestinal enzymes present in breast milk aid the immature digestive system of the newborn and ensure adequate absorption. Unsaturated fatty acids present in breast milk are essential to brain growth.

of good health, a helping husband who understands the relationship between rest and milk production, are the three most powerful contributors to the maintenance of the milk supply, apart from the baby's own demands (Stanway & Stanway, 1978).

Underfeeding is usually obvious with the hungry baby demonstrating to the world its feelings about milk quantity. However, not all babies are so vocal and regular weighing of breast fed babies in the first weeks is essential, if necessary, in the home on transportable scales (Davies & Evans, 1976). Those mothers who cannot or will not go to a clinic because of the problems of moving a pram, two toddlers and a baby up and down four flights of stairs are the ones most likely to run into the problem of underfeeding. Sometimes their fears are imaginary, but they cannot get to the clinic to weigh the baby and find out.

Equally common is the crying, fractious baby who is being satisfactorily breast fed but the anxious mother suffers. Dunn (1977) has found that this was the characteristic behaviour pattern of more than 50 per cent of breast fed babies in the first weeks. The mother then becomes discouraged and puts her baby onto the bottle, thinking that the breast has failed to satisfy. *Sustained* support is vital.

Mothers who do not want to breast feed or who fail to establish it in the first weeks are still the large majority in this country. It is important that adequate time be given to help them (see Ch. 3).

Vitamin supplements are thought necessary by most authorities but quite a lot of mothers never give them for more than a few weeks, despite recommendations that they should be given until the child is two years old. Evidence of their beneficial effect is hard to come by and with fortification of so much of the baby foods available, they are probably unnecessary for most children. However, the resurfacing of rickets in immigrant families from the Indian sub-continent, stresses the need for selective vitamin therapy in some populations.

Introduction of solids

The rule 'the later the better' is now universally taught. However, many mothers, unless advised to the contrary, have started solids by a month old and nearly all babies by three months (Shukla et al, 1972).

In the author's general practice with a *uniform* approach by health visitors and doctors, less than 20 per cent have started solids at three months, but nearly all have by four months. Occasionally, a breast feeding mother finds that solids are not needed even then and instead finds that not until well into fifth or sixth month does the baby's need for them become apparent. How to introduce solids, whether to offer a carbohydrate based solid as a starter or to introduce, instead, one of the fruit or vegetable based solids, depends on the individual preference of the mother and baby. The idea that babies need a 'transitional' carbohydrate solid can probably be discounted. Once solids are established, the mother should then be guided by the baby's preferences. From a cost point of view, it is difficult to show that homemade solid foods are cheaper than bought ones. Attention should be paid to vitamin content—most proprietary brands of solids have added ones and home preparation may destroy them, especially vitamin C. As well as starting solids from a spoon, the baby of four months should be allowed to hold a biscuit and to suck it, and the benefits produced by encouraging fine motor control are inestimable. Fears of choking can probably be ignored. The most important advice the health visitor can give to the mother about solids is how to read the label on the tin. 'Rice and meat broth' can contain 90 per cent of rice. The item listed first is always the major constituent, and mothers can be giving, unwittingly, large amounts of carbohydrates unless told; also it is important to ensure that the tin is emptied—food left behind is food uneaten.

A weekly weight gain between 150 and 180 g should be considered satisfactory for most babies over the first three months, thereafter a baby usually doubles his birth weight by six months and trebles it by 12. In the practice we advise mothers to continue breast feeding for as long as they want. In 14 years, a handful of mothers have breast fed their babies into the third year of life. In most cases the baby decides when to stop. Meals and orange drinks seem to signal the end. Most breast fed babies (90 per cent) are therefore off the breast by 12 months, the remainder having one token night feed that acts as a soporific and gives the mother and child some private intimate time together. Teeth, although often mentioned by mothers as a reason for stopping, do not seem to inhibit a minority from continuing. Certainly, some mothers happily continue unaffected by their baby's six or seven teeth.

Today, fashions are changing fast. Breast feeding at four months in our practice is now the rule, with more than 60 per cent still breast feeding at six months. Quite what has caused this shift is not difficult to pinpoint. A more dynamic approach by health visitors in the antenatal and mothercraft classes, more informed midwives in the obstetric unit who actively encourage the practice with support and understanding, publicity about its benefits in women's magazines, have all helped to promote the revolution, begun in the upper and middle classes, which is spreading with great rapidity through all social classes. Before long, I suspect our figures for breast feeding will be as high as 80 per cent at six months.

Prevalent myths and non-disease in early infancy

In the U.K. the growing infant is surrounded from the earliest days even in 1979, by a dense entanglement of myths surrounding his growth, development and upbringing.

Tongue tie

I have seen in the last 14 years, only three children who could be considered to have had a tight frenum. All sucked adequately and had no trouble speaking. In all three, the frenum lengthened as the child grew. I happened to see one of these children recently, now nine years old. He can protrude his tongue normally albeit with a slight indentation in the front of the tongue at extreme extension. Another ruptured the frenum in a fall when three years old. I do not believe that 'tongue tie' exists as a pathological entity and mothers should be discouraged from using the condition as a rationalisation to explain feeding or speech problems.

Wind

Experiments have shown that babies need a varying amount of time on their mother's knee after being fed. Often they are at their most wide-awake and sometimes in the evening, even when only a few weeks old, stay awake and are slightly fractious and difficult to pacify from one feed to the next (Dunn, 1977). Talking to the baby, giving plenty of auditory and visual stimulation, television, radio and even books with big pictures will continue to keep the baby awake and alert. So too, will back-slapping and some of the other tricks that mothers teach each other 'to get up the wind'. When a child stays awake and cries when put down into its visually and auditorily unstimulating cot, it is thought that the cause must be wind as yet unreleased. Father and mother become agitated as their efforts to bring it up end in failure. Their anxiety is transmitted to the baby who then becomes even harder to pacify. As Dunn has shown, what causes distress and what brings comfort are infinitely more complicated than that taught by health visitors and doctors.

In some other countries, the mother is not shown how to bring up wind. Instead, she is able to find out for herself that her baby needs varying amounts of time being talked to, cuddled and held until it can be laid down to sleep. I believe that swallowed wind, as an explanation of fractiousness after feeding, causes unnecessary anxiety to the mother, who, failing to appreciate the real reasons for her baby's wakefulness, sees the failure of her winding technique as a sign of her lack of experience and personal failure to manage her baby. If mothers could be shown that what is really needed is to match the baby's varying requirement for contact with time for holding, talking and cuddling, then she would see her effectiveness as a mother more realistically and with a greater sense of personal satisfaction.

Colic

It is often thought by parents, doctors and health visitors, that swallowed wind is the cause of violent explosive bowel actions that small babies sometimes have, accompanied by the signs of abdominal pain. Yet research has shown that the 'wind' is in fact methane released by the process of digestion in the small and large intestines (Jorup, 1952). Undoubtedly, babies do suffer from intense abdominal pain. The red face, the sudden scream and the drawing up of legs are familiar to nearly every mother. Questioning usually reveals that the mother notices an audible increase in peristalsis caused, possibly, as Illingworth (1954) suggests, by the gas trapped in loops of the colon. After minutes of pain the child quietens, only to start again. Usually, a noisy, bulky motion is expelled with explosive force, bringing the episode to an abrupt end.

The many preparations available for treatment attest the relative failure many doctors have in attempting to alleviate it. Sometimes a change of milk suggests that malabsorption plays a part and a switch to one of the non-cow's milk based milks—Velactin, Neutramigen or Prosobee is always worthwhile when it solves the problem. Their expense is prohibitive, however, and Allergilac, a specially prepared cow's milk powder with denatured whey, is cheaper, and should always be tried first. (Unhappily, it is not pre-scribable.) Sometimes, Merbentyl syrup, 5 ml diluted to half strength, 30 minutes, 15 minutes or even immediately before or after a feed can cause a dramatic reduction in colic. It is important to allow the mother to experiment with the timing of the dose and inadequate experimentation is often a cause of failure.

However, there are some children who, despite all efforts, continue to have severe colic. They become irritable and difficult to manage. The mother deserves a lot of support—just talking to a health visitor or doctor about how dreadful it is makes a lot of difference. More treatment is not usually required. The condition is essentially self-limiting and most have grown out of the habit by the time solids are begun at four months.

Breast fed babies are not immune from this condition and our experience of reducing the *mother's* intake of cow's milk (often greatly increased on the advice of the world at large) as suggested by Jakobsson and Lindberg (1978) has been most rewarding. The mother finds when she reduces her intake of milk, not only the baby's colic improves but his general mood improves and management becomes easier. Within 24 hours the improvement is noticeable which ensures the mother's acceptance of what appears at first sight, a somewhat bizarre method of treatment.

Evening crying

The majority (56 per cent) of breast fed babies, between two and three months old cry regularly in the evening (Dunn, 1977). For many it is intermittent fussing but some show extreme distress. There is much disagreement as to the cause. The fact that it occurs more commonly in breast fed babies who are reported to be more fractious overall, hints that an evening hunger peak is linked with it. However, ensuring that adequate food is given is no guarantee of stopping it. Luckily, most children grow out of it by four months and therefore support and explanation, not treatment, is required.

Spoiling

People still believe that it is possible to spoil a newborn baby by picking it up. Despite that, many mothers realise that the longer they leave their baby to cry, then the longer it cries once picked up, and that this has been amply confirmed by research (Thoman, 1975). In most households with a new baby there will be voices suggesting to the mother the dangers of spoiling. A hot, red, perspiring, sobbing baby manifests his distress to all when left to cry for longer than half a minute, and often continues crying for many minutes after being picked up. Moore and Ucko (1957) demonstrated that the babies of parents who were most afraid of spoiling them, tended, paradoxically, to wake most frequently. They also showed that 10 per cent of all babies slept badly in the first year of life. When a baby finally does cry himself to exhaustion and sleep, the mother's advisors declare a victory for their methods. Usually however, the mother hot, red and perspiring herself, effectively stimulated by the crying of her own baby, is made to merely feel anxious—knowing better.

The practitioners and propagators of many of the arbitrary upbringing practices, like fixed four-hourly feeding, consciously and unconsciously, proclaim the ancient concept of the baby being a *tabula rasa*, whose behaviour can be modified and controlled to produce the required image (De Mause, 1976).We now know how wrong this image is. Recent research into child behaviour shows what a complicated organism the newborn baby is. Much of the research demonstrates that the baby can never be considered in isolation. It is the study of the couple, mother and child which reveals by their complex interactions, cues and responses, the truths about baby behaviour. Truly, the baby maketh the mother.

Sleep

Sleep is one of the great variables that illustrates each newborn baby's individuality. Some babies, from the earliest days of life, sleep little. Recent research has shown the normal range of sleep patterns (Dunn, 1977). At one extreme, there are some babies who appear to sleep almost continuously in the first few weeks and mothers, taking the easiness for granted, expect to wake the baby to feed it and, furthermore, expect a full eight hours' period between feeds at night. At the other extreme, there are perfectly healthy normal babies, who, even in the first weeks of life, sleep scarcely more than nine hours in the 24. Mothers need to be persuaded that the range of normality is as wide as this. The exhausted, tearful parents who consult health visitor and doctor with a baby 'who never sleeps' is familiar to all in primary care. Careful history taking often reveals that the baby, in bounding good health, sleeps little in the day preferring to lie awake propped up to see the world around. Snatched naps of a few seconds or minutes restore flagging energies and peremptory demands for attention exhaust its care givers.

Worse, the pattern extends into the night with a wide-awake child after a 2 a.m. feed wanting to play and talk, and crying inconsolably if not getting it. Usually, all sorts of tricks have already been tried by parents to make the child sleep. Solids have been introduced early in a vain attempt to 'satisfy the hunger'. Gripewater and alcohol in various other forms, teething jellies and patent pain-relieving medicines 'for teething' have been applied to the baby. None works. What to do next is always a taxing problem. Treatment with antihistamines or antidepressants is usually doomed to failure. Antihistamines can, paradoxically, in some children, actually cause excitation and intense restlessness. If treatment is offered, follow-up reveals the lack of effect. Parents however, despite the patently obvious lack of effect, are sometimes afraid to discontinue the medicine for fear 'the sleeplessness worsens'. For these reasons, it is probably best not to treat the baby with drugs at all. Techniques, such as 'let him cry it out' have also been tried (see Spoiling) and normally have failed. Occasionally the baby has even to be admitted to hospital to allow the parents rest. A few days' separation quietens the child but once home, it quickly falls into its normal pattern (Bowlby, 1975).

A suggested technique of treatment is as follows. Take a careful sleep history to eliminate any (unlikely) extraneous causes, malaise, pain or hunger. Usually, the babies totally resistant to treatment are those that have been more active and needing little sleep from birth. They are often more fractious, demanding and curiously intelligent-looking. Family history sometimes reveals a similar sleep pattern in one of the parent's infancy which has continued into adult life. An explanation of the range of normal sleep and assurances that the baby will not suffer from lack of sleep and is not abnormal (a fear many parents have) and will eventually grow out of the habit, is the first step in treatment. Sympathy and understanding are most important and the doctor's own experience of his own children's sleeplessness helps. It is in fact likely that the doctor will have experienced the problem first hand. A survey, some years ago, carried out by one of the authors, showed that in a group of 30 paediatricians, 22 had experienced sleep problems with their own children.

It is important to realise that lack of sleep affects parents, sometimes severely and is a contributor to the non-accidental injury syndrome (Kempe et al, 1962). Realistic advice is then required. A shift system for the parents to get up in turn to the crying child is an excellent starting point. Moving the baby to the bedside of the parents certainly allows a parent to reach the baby the moment crying starts, raising the likelihood of quicker consolation. It is important to tell *both* parents that babies stir at frequent intervals through the night, sit up, look around and lie down to sleep more deeply again. Mothers whose changed sleep pattern towards light sleep allows them to respond to every move the baby makes, need to be warned of this. Taking the baby into the parents' bed is still condemned by some (Illingworth, 1977). It is a universal practice and when disapproved of, nevertheless is still carried out behind a doctor's and health visitor's backs. It frequently helps, as does a system whereby one parent sleeps with the baby and the other moves into a bed in another room to gain uninterrupted sleep. Fathers usually oppose this practice, so need to be assured of its lack of longterm effect. Sympathy, explanation, cautious prescribing of, for instance, small amounts of Diazapam 5 mg, half a tablet at night to the *parent* most in need of sleep, to be taken *occasionally*. The above stratagems certainly, in my experience, hold the situation long enough for time to solve the problem.

Teething

For many of the parishes in the City of London, in the 18th century, teething is given as the commonest cause of death in the parish records. Today, teething is still probably the commonest single misdiagnosis made by parents, and perhaps doctors, for changes of behaviour in children. Dribbling, malaise, temperature, earache, crying, sucking the hands, dummy or bedclothes (long before teeth are visible) are all ascribed to teething; so, too, are upper respiratory infections producing coryzal symptoms and gastro-intestinal disturbance. Usually, teething jellies and patent pain-relieving medicines have already been given before the mother finally consults the health visitor or doctor. From the moment the first tooth arrives, the process of dentition is fairly continuous. What could be more natural therefore to ascribe any change in the baby's behaviour to teething, when teeth are seen breaking through the gums? Most authorities now believe that at most, cutting teeth causes mild discomfort and the convenient, though erroneous, rationalisation if marked changes in a child's behaviour being ascribed to teething, should be strongly discouraged and instead a careful examination always made to search for the true cause.

Snuffles

Many babies develop extra mucus secretion from the nasal mucosa in the first few days after birth. it is more common in winter than in summer. The noise created by the baby when sucking on the bottle is often loud and worrying to parents who seek help to alleviate the condition. It is probably wise to avoid using even the mildest nasal drops. Parents given saline drops tend then to go and buy something stronger with undesirable effects of treatment rebound and habituation.

Instead, attention to humidity control, reduction of tobacco smoke in the air babies breathe, together with an explanation of the essential normality of the condition, are all that is usually required. Very occasionally, the baby actually has difficulty taking food, then treatment needs to be given *intermittently*. Unless mothers are shown how to give nasal drops they tend to be wrongly applied. It is important to show the mother how to take the baby onto her lap, head up and facing away from her and then, letting the head drop between her knees and gently holding firmly with her knees, put the drops into the nose.

It is important not to confuse snuffles with chronic bacterial infection in the nose. Swabs need to be taken before treatment, for, if the infection is picked up in hospital, it is likely to be penicillin resistant. Even infections contracted elsewhere are often notoriously resistant to treatment.

Growth and development

Physical growth is manifest but the change in the central nervous system, the enormous glial proliferation that takes place during the first four months, the rapid maturation of the brain and myelination of the main voluntary nerve pathways, is what influences the dynamic pattern of growth and development. The developing motor systems of the body are the most obvious indicators of this process. The unco-ordinated, helpless baby gradually gains ascendancy over motor function and by seven months has achieved considerable skills. The sensory systems of the body have evolved in parallel. Visual acuity has improved and the property space of the baby, the area inside which a baby is aware of things happening and takes notice of them, has enlarged from a few feet to many yards.

Hearing has developed fast and localisation of sounds is a skill that is easy to demonstrate. By seven months, even upward localisation is achieved by nearly 10 per cent of babies (and by most, if not all, by 10 months).

Language is developing as the purposeless sounds give way, first to cries for attention and then to the two syllable 'practice language' of the average seven month old.

This process of development has taxed the ingenuity of many who have tried to chart it. Many charts, forms and schedules are available that try to produce, in an easily understood form, a picture of this sweep of development across the four fields of behaviour. Their use is necessary when a doctor first starts to involve himself in the care of children so that he can make an estimate of the child's development and growth relative to his age every time he sees a child.

Most of the charts available are derived from the work of Gesell, who first described development across the four major fields. (See the Appendix to this Chapter.)

However, as an every day surveillance tool, it is far too complex and others have produced schemes more readily applied in clinical practice (Illingworth, 1972a; Sheridan, 1960). However, few systems give statistical norms based upon population studies but instead usually consist of an inventory of pass/fail tests. The 'wider knowledge' or 'experience' of the examiner is meant to be used to complete the final assessment. An alternative is an assessment where every item of history and examination is defined in terms of expected norms (Neligan & Prudham, 1969). This system has one great advangage; the majority of children pass an individual milestone over a relatively narrow age range and the few remaining over a relatively longer period. It is within this last group that the abnormally developing child is likely to be found. Both Starte's (1974) examination system and the simpler developmental paediatric research group system use this technique for isolation of the child 'in the tail'. Neither are fully statistically validated but both offer considerable sensitivity in detecting the abnormal child whose delay is often spread across several milestones—a fact made use of in the Denver scale. This has drawbacks in that it relies to a certain extent on what the mother remembers about her child's achievements of certain skills and can become cluttered if used as a continuous record (see Fig. 4.1—inside cover). It also takes too long a time to be used routinely in the clinical setting of a doctor's surgery. Gesell's key age schedules are still, although nearly 30 years old, probably the best of the records of development. They are certainly easy to refer to and use.

Why is it important to chart development?

Firstly, it teaches the doctor to observe the child.

Secondly, it enables the doctor to make an accurate estimate of the individual baby's developmental progress across the four fields of behaviour and to note any check that occurs for any reason.

Thirdly, it enables the doctor to detect quickly early deviation and delay which might become relevant later as part of an overall pattern of developmental delay.

Fourthly, and most importantly, it enables him to counsel the parents in an effective and realistic way about their child's progress.

By demonstrating to them the various aspects of developmental progress, the doctor can help the parents to be more effective at stimulating their baby to use existing skills and be aware when new skills are acquired and see their arrival as a positive affirmation of continuing healthy growth. Parents are accurate observers. They have ample opportunity, 24 hours a day, to compare their baby with others. Often they become concerned about their baby not achieving certain objectives, like holding a rattle, sitting up, crawling. Sometimes they become so anxious that they constantly seek advice for inappropriate or seemingly trivial complaints, and fail to bring themselves to talk about the unmentionable; that there is something wrong or different about their baby. If the doctor only wishes to keep the consultation on the 'medical' level then the opportunity to talk about these fears will never materialise. It always pays, even when in a busy surgery, to ask the open-ended questions 'how are things going' and 'what sort of person is your baby growing into?' 'Is he generally happy' is a question that is favoured by myself. The answer 'yes' is usually the truth. 'No' is usually the answer that opens a Pandora's box of problems that are worrying the parents and certainly need to be taken seriously by the doctor.

I believe it behoves every doctor involved in the care of children to have a sound knowledge of development and its range of normality. This can only be maintained by constantly using the knowledge gained effectively and appropriately—at every consultation. Constant practice with the normal is what enables the doctor to be quick to detect the variation or deviation which could signal disorder or delay.

By the seventh month, great advances across the fields of development are obvious to all. The alert, vocalizing, mobile baby able to sit unsupported, reaching out for toys and able to attract attention by purposeful sound and ready to play

Table 4.2 Starte's recording and examination system

Chart for grading responses to the tests

TEST	1	2	3	4	5
BRICK	No grasp	Palmar grasp	Mouthing	Transferring	Finger manipulation
SMARTIE	No interest	Whole hand scrabble No pick-up	Whole hand scrabble and pick-up	Fingers and thumb pick-up	Index finger and thumb pick-up
RATTLE	No interest	Transient interest and manipulation	Prolonged interest and manipulation	Manipulation and eventual limitation	Immediate imitation
BELL	,,	,,	,,	,,	,,
ROLLING	3/4"	1/2"	1/4"	3/16"	1/8"
BALLS	or larger				
6 SOUNDS	No hearing demonstrated	Response to 1–3 sounds or marked difference between two sides	Slow response both sides 4–5 sounds	Rapid response both sides 4–5 sounds	Rapid response both sides 6 sounds
PRONE	Head up not sustained	Head up weight on forearms	Head and shoulders up weight on hands	Head and shoulders up knee up	Crawls
SITTING	No sitting stability Hyper- or hypotonic	Sits briefly with support then unstable Back hypotonic	Sits upright needs Ex. hand on back	Sits upright steadily unsupported	Reaches each side without toppling
STANDING	No weight bearing	Stands with support. Full weight not taken	Full weight taken on legs	Shifts weight from one leg to the other	Walks supported
BABBLING	Silence or purposeless noise	Occasional purposeful babble	Frequent purposeful babble	Two syllable babble	Recognisable

games, has become a discrete individual to all who observe him. It is also a good age to make a routine assessment of this progress. At six months many babies are not sitting alone securely, and accurate pincer grasp and transfer are sometimes not easily observable. The standard tests of vision and hearing (Stycar) tend to be unreliable in that a substantial minority of children need to be recalled a month later for retest, because of the baby's immaturity of response.

Ideally, the examination should be done at a special clinic set aside for the purpose (see Ch. 6). The actual process of examination depends on the experience, skill and interest of the individual doctor and the aims and objectives of the programme. There are some excellent descriptions of the basics of the examination, and the Stycar tests of vision and hearing provide a cornerstone on which to build the rest (Egan et al, 1969; Starte, 1977). The present lack of any nationally approved system with a common method of recording is disgraceful, of course, but this has acted as an effective spur to some very imaginative and effective experiments (Starte 1974, 1976; Curtis Jenkins et al, 1978). Starte's recording and examination system (see Table 4.2), and analysis of 815 children seen at seven months (see Table 4.3a) can be compared to my own which uses a record system derived from his work and which has been modified by a

Table 4.3a   Results from developmental examination at seven months

a	*815 children*
13·7%	112 delay in development
3·3%	27 delay at 2 years still present
1·1%	9 referred for developmental problems, vision, hearing or retardation

From Starte G S 1976. Results from a developmental screening clinic in general practice. Practitioner 216: 311–

Table 4.3b   Results from developmental examination at seven months

b	*383 children*
7·6%	32 delay in development
6·0%	23 referred for developmental problems, vision, hearing or retardation

From Curtis Jenkins et al, 1978. Developmental surveillance in general practice. British Medical Journal 1: 1537–1540

PAEDIATRIC DEVELOPMENT RECORD

DR.

Surname _____ First Name _____

Date of Birth (14) | | | | | Birth Rank (20)

Father's Age (21)(22) Mother's Age (23)(24)

Father's Occupation _____ (25)

OFFICE USE

Dr's Code (1–2)

On Cols 3–13
Punch: First 8 letters of surname
First 3 letters of first name

(26) | | | | (31)

Exam. at **7 months** Date _____

		No	Yes	
Mother's Comments	Happy	No	Yes	32
	Sleeps	No	Yes	33
	Chews	No	Yes	34
Illness since last exam. (If yes specify nature of illness)		No	Yes	35

Breast Fed | | mos. 36
Solids started | No | Yes | 37

Nursery | No | Yes | 38
C. H. Minder | No | Yes | 39
Hours worked per week (mother) | | 40 41

Sitting	**No stability**	Sits supported	Sits un-supported	42
Standing supported	No weight Bearing	Full weight	Weight alternates foot to foot	43
Prone	No weight on hands, head up	Shoulders up on hands	**Knee up to crawl**	44
1" Brick	No grasp	Mouthing	Transfer	45
Pellet	Whole hand scrabble	Whole hand pick up	Finger-thumb pick up	46
Rolling balls	$\frac{1}{2}''$	$\frac{1}{4}''$	$\frac{3}{16}''$	47
Cover test	Squint	Doubtful	No squint	48
Hearing 3 ft.	Doubtful	Satisfactory	Good	49
Speech	Noise only	Purposeful sound	2 Syllables or more	50
Imitation rattle	**No interest**	Interest and manipulation	Imitation	51
Reaction to Examiner	None	Resists	Co-operates	52
Attention	Poor	Variable	Sustained	53

PHYSICAL EXAM.

Weight (54–6) | | . | | K.grms. Height (57–9) | | | Cms. H.C. (60–2) | | . | | Cms.

Abnormality   No/Yes (Specify below)

63

Appearance

Comments

Action

Card Code 79 | 2 |

If tests incomplete because of child's unco-operation put tick in box | | 80 | |

Fig 4.2 Recording card—7 months

developmental paediatric research group associated with the R.C.G.P. (see Fig. 4.2 and Table 4.3b) It can be seen that the overall abnormality rates are not exactly comparable; Starte's figures tend to stress the developmental ones, while my own give the full range of abnormality, both physical and developmental.

The following is an accurate description of my own technique of examination, and it is useful to follow the description on the actual recording form (Fig. 4.2). This is by no means a definitive technique. It does have the advantage though of being actually tested and used in general practice. Over the past seven years many thousands of children have been seen by myself and the other members of the developmental paediatric research group using both the protocol (Table 4.4) routine and examination.

Table 4.4   Routine examination at seven months

Sitting	*Equipment*	None
	Position	—
	Method	'C' is sat on firm flat surface with 'E's hand firmly in the middle of the back. If sitting appears stable 'E' takes his hand away.
	Score	'No'=unable to sit under any circumstances. It does not include falling over if the child reaches for a toy.
Standing	*Equipment*	None
	Position	—
	Method	'E' moves to front of 'C' and holding 'C's hands pulls him gently to his feet.
	Score	—accordingly.
Prone	*Equipment*	None
	Position	—
	Method	'C' is placed prone on firm flat surface. A toy is placed in fron of 'C' about 6–8 inches from the face to encourage activity.
	Score	—accordingly.
Brick	*Equipment*	One 1″square coloured brick.
	Position	'C' sits on 'M's lap on opposite side of table to 'E'. Table waist height to child.
	Method	'E' places brick on table directly in front of 'C' and midway between its hands, tapping it on table to attract 'C's attention. After allowing 'C' choice as to hand used, this hand is then gently restrained by mother and the other hand tested. Brick then removed.

Table 4.4 *(continued)*

	Score	—accordingly. Score highest either side. Note dominant side. Mouthing includes palmar grasp.
Pellet	*Equipment*	Smartie or similar size pellet.
	Position	As for brick.
	Method	'E' places pellet on table directly in front of 'C' and midway between its hands, tapping it on the table to attract 'C's attention. After allowing 'C' choice as to hand used, this hand is gently held by mother and the other hand tested. Pellet then removed.
	Score	Whole hand scrabble includes failure to attempt to manipulate pellet. Score highest either side.
Rolling Balls	*Equipment*	Nylon or polystyrene (N.F.E.P.) balls, size $1''$, $\frac{1}{2}''$, $\frac{1}{4}''$, $3/16''$.
	Position	'C' sits on 'M's lap facing wall at least 10 feet away. 'E' kneels on floor 10 feet in front of 'C' and to one side.
	Method	'E' attracts 'C's attention by suitable noise or $1''$ ball. 'E' then rolls balls across 'C's line of vision and observes 'C's eyes, to see if they follow the ball.
	Score—for smallest ball followed.	
Cover Test	*Equipment*	Point source of light, e.g. auroscope.
	Position	Light 'C' sits on 'M's lap within arms reach of 'E'.
	Method	The light is held near 'E's face in one hand. The fingers on the other hand steady 'C's head, while the thumb covers one eye. When the other eye is looking at the light the thumb is quickly moved to one side and the eye observed. If it moves to fix on the light then squint is present. Repeat for other eye. The test must be performed swiftly and accurately.
	Score	—accordingly.
Hearing	*Equipment*	'Nuffield rattle'
	Position	Child sits on mothers' lap opposite observer. Examiner holds rattle like a pen, slightly downwards, and rapidly moves it as if he is drawing an 'O' shape, so that the contents slide around inside the ball. Distance $12''$ from the ear. Hide rattle from child's head by keeping behind field of vision.

Table 4.4   *(continued)*

		Test from each side of 'C'. A response is when 'C' turns eyes or head towards side of sound. If 'H' is not present then 'M' has to encourage 'C' to face forward between each sound. (This is one of the most difficult tests to perform satisfactorily). Try each sound no more than 3 times, per ear.
	Score 1	Doubtful. Responds to the sounds in both ears, or marked difference between two sides. Note ear which appears to show deficiency.
	Score 2	Satisfactory. Eventual response to sounds. Both ears.
	Score 3	Good. rapid response to all sounds.
Speech	*Equipment*	None.
	Position	—
	Method	Observation of all sounds made by 'C' throughout examination.
	Score 1	No sounds or purposeless noises only.
	Score 2	Purposeful sounds made in relation to toy or person often repeated and accompanied by smiling.
	Score 3	Two syllable bable such as Da-da, Ba-ba.
Rattle	*Equipment*	1 coloured rattle with handle.
	Position	'C' sits on 'M's lap at table.
	Method	The rattle is shaken several times in a deliberate fashion with large movements in front of 'C'. It is then placed on table with handle towards 'C'. 'C' is encouraged to pick it up and rattle it. Allow no more than 2 minutes.
	Score	—accordingly.

Reaction to Examiner and Attention

	Equipment	None
	Position	—
	Method	Observation throughout examination.
	Score	—accordingly

Physical Examination
(Be sure to re-examine heart and hips)

E=Examiner
H=Helper
C=Child
M=Mother

Routine of examination at seven months (see Fig. 4.3–equipment used)

The health visitor or I call the mother and child from the waiting room and, talking in a quiet friendly voice to the mother, show them into the assessment room. The mother sits down with child on her lap and I put a small table in front of them, taking my seat opposite. While the health visitor is asking the mother the various questions needed to complete the social and personal history, I have plenty of time to observe the mother/child relationship. Often clues are given while taking the history and these must be remembered to be discussed at the end of the examination.

The child is by now usually quite used to me and I can go on to the developmental examination. Occasionally during the vision tests in particular the child becomes 'faced fixed' on me—this can easily be overcome by covering my face with my hand and looking through my fingers—this manages, effectively, to make me disappear from the child's view!

Fig 4.3 Equipment required to carry out developmental examination of the seven- and twelve-month-old child

On the bare table I now introduce the BRICK; once this test is completed I give it to the health visitor and replace it with the PELLET, for which I use a small sweet. I present the RATTLE next to observe the child's play with it and after this, I take the table away and retreat to three metres from the child to do the VISION test.

Mother and child are now moved into the centre of the room and I sit about one metre in front of them as the observer and the health visitor does the HEARING TEST, after which I do a COVER TEST to exclude squint.

I ask the mother to undress the child before the next part of the examination. This short break is another useful time to observe the interaction between mother and child, besides being a common time to hear the child's vocalization.

Once the child is undressed, I lie him PRONE on the floor, making quite sure that the mother is always in sight lest the child feels deserted. SITTING and STANDING follow naturally and the consultation is completed with a full physical examination.

When the child is undressed and during subsequent tests, I make a point of getting the mother to talk about any anxieties she may have about her child. They may be worries that she came with but found difficult to express, or anxieties raised by the child's performance. I always lay great stress on the wide spread of developmental progress within the range of normal. Often comparisons have been made by the mother with older siblings or next door children. Opportunity should be given for all this to come out and be discussed.

Any system or technique stands or falls on the motivation and experience of the doctor and the method of recording the data (see Ch. 5). Experience of the norm is vital to the early detection of the abnormal. A resolve to consider every child seen whether in illness or in health as a growing human being and a member of a family, is an excellent starting point on the road of discovery and revelation. I can recommend it.

Appendix

GESELL'S KEY AGE SCHEDULES: THE FIRST SEVEN MONTHS

4 weeks or less

Motor

Supine: side position head predominates
Supine: tonic neck reflex (assym) postures predominate
Supine: rolls partway to side
Prone: complete or marked head lag
Sit: head predominate sags
Prone: head droops, ventral suspension
Prone: placement, head rotates
Prone: lifts head momentarily
Prone: crawling movements
Supine: hand clenches on contact

Adaptive

Dangled ring, rattle: regards in line vision only
Dangles ring: follows to midline
Rattle: drops immediately
Bell: attends, activity diminishes

Language

Express: impassive face
Express: vague, indirect regard
Vocalises: small throaty noises

Personal-Social

Social: regards examiner's face, activity diminishes
Supine: stares indefinitely at surroundings
Feeding: 2 night feeds

8 weeks

Motor

Sit: head predominate bobbingly erect
Prone: head compensates ventral suspension
Prone: head in midposition
Prone: lifts head recurrently

Adaptive

Dangled ring: delayed midline regard
Dangled ring: regards examiner's hand
Dangled ring: follows past midline
Rattle: retains briefly
Bell: facial response

Language

Expressive: smiles (social)
Expressive: alert, expression
Expressive: direct, definite regard
Vocalizes: single vowel
sounds—ah, eh, uh

Personal-Social

Social: facial social response
Social: follows moving person
Supine: regards examiner
Feeding: only 1 night feed

12 weeks

Motor

Supine: head predom. half side
tonic neck reflex of arms
Supine: midposition of head and
symm. posture seen
Sit: head set forward, bobs
Stands: small fraction weight
briefly
Stands: lifts foot
Prone: head sustained lift
Prone: on forearms
Prone: hips low (legs flexed)
Supine: hands open or loosely
closed
Rattle: holds actively
Cup: contacts

Adaptive

Dangled ring: prompt midline
regard
Dangled ring: follows through
180°
Rattle: glances at, held in hand
Cube, cup: regards, more than
momentarily

Language

Vocalizes: coos
Vocalizes: chuckles
Social: vocal-social response

Personal-Social

Social: vocal-social response
Supine: regards examiner
Play: hand regard
Play: pulls at dress

16 weeks

Motor

Supine: midposition head
predominates
Supine: symm. postures
predominate
Supine: hands engage
Sit: head steady, set forward
Prone: head sustained lift
Prone: legs extended or semi-
extended
Prone: nearly rolling
Supine: fingers, scratches,
clutches

Adaptive

Dangled ring, rattle: regards
immediately
Dangled ring, rattle, cube, cup:
arms activate
Dangled ring, rattle: regards in
hand
Dangled ring: to mouth
Cube, cup: looks from hand to
object
Pellet: regards

Language

Expressive: excites, breathes
heavily
Vocalizes: laughs aloud

Personal-Social

Social: spontaneous social smile
Social: vocalizes or smiles, pulled
to sit
Feeding: anticipates food on sight
Play: sits propped 10–15 minutes
Play: hand play, mutual fingering
Play: pulls dress over face

20 weeks

Motor

Pulls to sit: no head lag
Sit: head erect, steady
Prone: arms extended
Prone: scratches surface
Cube: precarious grasp

Adaptive

Rattle, bell: 2 hand approach
Rattle, dangled ring: grasps near
hand only
Cube: holds 1st, regards 2nd
Manipulates cubes: grasps 1 on
contact

Language

Vocalizes: squeals

Personal-Social

Social: smiles mirror image
Feeding: pats bottle

24 weeks

Motor

Supine: lifts leg high in extension
Supine: rolls to prone
Prone: lifts head, assists
Sit in chair: trunk erect
Cube: grasps, palmarwise
Rattle: retains

Adaptive

Ring, rattle, cube, bell:
approaches and grasps
Rattle: prehension
Cube: regards 3rd cube
immediately
Cube, bell: to mouth
Cube: resecures dropped cube
Manipulates cubes: holds 1,
approaches another

Language

Bell, ring: turns head to bell
Vocalizes: grunts, growls
Vocalizes: spontan. vocal-social
(inc. toys)

Personal-Social

Social: discriminates strangers
Play: grasps foot (supine)
Play: sits propped 30 minutes

28 weeks

Motor

Supine: lifts head, forward on
hands
Sit: briefly, leans
Sit: erect momentarily
Stands: large fraction of weight
Stands: bounces actively
Cube: radial palmar grasp
Pellet: rakes (whole hand)

Adaptive

Rattle, bell: 1 hand approach and
grasp
Manipulates cubes: holds 1,
grasps another
Cube: holds 2 more than
momentarily
Bell: bangs on table
Rattle: shakes definitely
Dangles ring, cube: transfers hand
to hand
Bell: transfers adeptly
Bell: retains

Language

Vocalizes: m-m-m (crying)
Vocalizes: polysyllabic vowel
sounds

Personal-Social

Feeding: takes solids well
Play: with feet to mouth (supine)

REFERENCES

Balint M 1973 The doctor and his patient and the illness. Pitman, London, p 69–80

Bell S M, Ainsworth MDS 1972 Infant crying and maternal responsiveness. Child Development 43: 1171–1190

Bowlby J 1975 Anxious attachment. In: Separation attachment and loss. Penguin, Harmondsworth, England, ch 15, p 255

Brazelton T B, Koslowski B, Main M 1974 The origins of reciprocity in mother-infant interaction. In: Lewis M, Rosenblum L (eds) The effect of the infant on his care giver. John Wiley and Sons, New York

Brazelton T B, Tronick E, Adamson L, Als H, Weise 1975 early mother-infant reciprocity. In:Parent-Infant interaction. CIBA Symposium No. 33 New Series Elsevier, Amsterdam

Court   1976 'Fit for the Future'. The report of the Committee on Child Health Services. Command 6684 HMSO London, p 73

Curtis Jenkins, G H, Collins C, Andren S 1978 Surveillance in general practice. British Medical Journal 1: 1537–1540

Dalton K 1971 Prospective study into puerperal depression. British Journal of Psychiatry 118: 689–692

Davies D P, Evans T I 1976 Failure to thrive at the breast. Lancet 2: 1194–1195

De Mause L1976 The evolution of childhood. In: De Mause L (ed) The history of childhood. Souvenir press, London, ch 1

DHSS 1978 Local Authority Circular. Health Services Development. Court report on child health services. HC (78) S

Dunn J 1977 Distress and comfort. Fontana/Open books, London

Egan D, Illingworth R S, MacKeith R C 1969 Developmental screening 0–5. Clinics in developmental medicine. Heinemann Medical, London

Frommer E A, O'Shea G 1973 Antenatal identification of women liable to have problems in managing their infants. British Journal of Psychiatry 123: 149–156

Graham R 1977 Personal communication

Illick J E 1976 Child rearing in seventeenth century England and America. In: De Mause L (ed) The history of childhood. Souvenir Press, london, ch 7

Illingworth R S 1954 Three months colic. Archives of Disease in Childhood 29: 145, 165

Illingworth R S 1977(a) Basic developmental screening. Blackwell, Oxford

Illingworth R S 1977(b) The normal child. Churchill Livingstone, Edinburgh

Jakobsson I, Lindberg T 1978 Cow's milk as a cause of infantile colic in breast-fed infants. Lancet 2: 437–439

Jolly H 1978 Book of Child Care. Sphere, London

Jorup S 1952 Colonic hyper-peristalsis in neurolabile infants. Acta Paediatrica 85: 41, 1–110

Kempe C H, Silverman F N, Steele B F, Droegemenlter N, Silver H K 1962 The battered child syndrome. Journal of the American Medical Association 181: 17

Klaus H K, Kennell J 1976 Parent to infant attachment. In: Hull D (ed)

Recent advances in paediatrics. Churchill Livingstone, Edinburgh, ch 5

Le Chateau P 1977 Left-sided preference in holding and carrying newborn infants. Journal of Maternal and Child Care 2: 11, 418–421

MacCarthy D, Booth E M 1970 Parental rejection and stunting of growth. Journal of Psychosomatic Research 14: 259–265

Moore T, Ucko L E 1957 Night waking in early infancy. Archives of Disease in Childhood 52: 164, 333

Neligan G S 1974 Role of the paediatrician in the cycle of deprivation. Proceedings Royal Society of Medicine 67: 1055–1056

Neligan G S, Prudham D 1969 Norms for four standard developmental milestones by sex, social class and place in family. Journal of Developmental Medicine and Child Neurology 11: 423–431

Pringle M K 1974 Social adversity and its effects on the intelligent child's achievement. Proceedings Royal Society of Medicine 66: 1203–1204

Sheridan M D 1960 The developmental progress of infants and young children Reports on Public health medical subjects No. 102 HMSO, London

Shukla A, Forsyth H A, Anderson C, Marway S M 1972 Some aspects of infant nutrition in the first year of life. British Medical Journal 4: 507–515

Stanway P, Stanway A 1978 Breast is best. Pan original, London

Starte G D 1974 Developmental assessment of the young child in general practice. The Practitioner 213: 823

Starte G D 1976 Results from a developmental screening clinic in general practice. The Practitioner 216: 311

Starte G D 1977 Screening the seven month old child. Journal of Maternal and Child Health 1: 4, 16

Thoman E 1975 How a rejecting baby affects mother-infant syncrony. In: Parent-Infant Interaction. CIBA Symposium No. 33 (New Series) Elsevier, Amsterdam

Zander L I, Watson M, Taylor R W, Morrell D C 1978 Integration of general practitioner and specialist antenatal care. Journal Royal College of General Practitioners 28: 455–458

Zinkin P M, Cox C A 1976 Child health services and inverse care laws. British Medical Journal 2: 411–413

5.

From seven months to twelve months

By the beginning of the seventh month, the baby has begun to demonstrate the signs of character and personality that only the mother and other close care givers have so far attributed to him from the first few days after birth. Now they can be openly and directly observed. Curiosity, that most fundamental attribute that characterises all animal behaviour, has begun to take the baby forward into space and time. No longer content to just sit or lie and cry for stimulus until it appears, and cry for it when it vanishes, the baby can, with his new found mobility in rolling over and staying sitting up, observe and capture for himself much more of the world at large. His very mobility creates dangers that the mother learns to be on guard against. From now on the mother needs to be more aware, more alert than ever before and this accounts for her oft reported temporary failure to cope in this second half year, as the stresses rise and her fears that the child might hurt himself become very real.

The infant discovers with great rapidity the varieties of interactive play. Bruner and Sherwood (1976) have described the play-with-rules concept—for instance, peek-a-boo. This game is dependent on a mutual respect of each participant for the 'rules', i.e., their shared expectations concerning what happens *next* and their willingness to conform to the agreed procedures. By seven months, the child has usually learned to be the recipient—that is, will respond to the initiation of such a game. By a year, the child will initiate such a game himself.

It is important to realise that games with 'rules' have a natural history that begins when the child interacts with the people around him. The child needs to be 'taught'. At first,

114

the mother is the teacher; only much later can the child play games like these with strangers.

Learning to play games may seem to be so natural a part of a child's upbringing that it need not be given serious consideration. Yet, as Garvey (1977) has so compellingly argued, play can only emerge spontaneously if the very young child experiences some basic model of *non literal* treatment of resources. (Non literal behaviour is clearly signalled behaviour, tickling with the approaching hand producing screams of delighted anticipatory response in the child who has learned the game. This contrasts with literal behaviour, purposeful handling when the baby is bathed or attended to which does not produce the same response.)

As the child matures, play becomes more and more varied—but always initially interactive. For the doctor concerned with the care of children within the family, the lessons are obvious. Firstly, the health of the mother and her interest in her child dictate the stimulation that the child receives.

Play, a sign of the quality of that interaction, is a formative process in social and indeed in cognitive development. Play prepares children for life. Its absence when a depressed mother, a single mother attempting to do a job and bringing up a child, a mother struggling to keep a marriage together or a mother unable for any reason to spend the time with her baby 'teaching the rituals' of play, can cause often immediately obvious adverse effects on the baby and young child and should be watched for. Many of the examination techniques of the infant and young child depend on an assessment using changing forms of play which coincide with various stages in development. Their absence or dysfunction can give an erroneous impression of retardation in a child deprived of the experience of play. Their absence may account for the 'learned hopelessness' appearance of the grossly deprived child. Pollack (1972) has shown that three-year-old children living in an inner London suburb, who have delayed language development, had many fewer toys than the children with normal language development—24 per cent had no toys at all.

Behavioural problems

Prominent among behavioural problems in the second six

months of life are separation anxiety and stranger anxiety with the response of 'attachment behaviour'.

To the mother, the change in infant behaviour seems special and rewarding. The baby chooses, very positively, her company and smiles at her rather than at anybody else. A further development then occurs that seems to be the dark side of this change in relationship, namely, stranger anxiety. The baby begins to object violently when left and resents in particular, any contact with people he doesn't know and trust. It would be a convenient explanation if these two sorts of behaviour were both aspects of the same condition. However, the current view is that probably they are not. Many have observed that where the link to the mother is close, strong and confident, separation anxiety shows long before stranger anxiety. Secondly, where the child is surrounded by a few care givers to whom he is equally attached, then separation and stranger anxiety come together and neither is particularly strong.

The great problem for all who have either done research in this field or work with mothers and babies, is that babies vary enormously in the degree of anxiety they experience, and as Leech (1974) succinctly puts it, 'for practical purposes it is probably safest to assume that at some ages, on some days and in some circumstances, all infants will be made anxious by separation from the mother'.

Why is this important? Firstly, mother always notices the behaviour and in the company of critical strangers is usually blamed by them for 'spoiling' the child. Secondly, I have heard many times from mothers of older children 'I don't know what they did in that hospital, they spoiled him something chronic—all he wants, now he's home, is to be picked up'. Only careful explanation can defuse these two potentially serious situations. Thirdly, it is very tempting for doctors, faced with a crying struggling nine-month-old child, to attempt to take him from his mother into another room 'to examine him properly'. As a manoeuvre, it is bound to fail and, worst still, the child rarely forgets, greeting the sight of the doctor and his consulting room for months and sometimes years after, with signs of great distress. Instead, it is vital that the mother should be allowed to hold the child herself *whenever possible* as the tears on her lap are invariably less than the tears off it, caused by separation and stranger anxiety. Fourthly, badly handled situations where separation has to occur, as it does frequently in everyday life, can transform a placid calm baby into a neurotic frightened door-watching child, too frightened to play, instead, watching its mother's every movement, in case she disappears. Only careful history taking can signal the diagnosis. Even then, it is sometimes difficult to get a mother to change her behaviour as the child sometimes takes many days to forgive.

There is one additional manifestation of separation anxiety that, in my experience, causes particular problems and can only be diagnosed by the most careful history taking. If a baby who has started to show separation and stranger anxiety is left asleep in the care of a strange baby-sitter and wakes in the parent's absence, a most troublesome disturbance occurs. The first the doctor hears of it is when the child, usually eight or nine months old, is brought to the doctor. 'He suddenly won't go into his bedroom, let alone lie down and sleep in his own bed. You've got to do something'. Careful questioning frequently reveals an episode such as I have described. The parent's description of the child fighting off sleep, afraid to close his eyes and waking seemingly from deep sleep the moment he's left, is characteristic.

What should the doctor do? Most mothers usually understand the mechanism of the anxiety once it is explained. Techniques, such as always telling an older child that the mother is going away which will produce tears of loss but not of betrayal, or when the baby has to be left briefly, staying in voice range—the mother should talk continuously as she goes downstairs to collect a dry nappy or a bottle; all are helpful. Always leaving a child with a familiar baby-sitter helps too, as does asking the baby-sitter to come while the child is still awake to allow them to meet. (However, even this occasionally fails as mothers will tell you.)

The better the anxiety is handled, the shorter the period the attachment behaviour lasts.

A full discussion of this often fascinating and, for doctors sometimes extremely disconcerting behaviour, can be found in *Babyhood* (Pelican Books) by Penelope Leech, p 253–265, and in *Attachment* by John Bowlby, p 221–285.

Lastly, although the majority of mothers come to terms with and grow with the baby out of the problem, some do not. Resentment of the 'demands', an inability to understand what is going on and a violent nature, conspire together to produce an explosive situation, as the mother, becoming increasingly aggravated, lashes out and hits her baby in an attempt to 'knock some sense into it'. It is surprising how universal punishment is at a year old (Newson & Newson, 1965).

Motor function

The development of motor function produces the most obvious change that takes place in the second half of the first year.

Sitting up, reaching out, pulling to stand, crawling, or its normal variation, hitching, bottom shuffling (Robson, 1972) and finally walking, occur in a well-defined progression. There are, of course, wide variations in the pace at which this development proceeds. Non-sitting 14-month-old children are not very rare, nor is the walking eight month old. Illingworth (1977) reports wide variations in motor development in children who were subsequently quite normal—and it is very important that the doctor should never prognosticate unfavourably on the developmental delay of a child seen and examined once, particularly if only one field of development is affected.

Much confusion occurs about the terms 'developmental delay' and 'developmental diagnosis'. Development is very rapid in the first year of life and the picture can change from day to day as the child acquires skills and knowledge. Theoretically, therefore, delay in the process should be easy to detect. However, so many factors affect the process that serious mistakes can be made unless they all are taken into account. The first and most obvious factor is the age of the child. An allowance must always be made for any difference between gestational and chronological age. It is important to be as precise as possible over the exact difference. Prematurity, alone, is often blamed for causing a delay which in reality may be due to true retardation arising from factors surrounding the premature birth. These include birth asphyxia, infection and placental insufficiency affecting brain growth. This is obvious only when an exact estimate is made of gestational age.

Secondly, the quality of maternal care and, therefore, stimulation can make major differences to the pace at which development occurs in some fields, certainly in socialisation and motor function. A mother living on her own in a bedsitter who never talks to her baby and keeps him tied down in a cot 23 hours a day, can produce a profound effect. The baby, when seen with lack-lustre eyes and extreme immobility, gives an impression of being months younger than he really is. When a skilled foster mother has the same child for just a week or two, by handling, playing and allowing him freedom to move, an explosion of development occurs across all the fields of behaviour, making the baby unrecogisable to the doctor and mother, if they have not seen him for one or two weeks.

Thirdly, there are, as already stated, naturally occurring wide variations in the pace of normal development, dependent on the individual child and his genetic make-up (Robson, 1972).

Developmental diagnosis, therefore, must make an allowance for all these features (Holt, 1977). The factors that govern the arrival at a disgnosis are six:

(i) Delay in developmental pattern. The greater the delay the more serious it is. The Denver scale (Table 4.1–inside front cover) shows how the delay can be quantified. Any child who falls outside the scale of normal in one particular on one occasion should not necessarily be considered permanently abnormal—instead, he should be observed carefully, with perhaps an increase in the frequency of surveillance, until either the delay has disappeared or it has manifested itself across all the fields of development.

(ii) Distortion of developmental pattern. Variations can occur in the smoother integrated pattern of development at any time, and everybody responsible for the continuing care of children recognises them. It is important to take these into account before making a diagnosis of developmental retardation. Hence the golden rule 'never make a diagnosis of retardation after a single examination'.

(iii) Quantitative changes. As well as ensuring that the child does transfer a brick from hand to hand at seven months, it is important to ensure that at eight months he will tire of the brick, shed it, and wish to explore other conveniently near objects. So, too, infinitely repetitive play at a level inappropriate to the child's age should always alert the examiner to the possibility that abnormality might be present.

(iv) Qualitative changes. *How* the child looks at you is extremely important. A steady stare at the examiner's face whilst the examiner tries to carry out at seven months a Stycar rolling balls vision test at three metres is familiar to all who have tried. Fleeting glances or frank avoidance is of serious import if other factors in the child's life suggests a reason, such as the living conditions of mother and child.

(v) Application of abilities. The avid reaching out for toys that most one year old children show contrasts with the timid finger pointing that a shouted at and threatened child demonstrates in the same situation. This latter type of behaviour is typical of a child brought up in an abnormal environment, where the care givers notice *only* his positive behaviour, equate it instantly with 'wrong' and forbid it. This will cause alterations in developmental progress.

(vi) Other signs. Lack of use of a limb and gross motor delay accompanied by exaggerated tendon reflexes and rigidity in some muscle groups will carry a much greater significance than if the motor delay occurs on its own. Therefore, a full physical as well as a developmental examination should always be performed.

Once a diagnosis of developmental delay is reached, it is important to realise that it is not unchanging or unchangeable. The continuing assessment of the child at regular intervals never ceases to amaze those who perform it. Gloomy prognostications about a child's future abilities should be kept to oneself. Parents need firstly, confirmation of what, nearly always, they have observed already, and an open and frank explanation of the likely cause. Prophecy should be resisted. Instead, continuing surveillance demonstrates to the parents that the doctor and his team are maintaining interest in the child and his family. Ease of access to the doctor ensures that any new development noticed by the mother can be brought to the doctor's attention early, which minimises the parent's tendency to worry, sometimes for extended periods between fixed appointments.

It is important always to be positive about a child. The child is the centre of the parent's life, particularly when there is any suggestion of disorder that could lead to handicap. Never say 'he'll never go to a normal school' or 'he'll never see clearly'. It is much more likely to be heard correctly by the parents and understood, if phrased 'he'll be going to our special school where we can offer all the services he can't get in a normal school so easily' (speech therapy, physiotherapy, etc.) or 'we are going to give him special glasses which will help him to see much better, particularly if you, the parents, ensure that what he's trying to see is always well lit'.

The importance of good communication between doctor and parent is highlighted by the history given in Chapter 3.

At all times, the doctor should try and put himself in the parent's position and ensure by every possible means that he and the parents understand each other. In a recent survey of doctor/parent communication in a large paediatric unit in Los Angeles, the most important thing that the parents noticed was whether or not the doctor sat down to *talk* to them; the act of *sitting* was the most important thing the doctor did; what he had to communicate coming second! (Kotsch, 1978).

The development of vision, hearing and language parallels that of motor development. It is now known that a normal child can focus in the newborn period on an object more than 20 cm away from the face and also that he can be shown to focus on objects many metres away in the distance. By seven months his visual apparatus is fully developed and is used with ever-increasing precision in guiding, for instance, the hand to reach out and pick up objects. What is interesting is that the child can be persuaded by a variety of tricks to reach out initially in the wrong direction. The moment the hand is seen the trajectory is corrected, and the object picked up accurately (Bower, 1977).

Hearing also is developing fast. Babies, of course, can turn to sounds in the newborn period (Wertheimer, 1961), and by one year old can localise sounds, accurately through 360° both laterally and vertically. However, it is in his social behaviour that the maturity of his auditory system shows itself to best advantage.

The noises that babies make have been subjected to systematic research. It seems that the production of noise to order by the child occurs at about the sixth month. This explains, perhaps, why totally deaf children 'babble' until the sixth mouth in an apparently aimless 'practice' and then stop. Babbling, itself is dependent on the auditory environment of the child. Irwin (1960) has found that the quality and richness of babbling is closely related to social class, and Kagan (1971) showed that girls were less affected by this than boys.

So the aimless noises give way to aimed or 'practice' language—runs of two syllable babbling *ada ada ada aga aga abababa* are reported by parents lasting for minutes at a time. Usually *adadada* is produced first and *amamama* after a few days or weeks—yet in only one country in the world is a *'dada'* a mother. The mother, the world over, responds to the *'amama ama'* sounds produced later on and reinforces the message by showing delight every time the baby produces the sound.

Only when the preverbal child has seen and heard something a hundred times or more will he begin to 'speak to order', and only when he reaches one year old does he consistently name the mother 'Mama' and the father 'Dada'. Even then, careful questioning reveals that the child is often muddled, and many a newly qualified doctor has felt faintly embarrassed by the year old child strongly naming him Dada in the consulting room or in the street!

In all fields of behaviour, it can be seen that the mother's influence (or that of other primary care givers) is paramount in stimulating development. Learned helplessness is only one extreme example of this. Speech, games playing, confidence and the general synchronising of the mother's behaviour to the needs of the child are all facets of the good relationship called mother love. Unselfishness, tireless energy, patience and the ability to communicate with her child are all necessary for this most difficult of roles.

The family doctor observes the hopeless mother, the health visitor supports, the social worker undertakes case work, and the mother alas rarely changes radically. But it is never too late to effect some minor degree of change. Seizing the opportunity every time a baby is brought to you to look at the whole child, assuring the mother of the excellence of her skills as a mother, and showing her what the acquisition of new skills mean in the child's developmental progress, all help to encourage her. The doctor is often the one person the mother will listen to. All too often, we see the mother as a 'worrier', assure her at a superficial level without showing interest (let alone concern), and lose the opportunity of helping her to do a better job.

At around the first birthday is a good time to examine the baby again as part of the surveillance programme, the last

Table 5.1   Suggested technique of examination.

Twelve months

Gait	*Equipment*	None.
	Position	M places C on floor standing.
	Method	C is encouraged to walk after toy to M. If unable to walk M is asked to walk him holding one hand. Failing this C is sat at M's feet to see if he pulls to stand. Failing this C is watched moving on the floor after a toy.
	Score	—accordingly.
Brick	*Equipment*	One 1″ square coloured brick.
	Position	C on M's lap at table.
	Method	As for 7 months. Observe if C throws the brick and follows its trajectory with eyes.
	Score	—accordingly.
Pellet	*Equipment*	Smartie or similar size pellet.
	Position	C on M's lap at table.
	Method	As for 7 months. When C has picked up pellet, place a cup in front of him and encourage him to release pellet into cup.
	Score	—accordingly.
1Rolling Balls	*Equipment*	Plastic or polystyrene (N.F.E.R.) balls size $\frac{1}{2}$″, $\frac{1}{4}$″, 3/16th″, $\frac{1}{8}$″.
	Position	As for 7 months.
	Method	As for 7 months with addition of $\frac{1}{8}$″ ball
	Score	—accordingly.
Cover Test	As for 7 months.	
Hearing	As for 7 months.	
1Speech Observed	*Equipment*	None.
	Position	—
	Method	The observation of all words and speech made by C throughout the examination.
	Score	If no words are heard during the examination score 'None' even though M reports otherwise.
		Complete box in top section for reported speech using same criteria as for observed speech.

Imitation Rattle
Reaction to Examiner As for 7 months.
Attention

chance to detect congenital disorders and the first to confirm or deny variations in development spotted at the seven month examination.

The list of abnormalities detected or suspected at this age is short, but the seriousness of the disorders establishes decisively, I think, the need for an examination at this age (see Ch. 4).

What follows is a suggested technique of examination that many general practitioners and others are now using (Table 5.1). This can be used in conjunction with the proforma (Fig. 5.1) and covers all aspects of a year old's growth and development.

Whatever examination is carried out, it is essential to ensure that efficient examination of hearing, vision and motor function is included, otherwise, major abnormality will be missed—even with an efficient technique things are still missed in our programme, despite all our efforts.

One possible routine

When the mother comes in, ask her to sit down with the dressed baby on her lap and do not at first look at the baby. At 1 year visual alertness is marked and direct eye contact with a stranger can be threatening and result in the baby crying. It is best to look vaguely over the baby's shoulder and while talking quietly to the mother briefly look at his face from time to time It is important not to give him any toys that may be used in subsequent tests so as to avoid familiarising him with them and risk his disinterest later. However, a spatula or a brightly coloured paper-weight may serve to engage his attention.

Observe the mother-baby interaction, how the baby is dressed and his general appearance, whether he seems restless or placid on his mother's lap, how safely or securely she holds him. The presence of other older children may modify the interview. Ask the mother 'how is he getting on?", "are you pleased with him?" , and "is he pleased with you?" This latter question will encourage her to talk about his reactions to her and how she sees these as evidence of his personality. Be aware of her interpretations of normal stages of development such as whether she feels the earlier stage of putting things to the mouth is 'naughty' and how she deals with casting which may have begun. Does she think his constant need for her is evidence of his being spoilt? Has she begun to use physical punishment? How does she react when he cries? Many of these aspects are very delicate areas to explore and difficult to assess objectively, but will nevertheless give an idea of the relationship between mother and child and the quality of care.

Ask the mother 'is he happy?' and 'does he sleep well?' and 'does he eat well?' These questions are scored on a Yes/No basis but incidentally may reveal other information which can usefully be recorded. 'Has he been ill since he was last seen?' 'Does he go to a playgroup or nursery or have a child-minder?' and 'How many hours a week do you work?' If a child-

PAEDIATRIC DEVELOPMENT RECORD

OFFICE USE

Dr's Code (1–2)

DR.

On Cols 3–13

Surname _____ First Name _____

Punch : First 8 letters of surname

14

First 3 letters of first name

Date of Birth [ ][ ][ ][ ][ ] Birth Rank [ ] 20

21 22   23 24

Father's Age [ ][ ] Mother's Age [ ][ ]

26   31

Father's Occupation _____ 25 [ ]

Exam. at **12 months**	Date

Mother's Comments				
	Happy	No	Yes	32 [ ]
	Sleeps	No	Yes	33 [ ]
	Eats	No	Yes	34 [ ]

Illness since last exam.   No | Yes   35 [ ]
(If yes specify nature of illness)

Change in family circumstances   No | Yes   36 [ ]

Nursery No | Yes   37 [ ]
Minder   No | Yes   38 [ ]

Hours worked per week (Mother) [ ]   39 40 [ ][ ]

Reported Speech 1 2 3 4   41 [ ]

Gait	Creeps Crawls Hitches	Pulls to stand	Cruises Walks one hand held	Walks alone	42 [ ]
1" Brick	Withdraws	Transfers	Casts not looking	Casts looking	43 [ ]
Pellet	Withdraws or fails	Whole hand pick up	Finger Thumb Apposition	Releases	44 [ ]
Rolling balls	$\frac{1}{2}$"	$\frac{1}{4}$"	$\frac{3}{16}$"	$\frac{1}{8}$"	45 [ ]
Cover Test	Squint	Doubtful		No squint	46 [ ]
Hearing	Doubtful	Satisfactory		Good	47 [ ]
Speech observed	No words	2 words or less	3 words or less with meaning	3 or more words with meaning	48 [ ]
limitation rattle	No interest	Interest and manipulation		Imitation	49 [ ]
Reaction to Examiner	None	Resists		Co-operates	50 [ ]
Attention	Poor	Variable		Sustained	51 [ ]

PHYSICAL EXAM.

Weight   Height   H.C.

(52–4) [ ][ ] K.grms. (55–7) [ ][ ] Cms. (58–60) [ ][ ] Cms.

Abnormality No/Yes (Specify below)

61 [ ]

Appearance

Comments

Action

Card Code

79 [3]

If tests incomplete because of child's unco-operation put tick in box [ ]

80 [ ]

Fig 5.1 Recording card—12 months

minder is involved it is important to establish whether this is a close relative known to the baby, and if a registered minder, how many other children are minded at the same time. Ask about the number of words used and try to establish that they are used spontaneously and with reference to one object or person. Indiscriminate repetition of single syllables such as Da-da and Ma-ma does not count.

It is convenient to begin the examination with the 1″ brick, with the child sitting on his mother's lap set up to the table which is about waist height to the baby. The brick is placed on the table and the test performed. Next the pellet test is done, followed by the imitation with the rattle. By this time a rapport should be developing with the child and the examination will be fun. It is now convenient, with the child still sitting on his mother's lap, to do the cover test and this is followed by the hearing test. Some re-arrangement is now required for the Rolling Balls, such as removal of the table or the re-positioning of the mother and child in another seat and the movement of the examiner to a suitable position. At the end of the rolling balls test the child may want to get down to pick up the balls and this he is encouraged to do, giving a chance to observe his gait.

By this time the examiner may be in a position to record any speech heard and to ascertain if the sounds have any relation to an identifiable object. It will also have been possible by now to judge his reaction to the examiner and his attention span.

The physical examination

At some convenient time during the examination, the head circumference is recorded in centimetres. This must be estimated twice and the maximum recording is noted. At the same time the hands are passed lightly over the skull and the fontanelle palpated. The extent of the physical examination will depend as to whether the baby has been seen before. Generally at this age babies do not like lying supine and the examination is best done on the mother's lap. The examiner may have to compromise about the complete removal of all the clothes as this often leads to tears. As a minimum, the napkin must be removed, the hips examined and the testicles palpated in boys. Auscultation of the heart is important and is best done at an opportune moment when the baby is quiet. It may be resisted by plucking movements at the stethoscope, and these are best dealt with by holding the plucking hand firmly away or by giving the baby a brick to hold in each hand.

The examination ends with a chat to the mother about her beautiful child and if necessary a discussion about any doubtful results that may have been recorded and plans for future observation.

Appendix

GESELL'S KEY AGE SCHEDULES:

32 weeks

Motor

Sit: 1 minute erect, unsteady
Stands: maintains briefly, hands held
Prone: pivots
Pellet: radial raking

Adaptive

Cube: grasps 2nd cube
Cube: retains 2 as 3rd presented
Cube: holds 2 prolongedly
Cup, cube: holds cube, regards cup

Language

Vocalises: single syllable as da, ba, ka

Personal–Social

Play: bites, chews toys
Play: reaches persistently for toys out of reach

36 weeks

Motor

Sit: 10 minutes and stead
Sit: leans forward, re-erects from forward position
Stand: holds rail, full weight
Cube: radial digital grasp
Pellet: prehends, scissors grasp

Adaptive

Cube: grasps 3rd cube
Cube: hits, pushes cube with cube
Cup–cube: cube against cup

Language

Vocalizes: data (or equivalent)
Vocalises: imitates sounds
Comprehension: responds to name, no-no

Personal–Social

Feeding: holds bottle
Feeding: feeds self biscuit

40 weeks

Motor

Sit: indefinitely, steady
Sit: goes over to prone
Stand: pulls to feet at rail creeps
Cube: crude release
Pellet: grasps promptly
Pellet: inferior pincer grasp

Adaptive

Cube: matches 2 cubes
Cup–cube: touches cube in cup
Pellet: index finger approach
Pellet and bottle: grasps pellet
Bell: grasps by handle
Bell: spontaneously waves or shakes

Language

Vocalise: dada and mama
Vocalise: 1 'word'
Comprehension: bye and patacake

Personal–Social

Social: waves bye and patacake

44 weeks

Motor

Stands: (at rail of cot) lifts,
replaces foot
Bell: grasps by top of handle

Adaptive

Cup–cube: removes cube from
cup
Cup–cube: (after demonstration)
cube into cup without release
Pellet in bottle: points at pellet
through glass
Bell: regards and pokes clapper

Language

Personal–Social

Social: gives toy to person, no
release

48 weeks

Motor

Sits: pivots
Stands: cruises at rail
Walks: needs 2 hands held
Pellets: neat pincer grasp

Adaptive

Cube: sequential play
Pellet and bottle: takes pellet only

Language

Personal–Social

Play: carries toys

52 weeks

Motor

Walks: needs only 1 hand held

Adaptive

Cube: (demonstrated) tries tower,
fails
Cup–cube: (demonstrated)
releases 1 cube in cup
Pellet and bottle: tries insert,
releases fails
Ring–string: dangles ring by
string

Language

Vocalizes: 2 'words' (besides
mama, dada)
Comprehension: gives a toy
(request and gesture)

Personal–Social

Mirror: ball to mirror
Dressing: co-operates in dressing

56 weeks

Motor

Stands: momentarily alone
Cube: grasps 2 in one hand

Adaptive

Cup–cube: (no demonstration)
cube into cup
Drawing: vigorous imitative
scribble
Formboard: (demonstration)
inserts round block

Language

Vocalises: 3–4 words
Vocalises: incipient jargon
Comprehension: a few objects by
name

Personal–Social

Ball: releases with a slight cast
towards examiner

[Adapted from: Developmental Diagnosis. Gessell and Amatruda (by permission)]

REFERENCES

Bower T 1977 The perceptual world of the child. Fontana/Open Books, London

Bowbly J 1971 Attachment. Vol I Attachment and loss. Penguin Books, Harmondsworth, England

Bruner J, Sherwood V 1976 Peek-a-boo and learning of rule structures. In: Bruner J, Jolly A, Sylva K (eds) Play: its role in development and evolution. Penguin Books, Harmondsworth, England

Garvey C 1977 Play. Fontana Open Books Original, London

Holt K S 1977 Developmental paediatrics. Butterworth, London

Illingworth R S 1979 The normal child, 7th edn. Churchill Livingstone, Edinburgh

Irwin O C 1960 Language and communication. In: Mussen P H (ed) Handbook of research methods in child development. John Wiley and Sons, New York

Kagan J 1971 Change and continuity in infancy. John Wiley and Sons, New York

Kotsch L 1978 Personal communication

Leech P 1974 Babyhood. Penguin Books, Harmondsworth, England

Newson J, Newson E 1965 Patterns of infant care. Penguin Books, Harmondsworth, England

Pollack M 1972 Today's three year olds in London. Heinemann, London

Robson P 1972 Shuffling, hitching, scooting and sliding. Some observations in 30 otherwise normal children. Journal of Developmental Medicine and Child Neurology 12: 608

Wertheimer M 1961 Psychomotor co-ordination of auditory, visual space at birth. Science 134: 1926

6.

Developmental surveillance

Traditionally in general practice, doctors have been content to wait for the sick to come to them. Recently however, general practitioners have involved themselves in screening various segments of the practice population for which they are responsible (Hart, 1975).

The exercise has had varying results and many inside and outside the profession question the point of the effort. The time taken to find individual cases of diabetes or hypertension seems out of all proportion to the number of patients found with the illness compared to the numbers screened. In addition, the cost of such services and the untreatable nature of the conditions found has raised doubts as to its worth.

In the screening of the preschool child, many problems have been created by different interpretations put on the word 'screening'. I would prefer the word 'surveillance' and I take it to mean the acceptance of responsibility for the comprehensive care of children—routine medical care, immunization, developmental guidance and regular examination of *all* the children in the practice's care, at which certain screening tests are carried out, notably hearing, vision and speech, see Chapters 4 and 5. There are now many individual general practitioners working towards the goal of this comprehensive form of care. The Court Report estimated that 15 per cent of general practitioners were involved in this work. My* estimate is that the figure is now closer to 20 per cent. The actual work being carried out can vary from running one clinic a week to immunize children and see all-comers, to a sophisticated programme of care

*Dr G. Curtis Jenkins'.

involving health visitors, nurses, psychologists and general practitioner paediatricians (Stark et al, 1975). The one calls for minimal involvement and commitment, often with a large part of the work done by health visitors, the other involves a major commitment of time and effort within a radically different framework of family care.

Somewhere in the middle is a method of organisation and practice that can be effective and satisfying both to the doctor organising such a service and to the families lucky enough to benefit from it (Rowland, 1975).

In our six man, group practice, with nearly full lists; two medical officers from the Community Health Service and myself work the equivalent of five sessions weekly running the programme, four clinic sessions and one equivalent session for visiting all new babies in the home.

A nurse works two sessions weekly in the clinic with us. The secretary who administers the programme and runs the clinics, works 8 hours weekly. The four practice health visitors are usually on duty for each clinic and are available for consultation. What do we achieve?

(i) Near 95 per cent immunization rate.

(ii) 100 per cent coverage of the under five population for routine developmental examinations at under 20 days, 7 months, 12 months, 28–30 months and at $4\frac{1}{2}$ years, with a selective examination at 36 months dependent on the findings at the 28–30 month examination (See Introduction).

(iii) 30 per cent of clinic time spent on more frequent surveillance of children at risk for any reason and for more general problems, such as developmental guidance and the management of feeding problems, behaviour disturbance and other medical problems that the health visitors feel they are unable to handle.

(iv) A programme of practical support and help for the families with young children in our care run effectively by the health visitors who, because of the *very* high attendance rates, know virtually every family who, in their turn, know them and can call on them for help when needed.

My partners continue their traditional involvement in illness care and report that the parallel service causes few problems. Parents are quick to understand how to use each service and show considerable acumen in finding help at the appropriate level in the primary care team.

What is the point of the major part of the effort, the routine developmental surveillance programme?

The figures, (see Ch. 4) I believe, are justification enough and are mirrored by other workers who have learned the appropriate skills and who have ensured 100 per cent coverage of other child populations. Total coverage is extremely important as the non-users of such a service tend to have the most problems. (Zinkin & Cox, 1976).

Practice organisation is the key to success. The practice clerk responsible for new registrations and deletions should ensure that both are promptly notified to the health visitor or secretary running the programme. An age-sex register is vital initially to build the register of children under five in the practice but because it is filed alphabetically by year and for other reasons, it is unsuitable as the prime data base. Instead, 'year' books need to be constructed; stiff covered address books with the children registered in the practice listed in *month* order by birth date throughout the year. Five books will be needed, one for each of the age groups (nought to one, one to two, two to three, three to four and four to five year populations). Children can be entered in the books by the health visitors from their own notification system run by the Community Health Services when they are born into the practice. If the doctor intends making his initial visit when the new born baby reaches home, his involvement in the general practitioners obstetric unit or notification of discharge from specialist maternity units will enable him to visit in many parts of the country within 48 hours of discharge. (see Ch. 3).

New registration should be entered into the year books appropriately and deletions made in the same way. The books can also be used to record clinic attendance for surveillance examinations and for other items of importance, such as a note of handicap occurring, non-attendance for the examination and medically and socially at risk children. It is vital to ensure that no child is missed.

Initially, when these books are constructed, it is important to make an accurate count of the total number of children of each age. In a one or two man practice, the practice secretary can take on the task. In bigger practices, the task should be allotted more specifically. One person *only* should be responsible for the administration of the programme, and the maintenance of the year books. Often the Community Health Services can be persuaded to pay the salary.

Only when this is done can the doctor make an estimate of the likely workload. It is important to match time available to the workload. Starting with high hopes of seeing every child under five in the practice seven or eight times in the first five years of life has caused the downfall of many an ambitious programme.

Instead, it is advisable to calculate clinic workload in the following way. If *one* clinic weekly is to be run, assuming that *one* doctor *without* a deputy is going to staff it, allow for an average of 44 clinic sessions in the year. In a two and a quarter hour clinic it is possible to see eight to ten children for between 12 and 18 minutes per child (average 15 minutes). 75 per cent of the appointments need to be routine surveillance examinations but at least 25 per cent must be left to allow for other consultations, including 'emergencies' filled in by the health visitors.

In one year, over 250 surveillance examinations can be done. If all the new born children are visited in the home (so obviating the traditional six-week examination decreed by custom) then a practice with a birth rate of 50 per annum can ensure that *all* children in the practice can be seen five times in the first five years of life and also that any children and parents needing to be seen for any other reason can be fitted in.

In our practice,* the doctors are in attendance at the two clinics weekly and 18–20 children are booked for examination at each clinic. With a 10 to 15 per cent failure rate to attend for first appointments, about 1600 children are seen per annum, about 900–950 for routine examinations and 550–600 for extra consultations for a variety of reasons (see Table 6.1).

When a busy month is in prospect with a bulge in the numbers, the clinic secretary informs the doctors that one or two more children will be booked per clinic and over the year any drift away from the target dates can be quickly checked before the programme becomes hopelessly behind. After the last examination at 54–56 months, the child health records are transferred to the Community Health Services department to ensure that they are available when the child has his or her school medical examination 12 to 18 months later.

How can the information about the child's developmental

*From Curtis Jenkins et al 1978 Developmental surveillance in general practice. British Medical Journal 1 : 1537–1540

Table 6.1 Appointment failures at surveillance clinics in two years

Age at examination	7 months		12 months		28–30 months		3 years examinations		4½ years		number of examinations		Total
Sex	M	F	M	F	M	F	M	F	M	F	M	F	
Number	201	183	194	216	177	192	104	63	229	216	905	870	1,775
Failed first appointment	20	18	16	26	29	29	17	18	35	47	117	138	255
Failed 2 or more appointments	5	3	9	–	15	7	2	1	3	8	32	19	51

‡From Curtis Jenkins et al 1978 Developmental surveillance in general practice. British Medical Journal 1:1537–1540

(a)

PAEDIATRIC DEVELOPMENT RECORD

DR. ....

Surname _____ First Name _____

Date of Birth 14 [ ][ ][ ][ ][ ] 20 Birth Rank [ ]

Father's Age 21 22 [ ][ ] Mother's Age 23 24 [ ][ ]

Father's Occupation _____ 25 [ ]

Exam. at **24 months** | Date ....

OFFICE USE

Dr's Code (1–2) [ ][ ]

On Cols 3–13
Punch: First
8 letters of
surname

First 3 letters
of first name

26 [ ][ ][ ][ ][ ] 31

Mother's Comments

		No	Yes		
Happy		No	Yes	32	[ ]
Sleeps		No	Yes	33	[ ]
Eats		No	Yes	34	[ ]
Imaginative play		No	Yes	35	[ ]

Illness since last exam. (If yes specify nature of illness) | No | Yes | 36 [ ]

Changes in family circumstances | No | Yes | 37 [ ]

	No	Yes		
Play group	No	Yes	38	[ ]
Nursery	No	Yes	39	[ ]
Minder	No	Yes	40	[ ]

Hours worked per week (Mother) [ ] 41–2 [ ][ ]

		1	2	3		
Bowel	D				43	[ ]
	N				44	[ ]
Bladder	D				45	[ ]
	N				46	[ ]
Sentences	1	2	3	4	47	[ ]

Kick ball	No kick	Runs into ball occ. kick	Poor directed kick	Good directed kick	48	[ ]
Throw ball	No throw	2 hands poor direct.	2 hands good direct.	1 hand	49	[ ]
1" Brick column	3 or less	4–5	6–7	8+	50	[ ]
Screws on table	2 or less up	3 up	4 up	5 up	51	[ ]
Rolling balls	$\frac{3}{4}$"	$\frac{1}{4}$"	$\frac{1}{16}$"	$\frac{1}{8}$"	52	[ ]
Cover test	Squint	Doubtful		No squint	53	[ ]
6 Toy hearing	4 and under	5 – 6 with hesitation		6 Immediate	54	[ ]
Comprehension	Recognises 4 or less	Recognises 5–6	Spoon in cup and ball to mummy	Car on brick and brick under cup	55	58 . . .
Ladybird vocab.	2 or less	3 – 8	9 – 14	15+	59	[ ]
Sentences observed	None	Occasional connected words	3–4 words	5+words	60	[ ]
Form board	2 or less in	3 in after mistakes	3 in immediately straight	3 in reversed	61	[ ]
Attention	None	Poor	Variable	Sustained	62	[ ]

PHYSICAL EXAM. Weight Height

(63–5) [ ][ ] K.gms. (66–8) [ ][ ] Cms.

Abnormality No/Yes (Specify below) 70 [ ]

.... Dominant Foot	R	L	71	[ ]
,, Hand	R	L	72	[ ]
,, Eye	R	L	73	[ ]

Appearance
Comment
Action

Card Code 79 [4]

If tests incomplete because of child's unco-operation put tick in box [ ] 80 [ ]

Fig 6.1 Recording cards—(a) 24 (b) 36 (c) 54 months

PAEDIATRIC DEVELOPMENT RECORD

DR. ....

Surname _____ **First Name** _____

OFFICE USE
Dr's Code (1–2)
On Cols 3–13
Punch: First 8 letters of surname
First 3 letters of first name

Date of Birth — 14 ... 20

Birth Rank

Father's Age — 21 22

Mother's Age — 23 24

Father's Occupation _____ 25

26 ... 31

Exam. at **36 months**	Date ....

Mother's Comments

	No	Yes	
Happy	No	Yes	32
Sleeps	No	Yes	33
Eats	No	Yes	34

Illness since last exam.
(If yes specify nature of illness) — No | Yes — 35

....

Change in family circumstances — No | Yes — 36

Play group	No	Yes	37
Nursery	No	Yes	38
Minder	No	Yes	39

Hours worked per week (Mother) — 40 41

(b)

		1	2	3	
Eating Mode	Knife				42
	Fork				43
	Spoon				44
Bowel	D				45
	N				46
Bladder	D				47
	N				48
Dressing					49

Kick ball	Runs into Ball	Poor kick		Good direct kick	50
1″ Brick	Does not try	Tries but fails		Succeeds	51
Rolling balls	$\frac{1}{4}$″	$\frac{3}{16}$″		$\frac{1}{8}$″	52
Cover Test	Squint	Doubtful		No squint	53
7 Toy hearing	4 and under	5 – 6 with hesitation		7 Immediate	54
Ladybird Book	Speech	Less than 15 pictures	16 – 20 pictures	21 or more pictures	55
	Comprehension	Less than 5 actions	6 – 10 actions	11 or more actions	56
Articulation	Not Understood	Understood with difficulty words incomplete	Understood minor errors only	Clear and understood	57

Story answers	0	1	2	3	4	5	6	7	58

Questions to Child	Name	Sex	Age	Address	Number correct	1	2	3	4	59

PHYSICAL EXAM.

Weight Height

(60–2) ___ K.gms. (63–6) ___ Cms.

Abnormality No/Yes (Specify below) .... — 70

.... Dominant foot | R | L | 71

.... „ Hand | R | L | 72

.... „ Eye | R | L | 73

Appearance
Comment
Action

Card Code
79 | 5

If tests incomplete because of child's unco-operation put tick in box — 80

PAEDIATRIC DEVELOPMENT RECORD

DR. ....

OFFICE USE

Dr's Code (1–2)

On Cols 3–13
Punch: First
8 letters of
surname

First 3 letters
of first name

Surname _____ First Name _____

14

Date of Birth [ ][ ][ ][ ][ ]   Birth Rank [ ]   20

21 22   23 24
Father's Age [ ][ ]   Mother's Age [ ][ ]

Father's Occupation _____   25 [ ]

26   31
[ ][ ][ ][ ][ ]

(c)

Exam at 54 months   Date.....................

Mother's Comments

		No	Yes	
	Happy	No	Yes	32
	Sleeps	No	Yes	33
	Eats	No	Yes	34

Illness since last exam.   No | Yes   35
(If yes specify nature of illness)

Change in family circumstances   No | Yes   36

Play group	No	Yes	37
Nursery	No	Yes	38
Minder	No	Yes	39

Hours worked per   40 41
week (Mother)   [ ]

		1	2	3	
Eating Mode	Knife				42
	Fork				43
	Spoon				44
Bowel	D				45
	N				46
Bladder	D				47
	N				48
	Dressing				49

Heel-toe walk	Steps wider than 15 cms. or more than 1 step to side	Gap 5–10 cms. or 1 step to side	4 steps all less than 5 cms. gap	50
Matches in box	All in 3 or more corrections	All in less than 3 corrections	All in both hands	51
6 Brick pyramid	Fails	At least 3 bricks in relation	Succeeds after more than 1 attempt	Succeeds 1st attempt	52
Vision R	6/36	6/24	6/12	6/9	6/6	53
L	6/36	6/24	6/12	6/9	6/6	54
Cover test	Squint	Doubtful	No squint	55
Hearing Toy	4 and under	5 – 6 or hesitation	7 Immediate	56
Articulation	Not under-stood	Under-stood with difficulty Words in-complete	Under-stood min-or errors only	Clear and under-stood	57
Story answers	0	1	2	3	4	5	6	7	58
Questions to child	Name	Sex	Age	Address	Number correct	1	2	3	4	59
Draw a man	0 – 4	5 – 10	11 – 14	15+	60

PHYSICAL EXAM.

Weight   Height

(61–3) [ ][ ] K.gms.   (64–7) [ ][ ][ ] Cms.

Abnormality   No/Yes (Specify below)   70 [ ]

.... Dominant foot   R | L   71
....   „ hand   R | L   72
....   „ Eye   R | L   73

Appearance

Comment   Card Code

Action   79 [6]

If tests incomplete because of child's
unco-operation put tick in box   [ ]   80 [ ]

progress be stored? A half completed MC 46 (the most commonly used infant record card) of a child new to the area with its columns sometimes occupied with illegible scrawl has filled all of us involved in child care with dread. What can be put in its place?

It is essential, above all, to avoid the tendency to tick columns with headings like 'motor function' or 'vision'. It is best to avoid using 'inventory screening' forms with headings like 'goes to sibling in distress' (a category on a $4\frac{1}{2}$ year screening card used by a neighbouring borough council until recently).

Instead, try and describe *what* the child does. Does he walk alone or stand holding on at the age of one year? How many words is he putting into sentences at two years? Does he sit without assistance at seven months? And so on. A profile proforma is, I believe, the solution and the proformas illustrated in Chapters 4 and 5 for the seven month assessment and 12 month assessment which allow for a description of the child's specific skills in the four fields of behaviour, should certainly be favoured (Starte, 1974, 1976).

The advantage is that it demonstrates graphically the individual child's *level* of attainment at a set age but, in addition, each age examination card can also be used on children up to six months on either side of the 'target' date (Fig 6.1 a, b, c).

Once the programme is running and decisions have been made about examination frequency, it is important to test carefully the expertise of the agencies to whom seven per cent or thereabouts of the children seen are going to be referred (see Table 6.2).

Table 6.2 Referral rates from surveillance clinics

	(Annual percentage of all children in practice under 5 years).
Ophthalmology	3·0
Audiology	1·5
Speech therapy	2·7
General surgery	0·4
Developmental paediatric	0·7
General paediatric	0·15
Orthopaedic	0·15
Social Services	0·01

*From author's own practice 1975–1977

In some parts of the North of England, speech delay is a fact of life not a disorder, as no facilities exist in many places for its treatment. If the local hospital ophthalmology department examines a child with suspected squint once and discharges him, then it is necessary to try and find an ophthalmology department that will arrange at least one follow-up examination, even if it means parents travelling 30 miles to obtain it. If the Ear, Nose & Throat department is content to allow deaf children to wait 18 months or two years for treatment, try and find another with a shorter waiting list. If alternatives are not available, then follow up closely the individual child with suspected disorder *personally*, and re-refer when appropriate. Be prepared to take it up with the hospital paediatrician. Sometimes it is necessary. Do not wait to be proved right by events; suspicion is enough—certainly in the early days of such a programme.

Early discussions with the district community physician and the district nursing officer can do much to ensure the smooth start to a surveillance programme. Once the doctor has established his credentials by, for instance, accepting an approved training programme and is content to fit in with local organisation, a lot can be achieved. Communications with the local hospital's paediatric department by direct contact and attendance on ward rounds will quickly build up a relationship that will ensure early discharge of hospital paediatric patients to your care. The subsequently greater responsibility gives greater satisfaction. If an A4 system is in use in the practice the problem of note keeping is greatly simplified, with the sickness and developmental record being stored together.

With the existing Medical Record Envelope (MRE) system the problem of how to keep a comprehensive record is a great deal more complicated. It is my invariable custom to check the illness notes at routine examination and enter on the developmental record significant illness like measles, middle ear infection, febrile convulsions *etc.* in the space provided on my proformas. I also enter on the MRE a brief account of my developmental findings, limited in 80 per cent of cases to simply 'two and a half year assessment satisfactory', but fully listing abnormality suspected or detected and a note of referral. I would commend this system to all who are seeing not only their own but their partner's patients.

Comprehensive developmental notes are of great value

when a child is suspected (some 10 to 14 per cent) of having some developmental disorder. A quick check can reveal whether the disorder is isolated or forms part of generalised delay. Meticulously recorded information of children's performance at the 54 to 56 month examination enabled the author to discover a link with learning disorder occurring when the child was older. Certain findings at the preschool 54 to 56 month examination might have a predictive value (Curtis Jenkins, 1979).

Accurate description of the child's developmental progress to date is of great value to the developmental paediatric specialist when referral is made to him. The mother's memory is fallible and most likely to be inaccurate in those children with the most problems (Neligan, 1969).

Confirmation that overall development and hearing are normal saves the speech therapist a great deal of time when she makes her initial assessment of language of a child referred to her, although she will often want a more formal audiological assessment.

With the effort involved, all who run such programmes should only do it because they enjoy it. It is not a task for those whose interests are not child-centred. Nevertheless, as the Court Report suggested, only 30 per cent of general practitioners need commit themselves to the work to ensure an essentially general practice-based primary care paediatric service. With effective co-operation with the 'third force', the child care specialists and medical officers in the Community Health Services, so much can be achieved in the future.

Parents certainly find the comprehensive service helpful. When it is well run and can offer practical and realistic help, coupled with a routine of regular examinations, it allows parents to talk about their concerns and worries that they feel they cannot bother the 'illness doctor' with. Certainly, those who keep careful statistical records of all consultations in the nought to four age group can demonstrate a fall in illness rates when they carry out such a policy (see Table 6.3).

This shows, I believe, how parents reflect their reduction in anxiety by fewer consultations for sickness. As the nought to five age group at some times in the year can be causing up to one quarter of the total practice workload, a reduction of 10 to 15 per cent in the consultation rate for illness in this group has a marked effect on consultation rate generally.

Critics point out that until scientific evaluation of

Table 6.3 Episode of illness rate per patient per annum in 0–4 year age group in a group practice with each doctor caring for his own list of patients.

	Dr A.*	Dr B.	Dr C.	Dr D.	Dr E.
Episode rate all ages	1·8	1·8	2·0	2·1	2·3
Episode rate 0–4 year	2·5	2·7	2·8	2·9	3·9

*Dr A. runs the surveillance programme within the practice. Data derived from National morbidity survey 1970–71

surveillance has been done, it is wrong to proclaim it as a desirable policy for the nation's child health services. A comparison of randomly allocated children into surveillance and non-surveillance groups, thought so desirable as a first step in evaluating a programme's worth, has already unfortunately been carried out in most parts of the country. The dismal reports from those carrying out initial examinations of school children attest to the substantial amount of disorder that occurs undiagnosed and untreated until the child is properly examined at school entry or later (Rutter et al 1970).

Another criticism often raised is that no studies have yet been carried out on 'outcomes', i.e., the result of intervention. Parents, however, attest only too well to its good effects. The obvious effects of early stimulation of parent-infant interaction seen at later stages in the child's life when parents remark spontaneously 'what a difference it made' to their awareness, having been shown that their new born baby can see and hear. Other benefits of practical yet accurate developmental guidance are obvious to the doctor and parent when, for instance, life games, threatening to split a family, can be modified and made liveable with. The visually handicapped child fitted for the first time with glasses after initial diagnosis of loss of visual acuity at a surveillance clinic demonstrates joyfully his new found gift of good visual acuity. The depressed child seen at a routine surveillance examination, responding rapidly to antidepressants with parents at the end of their tether not knowing what was wrong produces an electrifying effect on the rest of the family quite apart from his own sudden switch from misery to delight. These are just some of the observed effects.

The concept of normality is another stumbling block to those who feel that its definition is a first essential to the evaluation of surveillance. It is a fact of life, however, that 'normality' cannot so easily be defined, except as a continuum with disruptions due to abnormality occurring at any time. The sudden onset of catarrhal deafness and the rapidly progressive loss of visual acuity that occurs so frequently in the first years of a child's life mean that two examinations a month apart will yield entirely different results, the first demonstrating normality—the next abnormality.

Repeatability of diagnosis is another stumbling block in the evaluation of such programmes. Critics point out that surveys of similar surveillance programmes in different practices would yield quite different results. Of course they will (as the Court Report stated) for the incidence of so many of the developmental handicapping disorders, squint, loss of visual acuity, hearing loss, even epilepsy, follows social class. So the argument that repeatability is important is a very weak one.

Some critics also believe that health visitors and family doctors are perfectly capable of testing vision, hearing and speech which form the bulk of the referrals from such a programme. Roberts and Khosla (1972) and Bain (1977) have shown, however, how unsubstantiated this pious hope is.

Surveillance is here to stay. Parents want it and the confirmation of normality in 85 per cent of children is for the average parent the programme's greatest advantage.

For the rest a close and sympathetic interest in the child with handicap suspected or detected, is also what parents want. A surveillance programme ensures they get this, too.

REFERENCES

Bain D J G 1977 Methods employed by general practitioners in developmental screening of preschool children. British Medical Journal 2: 363–365

Curtis Jenkins G H 1979 The identification of children with learning in general practice, Journal of Royal College of General Practitioners 29: 647–651

Hart C R (ed) 1975 Screening in general practice. Churchill Livingstone, Edinburgh

Neligan G A 1969 Potential value of four early developmental milestones in screening children for increased risk of later retardation. Journal of Developmental Medicine and Child Neurology 11: 423

Roberts C J, Khosla T 1972 An evaluation of developmental examination as a method of detecting neurological, visual and auditory handicap in infancy. British Journal of Preventive and Social Medicine 26: 94–100.
Rowland P 1975 Developmental assessment in general practice. Update 10: 379–388
Rutter M, Tizard J, Whitmore K 1970 Education, health and behaviour. Longman, London
Stark G, Bassett J J, Bain D J G, Steward F I 1975 Paediatrics in Livingstone new town. British Medical Journal 4: 387–390
Starte G D 1974 The developmental assessment of the young child in general practice. Practitioner 213: 823, 828
Starte G D 1976 Results from a developmental screening clinic in general practice. Practitioner 216: 311
Zinkin P M, Cox C A 1976 Child health services and inverse care laws. British Medical Journal 2: 411–413

Part II

Disorders and diseases

Part II

Introduction

The diseases and disorders which occur during the first year of life are discussed in this section of the book, under systematic headings for easier reference. It needs to be emphasised at the outset that the younger the child the less specific are the presenting signs and symptoms of illness. This is of particular note during the first year of life, the infant responding in similar ways to ill-health of varying aetiology. There may be a change in behaviour, either an unusual degree of lethargy or irritability, reluctance to feed, vomiting or loose stools. Mothers notice changes in their child's behaviour; it is essential to listen carefully as well as to enquire and examine.

One of the most important signs of ill-health during the first year of life is a reluctance to feed. This is often associated with the most common of non-specific symptoms—loose stools—and leads to the greatest hazard of this age group—dehydration, the assessment of which is a vital first principle of management.

Failure to thrive

This general term is widely used in paediatrics since adequate growth is the trademark of child health. There is such considerable overlap of symptoms, signs, methods of assessment and management of the varying conditions affecting the infant, that this separate account giving an overall view is included. Failure to thrive, of course, includes most of the problems of the sick child and will be discussed more specifically under the systematic headings.

When dealing with an infant, there is usually available

147

detailed information on growth and a few basic facts are useful and important, but too obsessional an approach needs to be avoided.

The normal full term baby loses up to ten per cent of the birth weight during the first four days and regains the birth weight by seven to 14 days. Weight is then gained at an approximate rate of 150–180 g/week (5-6 oz), the infant doubling the birth weight by six months and trebling it by 12 months. Usually, additional information is available from the infant's health clinic record. This will give the rate of growth which may be of greater significance and practical use than a single measurement. Attention to the baby's weight is important but too great an interest may create anxiety. In the breast fed infant, anxiety can influence lactation adversely (probably related to oxytocin release) and so a vicious circle is set up. Commonsense as well as science has a part to play. It is also essential to relate weight to other parameters of growth, such as length and head circumference.

Assessment of the infant failing to thrive will initially involve detailed information regarding food, particularly fluid intake, the enthusiasm or lack of it with which the child feeds and precise history of vomiting, bowel action and urinary output. It is important to know the quality as well as the quantity of loss from the bowel. There are two further basic facts:

(i) The fluid requirement of the infant is 150 ml/kg/24 h from the age of seven days to six months, then gradually falls to 120 ml/kg/24 h at one year.

(ii) The energy requirement is 110 cals/kg/24 h (milk contains 70 cals/100 ml (20 cals/oz).

Parents' ideas of vomiting, constipation and diarrhoea vary. A specific description must be obtained.

Assessment of hydration

The degree of hydration is one of the most important factors in assessing ill-health in infancy and deciding on appropriate management. A history of fluid intake over the recent feeds is necessary, together with loss from the gastro-intestinal tract and urine output. It is important to determine if the mother has witnessed urinary flow, as it is possible for profuse watery loss from the rectum to be misinterpreted as being urine. The most useful sign is that of skin turgor; a ridge of skin is gently pinched over the abdominal wall, axillary or neck folds, and released; normally the ridge immediately flattens. Weight loss rather than dehydration may result in loose skin but the turgor is normal. The appearance of the facies, particularly the eyes is useful. The tension of the fontanelle may be helpful but, of course, may be misleading if meningitis and dehydration co-exist. An accurately recorded recent weight may give the opportunity of precise assessment of weight loss. The clinical sign of dehydration becomes apparent at about five per cent of fluid loss; marked signs appear at 15 per cent loss, when the situation will be approaching the point of no return.

7.

The cardiovascular system

The normal heart rate at birth may vary between 90 and 140 beats per minute, the mean being 120/min. The rate rises to reach a maximum at the end of the first month and then falls gradually during the rest of childhood, reaching adult ranges at about 12 years, see Table 7.1. The normal blood pressure of an infant varies between 85–90 mmHg systolic and 50–70 mmHg diastolic. It is essential when taking the blood pressure that the special infant-type cuff should cover at least two thirds of the upper arm and similar proportion in the leg, and the inflatable part fully encompasses the limb.

The changes in the circulation at birth and the neonatal presentation of congenital heart disease have been discussed in Chapter 3.

Table 7.1 Heart rate and blood pressure in babies

	Heart Rate: Beats/Min			Blood Pressure: mmHg	
	Min	Mean	Max	Mean Systolic	Mean Diastolic
Newborn	85	119	145		
1–7 days	100	133	175		
8–30 days	115	163	190	$80 \simeq 16$	$46 \simeq 16$
1–3 months	115	154	205		
3–6 months	115	140	205		
6–12 months	115	140	175	$89 \simeq 29$	$60 \simeq 10$
1–3 years	100	149	190	$98 \simeq 30$	$64 \simeq 25$

Modified with permission from Shinebourne EA, 1974 In: Davis JA, Dobbing J (ed) Scientific Foundations of Paediatrics, Heinemann, London

Congenital heart disease (see Table 7.2)

Heart disease in infancy is rare in a general practice. When encountered, it is most likely to be congenital in origin, the incidence being in the order of six per 1000 live births. Congenital heart disease may present in three ways:

(i) congestive heart failure
(ii) cyanosis alone, and
(iii) during routine medical examination

(i) *Congestive heart failure* presents as respiratory distress, with tachypnoea and sternal and intercostal recession. The earliest symptom may just be difficulty in taking feeds, perhaps associated with an increased respiratory rate when feeding. Oedema may be difficult to assess in an infant, the principal sites being the dorsum of the hands and feet and particularly the skin over the tibia and around the eyes. Sudden weight gain may sometimes give a clue to excessive fluid retention, and accurate measurement of daily weight is invaluable in both assessment and management. A tachycardia, often with a triple rhythm and in the majority of cases a murmur, is usually detected although a murmur is not an invariable finding. The liver is palpable one to two cm below the costal margin in infants but becomes increasingly and often rapidly distended in heart failure. The spleen may also enlarge.

Appreciation of the normal physiological changes which occur after birth is particularly relevant to the presentation of congenital heart disease. If there is a potential left-right shunt (for example, via a patent ductus arteriosus or ventricular septal defect) then, as the pulmonary vascular resistance falls, a greater amount of blood will be able to flow through the pulmonary circuit. This will predispose to the development of heart failure. Particularly during the first two months of

Table 7.2 Classification of commoner types of congenital heart disease

Acyanotic	Cyanotic
Ventricular septal defect (VSD)	Transposition of the great arteries
Patent ductus arteriosus (PDA)	Fallot's Tetralogy
Atrial septal defect (ASD)	Severe pulmonary stenosis
Coarctation of the aorta	Persistent truncus arteriosus
Pulmonary stenosis	Total anomalous pulmonary venous drainage
Aortic stenosis	Tricuspid atresia

life, careful observation must be kept on an infant with a heart murmur. The larger the potential shunt, the earlier are symptoms likely to arise. The other important precipitatory cause of heart failure in these babies is a respiratory infection.

(ii) *Cyanosis.* This may accompany heart failure or respiratory illness. It may, though, occur as an isolated sign indicating cyanotic heart disease, particularly in the neonatal period—see Chapter 3. The commonest variety of cyanotic heart disease is transposition of the great vessels. This is more frequent in males, usually presenting in the immediate newborn period but sometimes during the early weeks of life; the infant develops cyanosis and heart failure. The other statistically most likely cyanotic condition to occur is Fallot's tetralogy (pulmonary stenosis, ventricular septal defect, over-riding aorta, right ventricular hypertrophy). In these babies, cyanosis may develop during the first three of four months of life. Heart failure is unusual but infundibular spasms may occur, these being acute, self-limiting episodes of pallor and cyanosis, resulting from acute obstruction of the abnormal pulmonary outflow tract. Congenital heart disease may be associated with other problems such as chromosomal abnormalities, particularly trisomy 21 (Mongolism).

(iii) *A frequent problem seen in general practice* is that of the well baby with a cardiac murmur. Successful management rests not so much with the baby as with the handling of the parents. Short ejection-type systolic murmurs may be heard during the first six weeks and these often disappear quickly. As discussed above though, a potentially large left-to-right shunt may be controlled initially due to the high pulmonary vascular resistance, so attention needs to be paid to the progress of the infant. Note the vigour with which the infant feeds, measure weight gain and carefully make a clinical examination, paying attention to the peripheral pulses of upper and lower limbs. Nothing need be said to the parents at this time; ideally, a watching brief is kept via the health visitor and another examination made at a later date. As soon as more attention is given to the baby (and this may be only a slightly longer time taken in auscultation of the chest) an explanation will be necessary for the sensitive mother.

Any suggestion that something is wrong with the heart causes considerable anxiety to parents and time will be required to reduce this anxiety to a minimum. A change from the routine given to other infants, such as measurement of the blood pressure or an earlier follow-up appointment, may lead to the mother suspecting something is wrong. If mother's suspicions are aroused, a full and open discussion is the best approach. If the murmur persists or becomes larger, filling systole, further assessment by chest X-ray and electrocardiogram should be arranged via specialist referral.

The commonest congenital heart lesions are patent ductus arteriosus and ventricular septal defect. The classical continuous murmur of the patent ductus may not be audible in infancy; sometimes only the systolic element is present. High pulmonary resistance, or just the infant crying, may prevent the diastolic murmur becoming apparent. The murmur of the patent ductus is best heard in the second left intercostal space with the baby supine. Treatment is by surgical closure.

There is now no doubt that a proportion of ventricular septal defects close spontaneously. Referral for specialist assessment will be needed, however; it is important to identify those with large shunts and the possibility of associated pulmonary vascular disease as management will be very different, further investigation being indicated.

8.

The respiratory system

Problems arising in the respiratory tract are a major cause of anxiety for parents and one of the most frequent reasons for seeking advice from the general practitioner. Though many of the problems are minor, respiratory infections are still among the principal causes of mortality in infancy (see Introduction). The frequency of upper respiratory infection does vary from infant to infant. Some of this variation will be due to environmental and social conditions and some, probably, to the individual child's quality of immunity. The baby who returns to a home where there are older children attending school is much more likely to start developing upper respiratory infections early compared with the first baby in a family who may escape until old enough to go to a playgroup or nursery. Since it is inevitable for parents and relatives to compare one child with another, these variations in circumstances need to be explained.

Upper respiratory problems

The common cold (coryza) affects babies chiefly by causing nasal obstruction. Since the young infant breathes through the nose preferentially, obstruction of the nares leads to difficulty, particularly during feeding. Treatment is symptomatic, clearing the nose using cotton wool sticks being the most effective. Nasal decongestant drops have a part to play but should be used sparingly and only for short courses; there is often rebound vasodilation as the drug wears off which may aggravate the problem. However, used intermittently before feeds, drops such as 0·05 per cent xylometazoline (Otrivine) can be effective.

The small preterm infant may develop lower respiratory tract infection in association with coryza. Though antibiotics have no part to play in the treatment of viral illness, one must be alert to associated infection with the pneumococcus or haemophilus influenzae and treat appropriately with penicillin or ampicillin respectively. Particularly in the newborn period, close supervision is important—and this means a daily visit from health visitor or doctor to every baby living in adverse circumstances.

Though rare in the infant compared with the toddler, the possibility of a foreign body in the nares must be considered if there is a persistent nasal discharge, particularly if it becomes offensive.

A minor degree of snuffles and noisy breathing in early infancy is not uncommon, reflecting as it does, the preferential use of the nasal airway. This is often heard in the immediate newborn period and gives rise to the erroneous idea in the mother that the baby has been 'born with a cold'.

Laryngeal obstruction

This is an important problem requiring patient and careful observation and at times urgent treatment. The upper airway is relatively smaller and the cartilage of the larynx more lax in the infant and young child compared with the adult, and obstruction can more easily occur. The most common causes of upper airway obstruction are infection and inhalation of foreign bodies. These problems are most frequent in the toddler age group but may present during the first year. Other important causes, though rarer, are congenital abnormalities leading to intrinsic or extrinsic narrowing of the larynx or trachea.

Symptoms and signs

The prominent feature is that of stridor, a harsh often high-pitched noise heard during inspiration. This is associated with sternal and intercostal recession. It is most important to assess the degree of airway obstruction and establish from the history and signs whether the respiratory difficulty is increasing. An infant with moderate or severe respiratory obstruction will tend to lie with the head retracted. Hypoxia causes restlessness, tachypnoea and tachycardia. If the obstruction is below the larnyx and involving the main bronchi, it is usually possible to observe inequality of chest movement. Variation in percussion note or air entry between the two sides of the chest may be less easy to detect. These latter findings particularly suggest a foreign body, a diagnostic feature being a localised persistent rhonchus. However, the smaller the chest size, the more difficult it is to pick up clinical signs and it is often necessary to back up clinical examination with radiography of the chest and upper airway. A missed foreign body may lead, eventually, to the need for a lung resection, so one cannot afford to take chances once suspicion is aroused.

Congenital laryngeal stridor

This sometimes frightening sounding condition is benign and self-limiting. The stridor is noted soon after birth and may vary in degree from a symptom only apparent when the baby cries to persistent stridor at rest with considerable suprasternal and sternal recession. It is due to the indrawing of an immature larynx and tracheal cartilage and improves spontaneously during infancy. It is important to consider other causes, such as laryngeal webs, haemangioma and extrinsic narrowing due to aberrant arteries. All are rare, but further investigation by X-ray and laryngoscopy may be indicated to eliminate the possibility of their occurrence. Upper respiratory illness may exacerbate temporarily the degree of airway obstruction and increased care of observation will be necessary at those times.

Laryngo-tracheitis (Croup)

This is a common problem of the two to four age group but may occur in the infant. It is due to an infection of the upper airway by either a virus (para influenza, adenovirus) or haemophilus influenzae.

Symptoms and signs

There may be evidence of an upper respiratory infection initially. There is sudden onset of upper airway obstruction giving rise to stridor and a hoarse barking cough, the stridor often waking the child during the night. The degree of obstruction varies and may become severe quite rapidly. The degree of suprasternal, sternal and intercostal recession is an important indication of the severity of the illness. Restlessness, anxiety and tachycardia are also features useful in assessing severity.

Management

Mild cases may be managed at home if the social and parental situation is suitable. Increased humidity is the most useful measure and taking the child into the bathroom and running hot water into the bath is the method of choice. Steam from an electric kettle may be tried but the presence of boiling water does increase the hazard of accidental scalds. The progression of airway obstruction has to be assessed carefully. There is no place for the use of antibiotics routinely in the mild case.

However, if it is known that the haemophilus influenzae infection is present already in other members of the family, then ampicillin is the best antibiotic to use. Sedation for this condition should be regarded warily and is probably best avoided. Triclofos (Tricloryl) is the safest drug to use; it has the advantage over chloral hydrate in being tasteless. Promethazine (Phenergan) may also be useful.

Signs requiring urgent admission

    (i) Cyanosis during coughing bout
   (ii) Pallor during coughing bout
 (iii) General restlessness
 (iv) Failure of improvement with first aid measures

Differential diagnosis

It is important to consider aspiration of a foreign body. Epiglottitis is very unlikely to occur in the first year; if suspected, urgent admission to hospital is essential. Croup occurs in all grades of severity and the changes are greatest in the youngest infants. Quite often the message reaching the general practitioner is insufficiently detailed or insufficiently reliable for a safe assessment without seeing the baby. If in any doubt at all, visit.

Acute bronchospasm

This is a common problem in late childhood but not one particularly affecting the first year. Confusion in terminology abounds. The term 'acute bronchospasm' is best confined to symptoms of acute reversible obstruction of the lower airway, whatever the cause. Other less satisfactory terms used are wheezy bronchitis, tracheo-bronchitis and asthma. The term 'bronchitis' suggests an infective inflammation of the bronchi which is not usually the case in these children; the condition is one that *affects* the bronchi by producing oedema and mucosal swelling. Asthma is, by definition, recurrent reversible airway obstruction. It is seldom practicable to make this diagnosis in infancy.

Symptoms and signs

The most frequent precipitating cause of bronchospasm in young children is an upper respiratory infection. The first symptoms are coryza or cough followed a day or so later by the onset of wheezing. The degree of airway obstruction may increase rapidly causing severe respiratory distress with tachypnoea, sternal and intercostal recession, tachycardia and restlessness. On auscultation of the chest there will be widespread expiratory rhonchi. It is important to assess air entry as in the more severe situations there may be a paucity of chest movement and breath sounds. The infant may have a history of eczema or cows' milk allergy and there may be a family history of atopy.

Management

This is directed towards relieving the bronchospasm and if appropriate, treatment of the precipitating infection. The problem as stated is more frequent after the first year of life which is in a way fortunate as the sympathomimetic drugs are not very effective in infancy. The bronchi become more receptive to β-stimulation during the second year. Clinical assessment of fluid loss and the ability of the child to take oral fluid are vitally important factors in management. It may be this aspect which determines the need for hospital admission. Promethazine (Phenergan) may be helpful in the infant with mild symptoms but care is needed as it will tend to dry the secretions which, in the more severe attack, may increase airway obstruction.

Aminophylline may be more effective than the sympathomimetic drugs and, with extreme care regarding dosage, may be used for the mild attack as aminophylline suppositories. It is essential to give the correct dose for weight. Suppositories must never be divided as the drug is not uniformly distributed. When given rectally, 3·5 mg/aminophylline/kg 12-hourly should not be exceeded (see Ch. 17). Corticosteroids may occasionally be required but this form of treatment should probably not be initiated at home in this age group. Antibiotics should not be used indiscriminately. The principal treatment required is the relief of the bronchospasm. Many of the infections are viral in nature and with these there is no place for an antibiotic. However, it may be difficult to exclude a bacterial chest infection clinically and an antibiotic may need to be given when there is doubt, and if practical, a chest X-ray arranged.

There are some infants that have considerable wheeze but are not ill or adversely affected by the symptoms. There may be associated upper respiratory catarrhal features. Symptomatic treatment may help but explanation to the parents and acceptance of the presence of some degree of wheeze may be necessary.

Differential diagnosis

In this group of infants with symptoms supporting acute bronchospasm this includes:
  (i)   Bronchiolitis
  (ii) Bacterial chest infection
  (iii) Cystic fibrosis

Bronchiolitis

This is an acute infection particularly of the infant causing respiratory distress which may rapidly become severe and life threatening. Babies under six months are particularly vulnerable. It occurs in epidemics, often in the autumn or spring. The cause is the respiratory syncytial virus (RSV).

Symptoms and signs

The most usual age group affected is two to six months.

Usually there are prodromal upper respiratory symptoms for 24–48 hours. The infant then starts to become wheezy and the degree of bronchospasm may progress rapidly leading to severe airway obstruction. There are signs of sternal recession, grunting respiration, tachypnoea and tachycardia in association with an over inflated chest. Fever is not a prominent feature. On auscultation, there may be a lack of sounds in the chest in the severe case, or more commonly, widespread rhonchi. Crepitations may be present though initially the signs of airway obstruction predominate. As the bronchospasm improves, moist sounds may be heard. The liver is often displaced by the over-inflated lungs. This can be a problem in diagnosing heart failure which may complicate the illness.

Management

All infants with bronchiolitis require admission to hospital. The condition tends to become worse over 24–72 hours, reaches a plateau and then gradually improves, lasting seven to ten days in all. Treatment is symptomatic, humidity and oxygen playing a significant part, but the most important aspect of proper treatment is good nursing of the child, with particular attention to hydration.

Pneumonia

Bronchopneumonia is the more common type to affect this age group, though lobar pneumonia may occur. The main causative organisms are the pneumococcus and haemophilus influenzae. Staphylococcal pneumonia is rare in general practice but its early identification is important because of the dangerous complication of abscess formation.

Symptoms and signs

There is variation in presentation and particularly in the young infant, non-specific symptoms are common. Classically, the child will present with tachypnoea, cough, fever, recession of the chest wall and grunting respirations. Signs of general toxicity are likely to be apparent; pallor, listlessness, and reluctance to feed. The onset of symptoms and progression to serious illness may be rapid. Failure to act quickly may be explained partly by the difficulty some parents experience in picking up the early signs of severe ill-health in babies. We should not be over-critical however, for all too often the earliest signs are overlooked or discounted by general practitioners too.

Management

Treatment in this age group is best supervised in hospital. The course of the illness is rapid and a vital aspect of treatment is attention to fluid balance. The choice of antibiotic will depend on the clinical picture. Penicillin or ampicillin are the first line choice effective against the commoner organisms, the pneumococcus and haemophilus. When the possibility of staphylococcal infection exists, flucloxacillin is the antibiotic to use. The route of administration is important as the sick infant may not take or absorb oral medicine satisfactorily. Oxygen is also a useful, often vital, adjunct to treatment. Thus the initial assessment and management is likely to be best achieved in hospital but once the illness is under control, recovery may be continued at home given adequate home care supervision.

Cystic fibrosis should be considered as a possible cause in every case of recurrent chest infection or staphylococcal pneumonia, see Chapter 9.

Differential diagnosis

It may be difficult to exclude bacterial pneumonia from bronchiolitis or in association with acute bronchospasm. A chest X-ray will often be necessary. It is important to remember that a metabolic acidosis may give rise to a clinical picture suggesting a chest infection. The most common cause of an acidosis in this age group is gastro-enteritis. Salicylate overdose, either therapeutic or accidental ingestion, may also need to be considered.

Whooping cough (Pertussis)

This infectious disease caused by *Bordetella pertussis* or *para-pertussis* may be a particularly serious illness in the infant, there being an appreciable risk of mortality from the pertussis infection at this age compared with the older child. Thirty years ago, the incidence of the disease started to decline and this continued until recently. This period of the falling incidence of the disease occurred in association with the introduction of immunisation against pertussis; there was, of course, also an improvement in the social and nutritional welfare of children at that time. Recently, following anxiety raised in 1974 concerning the safety of pertussis innoculation the incidence of whooping cough has risen abruptly (see Ch. 16).

It is a highly contagious disease spread by droplet infection. The incubation period is between seven and 14 days. The neonate does not receive any protection from the passive transfer of maternal antibodies.

The initial phase of the illness is a non-specific catarrhal state with coryza and cough. After 10 to 14 days the more serious illness develops in the form of the paroxysmal cough. The classical whoop occurring at the end of a paroxysm, as the child is at last able to take a breath, is not a feature of the disease in the infant. The paroxysmal cough is often associated with vomiting and this, with the exhaustion it causes, prediposes to the risk of inhalation pneumonia. This phase of the illness may last a number of weeks. The coughing bouts gradually becoming less severe and less frequent often becoming more of a problem at night. The severe episodes of cough may be associated with cyanosis or apnoea in the infant. During the height of the illness there may be considerable difficulty in maintaining adequate hydration and nutrition.

In spite of the severe cough, auscultation of the lung fields in the uncomplicated case remains remarkably clear. Attention, however, needs to be given to the important complication of involvement of the lower respiratory tract. Bronchopneumonia may develop during the paroxysmal coughing phase of the illness. There is also the long-term complication of the development of bronchiectasis.

The diagnosis in the severe case, particularly during an epidemic, is straightforward. The less severe illness may be more difficult to identify, particularly if the child has partial immunity or if the infection is due to para-pertussis which causes milder disease. It is important to make the diagnosis as parents need to have a positive explanation of a persistent symptom such as recurrent cough. The diagnosis is essentially a clinical one. The organism is difficult to culture and by the time the paroxysmal phase develops may not be present in the nasopharynx. It is necessary to take pernasal swabs, cough plates may be successful. Both, though, require the use of the special Bordet culture media. A white blood count may give helpful confirmatory evidence of the infection as there is usually a considerably raised total white cell count (20 000–40 000/mm³), 70 to 90 per cent being lymphocytes.

Management

This is mainly symptomatic, preventing undue stimulation which produces the paroxysmal cough and provision of adequate hydration and nutrition. Sedatives and antitussives do not have any significant therapeutic effect on the cough. Antibiotics are indicated if bronchopneumonia develops but are probably ineffective against the disease itself once the paroxysmal cough has developed (see below).

Nursing the infant with pertussis can be difficult and an extremely anxious time, day and night for the parents. It is, therefore, sometimes necessary for hospital admission for these infants during the severe phase of the illness where continual expert nursing care is available together with facilities for nasal-pharyngeal aspiration and oxygen.

Careful follow-up is essential. The major complication of the pre-antibiotic era, bronchiectasis, is now rarely seen but it can be difficult to determine small areas of persistent collapse of the lung clinically. Therefore, once the paroxysmal cough has resolved and clinical recovery occurred in the severe case a chest X-ray should be arranged to ensure normal lung fields.

Prophylaxis

The principal measure advised is that of innoculation (see Ch. 16). The *Bordetella* organism is sensitive to chloramphenicol, erythromycin and cotrimoxazole. Immunisation schedules start at three months and therefore the infant may have little protection under six months. During an epidemic, it is worth considering the use of erythromycin or cotrimoxazole as a prophylactic measure in the infant, particularly if the older children in the family contract the disease.

9.

The alimentary system

The Mouth

Candidiasis (thrush) infection is a common problem causing difficulty with feeding during infancy. The mouth, oesophagus and perineum may be affected. The tongue and buccal mucosa become coated with greyish-white patches which are difficult to remove, this feature differentiating the condition from white areas due to milk curds. Confirmation may be obtained by culture of the fungus in the laboratory. The condition rarely occurs in breast fed babies. Nystatin suspension, 100 000 units after feeds or amphotericin B (Fungilin) 100 mg will quickly control the oral infection. It is also very important to ensure that the method of bottle and teat cleansing and sterilization is effective. *Candida* infection may follow the use of broad spectrum antibiotics in the infant. Prophylactic use of nystatin may prevent this complication.

Aphthous stomatitis. This usually affects the toddler age group but may occur at the end of the first year. It is primarily a fungal infection of the genus *Candida* causing ulcers on the palate, tongue and buccal mucosa. The discomfort and irritability may lead to inadequate hydration because of reluctance to take nourishment. The condition is self-limiting, lasting about 10 days. Effective management consists of ensuring adequate fluid intake which may occasionally necessitate admission to hospital. Once established, the *herpes simplex* virus remains present (though latent) in the host throughout life, and during exacerbations of infection, recurrent outbreaks of stomatitis may occur, usually on the lips at the junction of skin and mucosa.

Oesophageal reflux, hiatus hernia

The vomiting baby is a common problem of infancy. The comments at the start of this section are particularly relevant in making the decision as to whether further investigation is warranted or not (Ch. 7).

Infections of the middle ear and urinary tract should always be considered in the infant with a short history of vomiting. On the other hand, when the condition persists or becomes recurrent, a barium swallow may be needed to differentiate between such structural problems as intrinsic and extrinsic oesophageal obstruction, gastro-oesophageal reflux (achalasia), hiatus hernia and diaphragmatic hernia. Often no specific abnormality is detected on X-ray, or only a minor degree of oesophageal reflux. Treatment then consists of:-

(i) Sitting the infant up following feeds

(ii) Thickening the milk feed using nestargel or gaviscon, the latter being an alginic preparation which works by reducing the symptoms of oesophageal reflux by formation of a gel in the stomach. It should be noted that gaviscon powder contains four milli-equivalents of sodium in each 2 g sachet which may be a significant salt load in an infant. Oesophageal reflux is self-limiting, improving as the infant matures and attains the upright posture.

Hypertrophic pyloric stenosis

This is a condition of unknown aetiology, not certainly congenital as it is rarely found in the newborn, occurring in about 0.3 per cent of infants and being commoner in boys than girls (four to one).

Symptoms and signs

The usual age at presentation is four to six weeks. Most babies present with a history of abrupt onset of projectile vomiting. The degree and rapidity of malnutrition and dehydration which develop will depend on the severity of the symptoms. The vomitus may contain stale curds or altered blood due to a gastritis. The appearance of bile in the vomit would strongly suggest an alternative diagnosis (see below). The diagnosis is made by observing and palpating the abdomen whilst the infant is taking a milk feed. There is little chance of feeling the pyloric mass if the baby is only given a dextrose/water feed, or following the use of atropine methonitrate (Eumydrin). The baby is held on the mother's left arm and the examiner's left hand is placed across the infant's upper abdomen dipping down with the middle finger immediately to the right of the mid-line. The pyloric mass is felt as a small, smooth, rounded mass, the size of an olive, the palpation of which characteristically varies as the pyloric muscle contracts and relaxes. The other important observation is that of visible gastric peristalsis.

Management

The treatment of choice is operation (Rammstedt's procedure) carried out after any necessary correction of electrolyte imbalance. Where a definite tumour has been felt this approach is to be preferred rather than attempts at medical management. In experienced hands, the surgery and post-operative progress is straightforward. The infant is able soon after surgery to tolerate full strength feeds so that chronic under-nutrition is avoided. There are no long-term sequelae.

Intestinal obstruction

The conditions causing obstruction are considered together as the differential diagnosis will necessitate admission to hospital.

The earlier in life symptoms of intestinal obstruction develop, the more likely it is that they are due to a congenital abnormality. The commoner problems presenting in the newborn have been discussed in Chapter 3. The importance of prompt assessment and treatment of these infants cannot be overstressed. Severe electrolyte and fluid imbalance can occur rapidly and the viability of the gut soon jeopardized by impairment of the blood supply associated with abdominal distension.

Symptoms and signs

Vomiting and abdominal distension are the cardinal signs.

Vomiting is a common symptom in infants, but if there is bile-staining of the vomitus, urgent assessment is indicated. Decrease in frequency in bowel action may also be an important symptom. Examination should concentrate on hydration, degree of abdominal distension and in particular, attention to hernial orifices. The clinical diagnosis of probable obstruction will need to be followed by erect and supine abdominal X-rays.

Differential diagnosis

Bowel atresias present in the neonatal period but stenosis or obstruction due to external constriction of the lumen by peritoneal bands or malrotation secondary to congenital lesions may present later. As a group, they are rare, an infrequent but important and treatable problem for the general practitioner to encounter.

Inguinal and femoral hernias are more common problems. The latter is more likely to give rise to immediate trouble, due to the narrow neck of the sac, but it occurs much less frequently than the inguinal hernia. Hydrocoele of the cord or an enlarged lymph node is occasionally confused with inguinal hernia but this will be sorted out on referral. The timing of routine repair of a hernia varies with individual surgeons, but the tendency is for the repair to be carried out as soon after diagnosis as can be conveniently arranged. It is best to refer at diagnosis rather than risk incarceration or strangulation of the bowel.

Umbilical hernia only extremely rarely causes an acute problem. The true umbilical hernia with the circular central defect will almost certainly resolve spontaneously. There is no need to bind the abdomen or strap on a penny; a plaster rash is a more likely outcome of such treatment than any structural benefit. The supra umbilical hernia, with a crescenteric defect will probably need surgical repair.

Intussusception

This is the most important commonest cause of intestinal obstruction in infancy. The incidence is between 0·1 and 0·2 per cent and the condition occurs more commonly in males than females in a ratio of two to one.

Symptoms and signs

It is rare in the neonatal period, commonest in the second half of the first year. The aetiology is still debated. Sometimes there is an anatomical reason such as a polyp or lymph node which may induce the intussusception, which most commonly is ileocaecal. The condition sometimes occurs in association with gastro-enteritis and it has been suggested that introduction of mixed feeding may be a causative factor.

Classically, the mother describes the infant suddenly screaming, drawing up the legs and becoming pallid. The episodes are short but recurrent. Vomiting is not a prominent early symptom. If the condition goes unreported or unrecognized, then the picture changes to one of intestinal obstruction; the child then may become quiet, toxic and have signs of peritonitis. It may be possible to feel the rounded mass of the intussusception. An important and often early sign (in about 65 per cent) is the passage of blood and mucus per rectum. A rectal examination may reveal blood on the finger stall and commonly an empty rectum. Occasionally, the apex of the intussusception can be felt.

Management

This condition requires urgent hospital referral. It is possible for the intussuscepted bowel to reduce spontaneously but even if this is suspected as having taken place, close observation is necessary as the blood supply to the bowel wall may already have become jeopardized. Confirmation of the diagnosis, if not obvious clinically, is made by barium enema examination. It is sometimes possible to reduce the intussusception during the enema, but more usually laparotomy is required. This has the advantage of direct inspection of the bowel. With prompt treatment, the prognosis is excellent though recurrence can occur.

Appendicitis

Though very rare in infancy, this common condition of later childhood warrants mention. Mortality of 50 per cent has been reported in infants and though only seven per cent of cases of appendicitis occur in children less than five years old, the mortality in this age group accounts for about a third of the total deaths from the condition. It is difficult to diagnose in infants as the classical history of older childhood is absent. Young children localize peritoneal inflammation poorly and so presentation is usually late with signs of toxaemia and peritonitis. To achieve early diagnosis, a high index of suspicion is necessary with careful observation and early referral of babies who go off their feeds and show early signs of dehydration and abdominal distension or tenderness.

Gastro-enteritis

This infection leads to loss of salt and water and in the infant this can rapidly lead to severe illness. It has been a common cause of mortality and morbidity in the United Kingdom until the last decade, but the incidence and complications following dehydration have now fallen due to improvements in the standard of living and health care and more recently, modification of artificial milk feeds.

The precise aetiology in infancy is often not established, partly due to the varying enthusiasm and facilities available for investigation. Over half the cases are probably viral in origin and in the last few years the rotavirus has been specifically identified as the commonest agent. Bacterial causes include the pathogenic strains of the *E. coli*, the shigella and salmonella species and campylobacter.

Symptoms and signs

Frequent loose watery stools are the usual prominent feature in infants. There is often a reluctance to take feeds; vomiting may also occur and, if persistent, should raise suspicion of some other cause. It is necessary to enquire carefully into the fluid intake and assess the loss from the bowel and the quantity of urine passed. Careful weighing of the sick infant and comparison with known previous weights or the expected weight judged by the birth weight, will help to give an idea of the severity of the illness. The clinical assessment of hydration has already been discussed. Infants can rapidly become seriously dehydrated and careful supervision is necessary in the early stages. The younger the infant, the closer the observation required.

Management

The essential aim of treatment is to rest the gastro-intestinal tract; the safest way to do this is to substitute water for the milk feeds and in the older infant modify or stop solid feeding. There is no need in the mild case to give an electrolyte solution, though now this has been made easier and safer by the commercial availability of Dioralyte (four per cent dextrose, 35 mmol of sodium, 20 mmol of potassium, 18 mmol bicarbonate). The instruction to give sugared water or a 'little salt' is very dangerous and this should not be given. It is easy for the mother to prepare a hyperosmolar solution which will further dehydrate the child. After 24 hours the diarrhoea has usually stopped with this simple treatment. Milk feeds may then gradually be re-introduced, starting with quarter-strength feeds and gradually building up to full strength feeds by increasing to half-strength, then three-quarter strength at 24 hour intervals. Progress must be monitored and if the diarrhoea persists or the infant fails to take feeds, referral to hospital has to be considered. During the illness daily assessment of hydration will be necessary whenever practical including the baby's weight. Most cases will respond to this regime and there is no place for drugs such as diphenoxylate (Lomotil) nor the use of antibiotics; the latter only have a place in treatment of associated septicaemia, in which case the infant should be in hospital. A complication of gastro-enteritis in infancy, is a temporary lactose intolerance or a malabsorption state (see later), so attention to how the infant thrives over the ensuing weeks is of great importance.

Differential diagnosis

It must be remembered that vomiting and diarrhoea are non-specific signs of ill-health in infancy. It is important to consider the acute infections such as otitis media, urinary tract infection and meningitis. Viral illnesses causing laryngeal symptoms in the parents may be associated with loose stools in the infant and bronchospasm in the toddler.

Malabsorption states

There are three main causes of malabsorption states in the infant: post-infective, coeliac syndrome and cystic fibrosis. There are other rarer causes which need not concern us here.

Symptoms and signs

These are of an infant failing to grow, particularly making poor weight gain. The stools will be bulky, pale and offensive and the abdomen distended. The important points to note in the assessment of these infants are the age at which the infant started to show symptoms, particularly failure to gain adequate weight, the dietary history with reference to the introduction of wheat-containing foods, and specific enquiry concerning an acute episode of gastro-enteritis.

Post infective malabsorption may give a secondary lactose intolerance or steatorrhoea. Lactose intolerance is secondary to loss of the enzyme lactose which splits lactase prior to its absorption. This enzyme is normally present in the brush border of the jejunal villi, and in cases of partial villous atrophy, there will be a more widespread impairment of absorption. The problem may last a few days or weeks. The diagnosis may be suspected when there is recurrence of loose watery stools as milk feeds are re-introduced after treatment of a diarrhoeal illness, along the lines previously described. Confirmation may be made by identifying lactose (a reducing sugar) in the stool. The treatment is to change the milk feed, using instead a special milk that excludes lactose, such as galactomin which is a modified cow's milk or a soya bean preparation.

Coeliac syndrome

The aetiology of this condition is still undetermined. There are two main lines of research, one involving an immunological basis, the other related to 'toxic' damage of the intestinal mucosa secondary to the absence of a specific enzyme responsible for the degradation of gluten. The infant thrives initially, but a few weeks after the introduction of gluten, signs develop of malabsorption, usually associated with irritability and anorexia and delayed motor milestones. The diagnosis, once suspected, requires referral for investigation, the definitive finding being villous atrophy determined by jejunal biopsy. Treatment is *total* exclusion of wheat and rye from the diet, following which the child should show clinical improvement. The stools may take a few weeks to return to normal as the villi take time to recover. The child requires close supervision during the growing period. The diet needs to be continued for life.

Cystic Fibrosis

This is an inherited condition affecting the exocrine glands, those principally involved being the pancreas, mucous secreting glands of the respiratory tract, and the sweat glands. It is an autosomal recessive condition; both parents must carry the gene, the frequency of which is one in 25 of the population. The risks of an affected child for those parents are one in four for each pregnancy. The incidence of the condition in the United Kingdom is one in 2000.

Symptoms and signs

There is no satisfactory screening test, though one based on testing the initial specimen of meconium has been tried recently. Since 20 per cent of babies with this condition do have reasonable pancreatic function, this test is not ideal. Even more important, it has a tendency to produce false positive reactions. About 10 per cent of affected children present with neonatal obstruction due to inspissated meconium in the small gut—meconium ileus (for details the reader is referred to paediatric texts). There is an increased incidence of rectal prolapse.

It will be appreciated that a clinical diagnosis of this condition is important. The failure of adequate pancreatic function will lead to steatorrhoea and failure of the infant to thrive. This tends to be apparent from birth. In contrast, the child with coeliac syndrome develops symptoms only after the introduction of gluten to the diet. The child with cystic fibrosis tends to be hungry and feeds well, unlike the child with coeliac syndrome. Another important reason for making the diagnosis of cystic fibrosis early, is because the child is susceptible to respiratory infection. The early signs may be just a raised respiratory rate, possibly associated with some degree of bronchospasm. Ideally, the diagnosis should be made before severe respiratory illness develops as there is evidence that the prognosis is improved in those children diagnosed early. There is a predisposition for the respiratory tract of these infants to become colonised by the staphylococcus, and this should alert one to the diagnosis when a pharyngeal swab detects this organism. Once suspicion is aroused, the definitive investigation is the sweat test, the sodium content in the sweat being raised above 60 mmols/litre.

Management

This is complicated. Treatment is directed towards
- (i) prevention of respiratory illness, the mainstay of which is regular chest physiotherapy with appropriate use of antibiotic therapy by nebulizer and systemically
- (ii) attention to dietary problems with the use of pancreatic extract and vitamin supplements
- (iii) counselling and support of the family

Nebulizers can be provided by the hospital or by the Cystic Fibrosis Association. Parents of affected children should be introduced to this excellent organisation as soon as the diagnosis of the condition has been fully discussed with particular emphasis on the variation of prognosis being explained.

10.

Endocrine and metabolic disorders

Problems of the endocrine glands will only rarely be encountered by the general practitioner.

Hypothyroidism (cretinism)

This is the most common endocrine disorder to present in infancy. Lack of thyroid hormone may be due to:
- (i) failure of the normal formation of the thyroid gland, the extreme being athyroidism, or
- (ii) failure of production of the active hormone, thyroxine, due to enzymatic defects (dyshormonogenesis).

Symptoms and signs

Severe cretinism is apparent at birth. Affected babies are lethargic, feed poorly and have difficulty in breathing—both these latter symptoms being related to the enlarged tongue. The facies are coarse, the nasal bridge poorly formed and the neck thick. The skin is rough and thickened and often the limbs are cold, with poor superficial circulation. An umbilical hernia is often present, and constipation a problem. The pulse rate is slow. Those babies with an abnormality of thyroxine metabolism will normally have a goitre.

The milder degrees of hypothyroidism may be less easy to diagnose. A clue to the condition in the neonatal period is prolonged neonatal jaundice. Those presenting later will show delayed motor and social development, associated with slow growth.

The diagnosis is confirmed by measurement of the thyroxine (T_4) level in the blood which will be low, and there

174

will be a raised level of thyroid-stimulating hormone (T.S.H.). The earlier the diagnosis is made, the better the chance of achieving a satisfactory result, particularly in terms of intellectual development. However, in severe cases results of treatment are often disappointing in spite of prompt diagnosis, and this may be because there has been severe deprivation of hormone during intra-uterine life.

Treatment

This should be initiated in hospital when the condition presents in infancy. The replacement of thyroxine must be approached with great caution to avoid putting the child into heart failure. Treatment will, of course, be life long and there is always the risk that the adolescent will find the continual taking of regular medication irksome.

It is likely that a satisfactory screening test will be developed (Walsh, 1979).

Hyperthyroidism

This rare condition may occur transiently in babies born to mothers with exophthalmic goitre. The baby is agitated with tachycardia and exophthalmos and usually fails to gain weight. Treatment may be necessary for a few weeks.

Adrenogenital syndrome

This is a rare autosomal recessive disorder in which there is absence or reduced activity of one of a number of enzymes necessary for the synthesis of the adrenocortical hormones. Control of the adrenal hormones is via the feed-back mechanism regulating adrenocorticotrophin (A.C.T.H.) production from the pituitary gland. Failure of production of cortisol during intra-uterine life results in excessive stimulation of the adrenal gland leading to hyperplasia and over production of the hormones with intact metabolic pathways and the formation of abnormal metabolites consequent upon the blocked pathways. The commonest defect is failure of the enzyme C_{21}-hydroxylase necessary for the conversion of 17α hydroxyprogesterone to 17α, 21 dihydroprogesterone in the cortisol pathway and the conversion of progesterone to 21 hydroxyprogesterone in the aldosterone pathway.

Symptoms and signs

The precise presentation, timing and characteristics vary depending on which enzyme is lacking. The commonest of the varieties will present in the neonatal period as an adrenal crisis. The infant loses salt and water, presenting as an ill, dehydrated baby and possibly also hypoglycaemic. It may be that this acute presentation can be anticipated in the female infant as, due to the excess androgen production during intra-uterine development, ambiguous genitalia may be present. The male infant may show virilism though this is more likely to develop postnatally. The diagnosis is confirmed by biochemical investigation.

Treatment

Replacement of glucocorticoid in the form of cortisone may be sufficient but it may also be necessary to give mineralocorticoid usually as fludrocortisone. The dose has to be carefully adjusted to achieve suppression of adrenal hyperplasia without depressing growth due to excess treatment. There may be a considerable problem with regard to the degree of intersex in the female infant. The child will be at risk during intercurrent illnesses or if there is difficulty for any reason in the administration of the replacement hormones, which will be life long. Parents should be advised that the risks of further affected children are one in four for each pregnancy.

Diabetes mellitus

Though rare, diabetes mellitus may present during the first year of life. The symptoms and signs are the classical ones of polydypsia, polyuria and weight loss; the polyuria will, of course, be less apparent whilst the child is in napkins. Confirmation of the diagnosis will be made by examination of the urine for sugar and ketones. Once diagnosed, referral to hospital for treatment is a matter of urgency and must not be left until the next available outpatient appointment. The control of diabetes in infancy and childhood always requires insulin.

Metabolic disorders

There are many disorders now identified which affect growth

and development adversely and which may become apparent during the first year of life. Individually, these conditions are rare, only very occasionally being seen by a general practitioner. A few general comments follow. For detailed information concerning a specific condition, referral should be made to the appropriate text.

Disorders of *amino-acid metabolism* constitute the largest group; each is associated with specific enzyme deficiency. Some can be treated by dietary measures but exclusion diets may be difficult to construct. Often some complication of the condition, usually a severe metabolic acidosis, arises too soon even for a diagnosis to be made, let alone treatment started. Since most of these illnesses arise from autosomal recessive conditions, anticipation of a problem may be possible. The clue may be in a history of unexplained neonatal deaths.

An example of this group is *phenylketonuria*, the incidence being one in 20 000. Here there is a deficiency in the enzyme phenylalanine hydroxylase, which converts phenylalanine to tyrosine. There is a consequent failure of the metabolic pathway beyond tyrosine, resulting in abnormal metabolites of phenylalanine which are toxic to the brain. The result is mental deficiency often associated with epilepsy, eczema and a characteristic pale complexion. If diagnosed early, a diet with very low phenylalanine content can be prescribed and the child may then develop normally. The diet may be relaxed in later childhood, possibly due to alternative metabolic pathways developing. As with all inborn errors of metabolism, inheritance is autosomal recessive giving a one in four chance of an affected child.

A screening test is used in the U.K. for all neonates to diagnose this condition. This is the Guthrie test which is a biological assay of a spot of blood to determine excess of phenylalanine at six days as soon as the infant has been established on milk feeding. It is important to remember that infants born in other parts of the world and then coming to this country, whether the indigenous population returning or as immigrants, may not have had the Guthrie test.

The aim of management of these disorders in the future is three-fold:

(i) to expand the number of defects which may be conveniently screened in a simple economic fashion and for which treatment is available

(ii) to develop means of detecting the heterozygote (the

carrier state) which can already be done in phenylketonuria (half of the siblings of an affected child will be
carriers)

(iii) to develop methods to detect affected fetuses by
antenatal examination of the amniotic fluid.

Other examples of these inborn errors are to be found in
association with carbohydrate metabolism (e.g., galac-
toseaemia), mucopolysaccharide metabolism (e.g., Hunter's
syndrome, Hurler's syndrome—known as gargoylism), lipid
metabolism (e.g., the denerative central nervous symptom
disorders, Tay-Sach's disease, Gaucher's disease). For
further information, refer to the appropriate paediatric texts.

Rickets

This condition is the result of vitamin D deficiency. Vitamin
D is uncommon in natural foodstuffs, the principal source
being by the formation of the vitamin in the skin by the action
of ultra-violet light. Rickets affects growing bone, it is now
rare in the indigenous population of the U.K. but still occurs
in certain areas and particularly may be seen in the immigrant
children with skin pigmentation living in areas where there is
limited sunshine or poor nutrition or both. The most usual
form is nutritional rickets where there is deficient intake of
vitamin D, calcium or both. Rarer forms occur such as rickets
secondary to renal disease.

Symptoms and signs

Infants of any age may be affected, the low birth weight baby
may be especially vulnerable if vitamin supplement is
omitted. The classical features are swelling of the epiphyses
particularly wrists, lower ends of the femur and tibia and the
costochondral junctions (ricketty rosary). There is often
bowing of the tibia which if the child is weight-bearing can
lead to marked deformity. The skull bones may be soft and
the sutures prominent. The infant is often irritable and the
epiphyses tender. There may be an associated iron deficiency
anaemia.

Confirmation of the diagnosis is made by radiological and
biochemical investigation. The epiphyses on X-ray show a
ragged appearance due to failure of calcification of the
epiphyseal cartilage and widening of the metaphyses. The

characteristic biochemical change is a markedly raised alkaline phosphatase, a low plasma phosphate and rarely a low plasma calcium.

Management

Nutritional rickets responds to vitamin D oral supplement. Care must be taken not to cause overdosage, an initial dose of 3000 units is acceptable with careful follow-up and monitoring of progress by clinical, X-ray and biochemical means.

Prevention is the most important aspect of management. The recommended dietary requirement is 400 units vitamin D per day.

REFERENCE

Walsh M P 1979 Screening for neonatal hypothyroidism. British Journal of Hospital Medicine 21 : 28–36

11

Urogenital disorders

The neonatal and infant kidney is both anatomically and physiologically immature, maturation taking place during the first two years of life. Glomerular filtration and tubular function are less efficient than in the adult kidney; the infant's kidney is less capable of concentrating urine and less able to cope with high sodium, high solute loads and acid-base homeostasis.

The principal problems during the first year of life are those of congenital origin and urinary tract infection.

Hypospadias

The incidence of this malformation is about 0·3 per cent of male births. There is failure of the urethra to develop, resulting in an abnormal position of the external urinary meatus. This in some cases is associated with a curvature of the penis—chordee. Most commonly, there is only slight ventral displacement of the meatus, which may be sited as far back as the penoglandular sulcus associated with a ventral deficit of the prepuce—the so-called 'hooded prepuce'. Only about 10 per cent of cases have the meatus situated along the shaft of the penis and these have more marked degree of chordee. Rarely, the meatus is on the perineum but if this occurs, the differential diagnosis of intersex becomes an important consideration.

Management

The first step is the assessment of the urinary stream, for if there is meatal stenosis, this will require relatively urgent treatment; the second, counselling the parents. Correction of the malformation will need to be carried out in stages, the first operation being to correct any degree of chordee, and subsequent operations being directed towards moving the meatus towards the glans. Early referral is beneficial so that the parents may learn from the start details of treatment directly from the surgeon responsible. Circumcision must *not* be carried out, as the residual preputical skin may be useful for the surgical reconstruction. There is an association, particularly in the more marked anomalies, with upper renal tract malformation. This will necessitate radiological investigation. It is necessary, therefore, to watch for evidence of urinary tract' infection (see later). The prognosis in the majority of cases is excellent—normal function of micturition and reproduction, a fact which often needs to be stressed to the parents.

Hydronephrosis

This may present at any age, rarely by a distended abdomen at birth or with a palpable mass, most frequently by urinary tract infection (see later). There may be obstruction at the pelvic ureteric junction or at the lower end of the ureter by, for example, a ureterocoele or, in males, by urethral valves. The ureterocoele is associated with duplication of the renal pelvis and ureter. For more detailed accounts, reference should be made to paediatric texts.

Management and successful treatment depend to a great extent on early recognition before secondary renal damage has occurred.

Urinary tract infection

This is an important problem in infancy for two reasons; firstly, the non-specific nature of presentation in this age group and, secondly, the relationship between infection of the urine and congenital malformation of the renal tract. The incidence of radiological abnormality in children presenting with urinary tract infection lies between 30 and 40 per cent. Opinion varies, but most agree that the first infection in a boy and at least the second, if not the first, in a girl, should be investigated radiologically. Saxena and his colleagues (1975) recommend investigation by intravenous pyelogram and micturating cystogram after the first infection in every child.

Symptoms and signs

The classical symptoms of urinary infection in older children are not applicable to infancy. Neonatal urinary infection may present with a failure to gain weight, poor feeding or hyperbilirubinaemia. The normal neonate may lose up to 10 per cent of the birth weight by the fourth day and then regain the birth weight by 10 to 14 days. A more profound initial weight drop, or a secondary fall during the second week, may be the presenting sign of urinary infection. During infancy, reluctance to feed, vomiting and poor weight gain, may be due to urinary infection. The onset may be more acute with an ill infant who may have pallor, fever and not infrequently, loose stools. Towards the end of the first year, urinary infection has to be considered in the differential diagnosis of a febrile convulsion.

Management

The acutely ill infant will need full investigation to determine the specific diagnosis and this is likely to require admission to hospital. The infant with symptoms but not ill, needs less urgent but no less careful investigation. In such babies, it is important to obtain adequate urine samples to be *absolutely* sure of the diagnosis, rather than to treat and then find the laboratory report does not confirm unequivocally the diagnosis. A definite urinary infection is likely to involve the child in radiological investigations, and long term follow-up will also be necessary to exclude recurrent infection. *It is irresponsible to treat without obtaining adequate urine examination.* Both microscopic examination and culture of the specimen are necessary. Interpretation of pyuria may be difficult, more than 10 pus cells per cm^3 suggesting infection in a boy (higher numbers, 50 to 100 may occur normally in girls) but pyuria may not always be present. A significant culture is more than 100 000 organisms per ml and this is likely to be a pure growth. Less than 10 000 per ml is likely to be due to contamination of the specimen, particularly if mixed organisms are present. Repeat samples should be obtained when 10^4 to 10^5 organisms/ml are cultured.

The collection of specimens in infants is a problem. The ideal is a mid-stream clean catch specimen. The use of 'uribags' may be necessary and the urine *must* be emptied as soon as possible after voiding. It is essential that the urine is transported promptly to the laboratory and ideally it should be kept cool. The use of the dip culture technique has helped to solve the problem and this should be more widely available to general practitioners than is the case at present.

The most common organism causing infection is the *Escherichia coli*. Other important organisms are *streptococcus faecalis*, *proteus mirabilis* and *pseudomonas*, the latter two particularly should alert the clinician to the possibility of an anatomical malformation of the renal tract.

Treatment

The ill infant with a urinary infection should be referred to hospital. Biochemical investigations will be required and septicaemia may complicate the illness. Since most of the infections are due to *E. coli*, the antibiotic of choice lies between one of the sulphonamide preparations (including those combined with trimethoprim) and ampicillin. All will require treatment for 10 to 14 days and it is obligatory to follow up treatment by regular urine examination for at least 12 months at monthly intervals, or more frequently, if the infant's progress is not satisfactory.

During infancy, a proven urinary tract infection, whether in a male or female, should have radiological investigation and close follow up.

Nephroblastoma (Wilm's tumour)

This, though rare, warrants mention as those tumours presenting and diagnosed early have a much better outlook; survival of up to 60 per cent is now being recorded. The usual presentation in infants is with an abdominal mass. Haematuria is rare; hypertension may occur.

Haematuria

This is not a common symptom in infancy, but when it occurs, it requires full investigation of the renal tract. Acute nephritis is extremely rare in this age group. The most usual cause of blood on the napkin is local bleeding either from the prepuce or an anal fissure. Red staining of the napkin, resembling blood on cursory inspection, may be due to a deposit of urates. (In older infants, red urine is commonly caused by eating beetroot).

Circumcision

The only medical indication for circumcision is that of phimosis which may be congenital or acquired. The former is very rare and the latter unlikely to occur during infancy. The prepuce of the infant is not retractile and any attempt to make it so is meddlesome.

There are religious and emotional reasons for circumcision and these should be discussed rationally with the parents. A circumcision after the first week of life must be carried out as a formal surgical procedure. Any surgical treatment carries a risk of morbidity and mortality; circumcision is no exception. If carried out whilst the infant is still in nappies, the operation leads to an increased risk of meatal ulceration.

Balanitis

Probably the commonest urogenital disorder in male infants, this responds readily to simple hygenic measures. The foreskin is not retractile in the infant.

Undescended testicle

The testes normally descend into the scrotum at 38 weeks of intra-uterine life. In the normal neonate, the testes are therefore palpable in the scrotum and examination and recording of this fact in the neonatal period is a useful exercise. The testes may become retractile during later childhood but if they have once been in the scrotum, there will be no necessity for interference. If the testicles are not present in the scrotum at birth, they may descend spontaneously during infancy but if there is no indication of this happening by the second year, then operation is usually necessary, and is best performed before school age. Early referral is therefore advocated.

REFERENCE

Saxena S R, Laurance B M, Shaw D G 1975 The justification for early radiological investigations of urinary-tract infection in children. Lancet 2: 403-404.

12.

Skin disorders

The skin of a healthy newborn baby is translucent and elastic. It is easily injured, but quick to heal, usually without scarring. It is more prone to infection and more sensitive to irritants than in later childhood.

Congenital lesions

The commonest congenital lesions encountered are vascular malformations. There are two main types: the cavernous haemangiomata which resolve and the capilliary haemangiomata which persist. *Superficial cavernous haemangiomata* may present at birth but more frequently appear during the first few weeks of life. They are found most commonly in preterm infants. The presentation is a raised fleshy red lump and the synonym strawberry naevus describes the appearance appropriately. These naevi may occur in any site but are often on the face or trunk. They may involve the perineum which can cause problems with management. The natural history is for the lesion to increase gradually in size during the first year and then slowly resolve. As resolution occurs the centre becomes greyish white. Complete disappearance occurs (except occasionally in the very large ones) and they should *not* receive active treatment. The policy of non-interference may be difficult for some parents to accept, particularly with the larger lesions or in more awkward sites. Secondary infection may accelerate the resolution.

Deep cavernous haemangiomata are less common. They present as a fleshy swelling, part of which may appear vascular. A complication which may arise is thrombocytopaenia. These lesions will also resolve spontaneously over a number of years.

The *superficial capilliary haemangiomata* (naevus flammeus, port wine stain) are macular or minimally raised lesions of variable size, of deep purplish colour and present at birth. They most commonly affect the face and sometimes the limbs. They do not blanch on pressure but sometimes dramatically do so when the child goes faint. This lesion does not fade or regress and so has significant implication regarding cosmetic appearance. It is possible to obtain specialist advice on cosmetic masking and it is important to mention this at the first consultation, to help the parents in accepting the deformity. The rare Sturge-Weber syndrome is the association of intracranial angiomata and a superficial capilliary angioma in the distribution of the trigeminal nerve.

Neonatal problems A number of common minor neonatal skin lesions, (erythema toxicum, fat necrosis, milia, staphylococcal infections) are discussed in Chapter 3.

Seborrhoeic dermatitis

This is a scaly condition which arises in early infancy. The aetiology is uncertain though there may be a genetic predisposition. The onset corresponds to the increased activity of the sebaceous glands which occurs postnatally.

Symptoms and signs

The condition first appears around four weeks. The skin becomes erythematous and scaly, often producing greasy yellowish plaques which may coalesce on the scalp (cradle cap). All areas may be affected, the trunk, perineal region and skin folds, particularly around the ears being most frequently involved. The infant remains well, there is no pruritus, but the appearance may be extremely distressing for the parents.Secondary infection may occur with candida or bacteria, and napkin dermatitis may be an associated problem (see below).

Treatment

Scaling of the scalp may be improved by washing with neutral soap, one per cent cetrimide solution. Care with hygiene of the skin is important and if candida or bacterial infection is present, this will need specific treatment. Topical steriod ointments are effective but should always be used with care, the weakest preparation that is effective being used for the shortest period possible. Avoid woollen garments. The condition tends to be self-limiting and does not indicate increased risk of eczema. Support for the mother is essential, since the condition, as with napkin dermatitis, gives mothers an inappropriate sense of failure and guilt.

Napkin dermatitis

This is one of the commonest problems in infancy. It is due to ammoniacal burning of the skin. Ammonia is released by urea splitting organisms, which are present in the stools, acting on the urine.

Symptoms and signs

It principally affects the napkin area, and occurs at any time during the first year but most frequently between two and six months. The skin becomes erythematous often associated with papules and desquamation, sometimes excoriation. The flexures are spared. The pungent smell of ammonia may be present as the napkin is removed.

Management

Attention to the care of the child and laundering of the napkins is necessary. This being a contact dermatitis, the best treatment is to avoid the irritant which can be achieved by nursing the infant without napkins. This approach is only easily applicable in hospital where there is no problem with laundering, and a constant temperature. However, even at home, it is possible to expose the affected area at times and to try to ensure that soiled nappies are not left on for long periods. The perineal skin must be well cleaned and dried, fresh nappies must be dry and plastic pants avoided as completely as is practicably possible. Attention to the laundering of the napkins is essential, with use of simple soaps and avoidance of some of the softening agents at least whilst the skin is affected. The nappies should be rinsed in a mild antiseptic such as benzalkonium chloride 1:1000

(Roccal), or a dilute acetic acid solution (made up as one oz (30cc) vinegar in a gallon (4·5 litres) of water) used as the final rinse. Barrier creams are often effective. Topical dilute steroid preparations with an antibacterial or antifungal agent may be used if simple measures fail. Drapolene cream (containing benzylkonium chloride) applied over the entire napkin area usually eradicates the condition.

Atopic dermatitis (infantile eczema)

This is an allergic response of the skin and is often associated with a family history of atopy (hay fever, eczema, asthma) and may herald atopic manifestation in the future for the particular infant.

Symptoms and signs

It is unusual for the condition to start before three months. An erythematous rash develops, often starting on the face, on the cheeks, forehead or ears and involving the rest of the body to a greater or lesser extent. Both the extensor and flexor aspects of the limbs may be affected. The rash is papular and vesicular though the blisters may be only transient. The affected areas of skin may weep and become crusted. The infant is miserable and pruritus prominent; this may lead to excoriation by scratching, secondary infection may occur and consequent local lymphadenopathy. In some cases there is a co-existent ichthyosis.

Management

This is directed towards alleviating the skin lesion, the pruritus and the anxiety and disruption the condition may cause to the family. Weeping areas should be treated with calamine lotion, and the lichenified areas with one per cent coal tar in zinc ointment. An emulsifying ointment is used for bathing, avoiding the use of ordinary soap.

Steroids have an important role in controlling the condition but must be used carefully, the most dilute and least toxic preparation being used as sparingly as possible and every attempt made to avoid using fluorinated corticosteroid ointments and creams. Absorption of steroid occurs through damaged skin and this is accentuated if the skin is bandaged.

Continuous use will also damage the skin, hardening and destroying the subcutaneous fat, which causes the skin to thin and provokes telangectasia. Secondary infection will require local antibacterial or antifungal ointment, preferably after swabs from the skin have been taken for culture. Pruritus needs to be treated by attention to the nails and the use of an oral antihistamine or a sedative such as triclofos (Tricloryl).

The other important aspect of management is to consider a possible allergic aetiology. Careful history taking is necessary to determine whether or not an item in the diet exacerbates the eczema. The question of milk allergy continues to be debated. The diagnosis is a clinical one. If withdrawal of cow's milk improves the skin and reintroduction is associated with recurrence, then exclusion of cows' milk protein from the diet is certainly worth a trial. There are adequate substitute preparations (Nutramigen, Velactin) though some require vitamin supplements which can be supplied in the form of Ketovite liquid and tablets. They are also very expensive. In recent years, the exclusion of cows' milk protein in possibly susceptible atopic infants, based on a family history of allergy has been tried (Matthew et al, 1977). There is some evidence in favour of excluding cows' milk for six months; if breast feeding is successful, this may quite easily be achieved. There may be a place for admitting the more severely affected infant to hospital; nursing the child exposed aids the recovery of the skin, and temporary relief for the mother may be of vital importance. However, this should be an absolutely last resource. The involvement of the health visitor and community nurse in home treatment rarely, if ever, fails.

REFERENCE

Matthew D J, Taylor B, Norman A P, Turner M W, Soothill J F 1977 Prevention of eczema. Lancet 1: 321-324.

13.

Diseases of the nervous system

Congenital and inherited diseases of the central nervous system present at varying times during the first year of life.

The major malformations will be apparent at birth and may require immediate decision on management. Gross deformities such as anencephaly and encephalocoele are likely to cause stillbirth. The major problem is the management of the open spinal cord defect—the myelomeningocoele; the overall incidence of these severe neural tube defects in the U.K. is about one in 200 births.

Spina bifida is the general term used to describe these malformations and it may be associated with *hydrocephalus*, though each may exist independently. The minor degree and a common incidental finding on X-ray is *spina bifida occulta* where there is simply a failure of fusion of the bony element of the spinal column, with nervous tissue development and skin closure being normal. *Spina bifida cystica* is a more extensive malformation, the bony defect is likely to be larger and there is protrusion of the contents of the spinal column. If the spinal cord has developed normally, then the protrusion will consist only of the membranes retaining the cerebro-spinal fluid—a meningocoele. If the spinal cord itself is involved in the malformation, then the nervous tissue is visible as a red fleshy mass, this being the myelomeningocoele.

Meningocoele

It is important to recognize this defect as it may be associated with a fibrous band extending into the spinal column and resulting in tethering of the spinal cord, diastematomyelia.

191

During growth, normal development and migration of the cord is inhibited and this may give rise to neurological deficit in the lower limbs. The meningocoele may only be small or even appear as a trivial mid-line abnormality, such as a haemangioma, lipoma or hairy naevus. All these mid-line lesions must be referred early for specialist opinion so that adequate investigation and treatment to prevent later complications can be carried out.

Myelomeningocoele

This malformation can be very difficult to assess and treat. Historically, following the introduction of the Spitz-Holter valve which made treatment of hydrocephalus possible, tremendous enthusiasm resulted in early treatment of many children with all degrees of myelomeningocoele. Over the years, it has become apparent that this aggressive approach to treatment has led to many seriously handicapped children surviving. It is now realized that before embarking on treatment, careful consideration has to be given to the quality of life being offered to that child. This demands diligent assessment and thought by the doctor caring for the child and the family, including discussion with, and as much under-standing as is practicable by, the parents themselves.

The commonest site of the myelomeningocoele is the lumbo-sacral region, though dorsal lesions occur. The effect of the malformation is a flaccid paralysis of the lower limbs, the degree of which depends on the extent of the defect. This paralysis is likely to be associated with deformity of the limbs usually talipes equinovarus, which may be extreme, and congenital dislocation of the hip. There is usually impaired control of bowel and bladder function and often an associated hydrocephalus. Treatment involves closure of the defect as soon as is practicable, and possibly later insertion of a ventricular shunt to manage the hydrocephalus. The shunt may require revision during childhood.

There will also be the need for orthopaedic and often urological treatment. The management requires considerable dependency on hospital attendance. There will be problems with home and school life, and stress on all members of the family, parents and siblings. The decision to embark on treatment is often difficult, sometimes straightforward. The small defect with otherwise normal development and good movement of the lower limbs should be referred promptly for treatment.

On the other hand, there would seem no justification for striving to keep alive the severely affected baby with a large open defect, kypho-scoliosis of the spine, deformed and paralysed lower limbs and hydrocephalus. Many infants will, of course, fall between these two extremes in which case specialist opinion will be indicated. The immediate management is to cover the defect with a warm saline dressing and give the usual neonatal attention to maintaining the infant's airway, temperature and blood glucose. Prevention by antenatal diagnosis and genetic counselling has been discussed in Chapter 2.

Hydrocephalus

This may be apparent at birth or develop during the first few months of life. Once recognized, referral should be made for full investigation and treatment. The earlier raised intracranial pressure is diagnosed, the better the chance of successful treatment though the outcome will, of course, be partly determined by the aetiology. There may be associated malformation of the brain or the condition may be secondary to intra-uterine infection, in which case the outcome will be dependent on the primary cause.

The routine attendance of the infant at the baby clinic should ensure that abnormal rate of growth of the head is picked up by regular measurement of the head circumference. The variation in size and shape of the infant skull may make interpretation of the measurement difficult, so attention should also be given to the other parameters of growth, length and weight and the child's general development, particularly that of head control. Raised intracranial pressure may be reflected by a tense anterior fontanelle, impaired upward gaze giving the 'sun set' appearance of the eyes and dilated scalp veins. When pressure is raised markedly respiratory difficulty, stridor and vomiting may also occur. Prolonged raised pressure may give rise to papillodema and consequent optic atrophy.

Cerebral palsy and the degenerative diseases of the nervous system are discussed in Chapter 18.

Epilepsy

The emotional aspects of epilepsy in childhood are often as confused as the terminology. Epilepsy should be considered as a symptom and can be defined as 'paroxysmal recurrent involuntary alteration of motor or sensory function originating from abnormal discharges within the brain and often accompanied by alteration in consciousness'. The terms 'convulsion' and 'seizure' are used synonymously, as is 'fit', though the last is less precise and best avoided in this context.

A full description of the types of epilepsy is not relevant in a book on the first year of life, and the reader is referred to paediatric texts for a more complete account than the one that follows.

No apology is made for reiterating the fact that epilepsy is a symptom. During infancy and early childhood, the most important precipitating cause is infection of the central nervous system, meningitis or encephalitis—not the commonest overall cause, but the most important since it can lead to the early diagnosis of meningitis and so gives the greatest chance of reducing the mortality and morbidity from that disease.

Grand Mal epilepsy

The classical attack of aura, cry, tonic and clonic movements is not characteristically seen during infancy. In the neonate, movement of the trunk may be the only manifestation though generalized clonic movement of the limbs may occur. Similarly, during infancy, there may simply be loss of consciousness and tonic movement, followed by lack of response to stimuli. The question of tongue biting and incontinence is not particularly relevant to this age group.

Neonatal convulsions require referral to hospital for full investigation and this will include examination of the cerebro-spinal fluid. These babies need close follow-up with regard to their development.

Febrile convulsions

A Grand Mal attack occurring in association with fever is a common problem in early childhood and occurs most commonly between the ages of one and three years. It may occur between six and 12 months but great care is needed in assessing the younger child, particularly with the first convulsion. It is the sudden onset of high fever in association with a relatively immature brain that is broadly responsible for a febrile convulsion, but the exact aetiology, as with epilepsy generally, is not yet known. There do appear to be genetic factors involved as there is, at times, a strong family history.

Management

The convulsion may be self-limiting within minutes but if not, should be controlled as soon as possible. The treatment of choice is diazepam 0·25 mg/kg body weight given by slow intravenous injection, the injection being stopped once the convulsion has ceased. Diazepam may be administered rectally or intramuscularly, but these routes give less precise absorption, the latter being particularly unreliable and, if possible, avoided. Rectal infusion using the intravenous solution direct from a 2 ml plastic syringe is certainly effective when a vein cannot be found; it also can be considered as a method for use by a competent parent. As a second line drug, paraldhyde still has a place, 0·15ml/kg body weight by deep intramuscular injection. A plastic syringe may be used if the injection is given immediately. Management is also directed towards airway maintenance and reducing the body temperature. Once the convulsion has been controlled, attention must be directed towards determining the cause and this will require full examination with particular attention to the ears and throat. The question of referral to hospital for lumbar puncture is a debatable point but it is the authors' view that when a convulsion occurs for the first time in a child less than one year old, then the cerebro-spinal fluid must be examined. Remember that otitis media and meningitis may co-exist and if it is proposed to treat the child with antibiotics, this makes full investigation of even greater importance.

Many parents assume that their child is dying when they witness a convulsion, particularly for the first time and due attention must be paid to their anxiety in deciding on home or hospital management. The parents will also need to be instructed in how to deal with any future fever and/or convulsions. The most important advice is that directed towards ensuring a patent airway, staying with the child and calling the doctor urgently if the convulsion does not subside within two minutes, or if it recurs. It needs to be emphasised that removal of clothing and reducing the body temperature is the correct treatment of a fever. If further antipyretic treatment is needed, then tepid sponging may be advised with emphasis on tepid, not cold, water and the use of paracetamol (15 mg/kg/dose up to four times a day). The long term management of children with recurrent febrile convulsions will not be pursued. However, in the short term, any convulsion which is outside the usual definition of a febrile convulsion, such as one lasting longer than two minutes, or associated with any localizing signs, such as a temporary hemiparesis or prolonged alteration of consciousness or behaviour, should be referred urgently for further investigation. The danger of permanent brain damage from temporary hypoxia is ever present.

Infantile spasms (jack-knife epilepsy, salaam spasms)

This rare form of epilepsy characteristically presents during infancy, usually after the age of two months. It is often associated with severe neurological disorder such as the degenerative diseases of the nervous system, or tuberous sclerosis.

Symptoms and signs

There are sudden episodes of flexions of head and trunk and lower limbs, the classical attack giving the synonyms above. There is often a cry associated with the attacks which frequently occur in bouts. The atypical attack, and particularly those occurring before the child is sitting up, may be more difficult to identify. There may be associated developmental delay.

Management

Referral to hospital is best arranged immediately as there is some but slender evidence that prompt treatment improves prognosis. The clinical diagnosis is confirmed by electroencephalogram which typically is a bizarre tracing of grossly abnormal activity—hypsarrythmia. Treatment is by daily intramuscular injections of ACTH for six weeks or nitrazapam (Mogadon) or a combination of the two. It is usually possible to stop the epilepsy, though it may recur on completion of the course of injections, but the prognosis will depend on the underlying pathology.

Breath-holding attacks

These alarming but entirely benign episodes may start towards the end of the first year of life. The child suddenly holds his breath, becomes cyanosed and may then lose consciousness and even convulse. If a careful history is taken, a precipitatory injury or episodes of frustration can be obtained. The child's condition immediately following an attack, his development and neurological examination will all be normal.

Management

This is directed towards the parents by allaying, as far as possible, their anxiety and giving advice on handling the child. As little attention as possible should be directed towards each incident and the child should not be allowed to achieve benefit from the attacks. There is no place for giving medication to the child.

Meningitis

Neonatal meningitis has been discussed in Chapter 3. *Haemophilus influenzae* is the commonest causative organism of bacterial meningitis in infancy. Meningococcal, tuberculous and viral infection may occur.

Symptoms and signs

The classical signs of neck stiffness, tense fontanelle and opisthotonus occur late and the diagnosis of meningitis in infancy must be made before these signs develop, to avoid the sequelae of death or handicap. The early signs are non-specific—irritability or lethargy, reluctance to take feeds, vomiting, fever and general malaise. The physical signs may be little in addition to irritability, but a rash may occur; this is classically purpuric in meningococcal infection but may also be present with *haemophilus influenzae*.

Management

Immediate referral to hospital for lumbar puncture is indicated. Careful observation will be needed for other children in the family; in the case of meningococcal infection, the administration of prophylactic antibiotic to the other members of the family is advocated. Early diagnosis carries a good prognosis but follow-up to assess development and particularly any damage to the VIII nerve will be needed.

Squint

The newborn infant does not have accurate conjugate eye movement and so a squint is not necessarily abnormal in the first two months. When suspected, the eyes should also be examined for cataract, and an attempt made to visualise the retina.

The examination for a squint is best assessed by the corneal light reflex and cover test. The infant sits on the mother's lap facing the examiner and a point of light from an auriscope without the speculum, used to attract the infant's attention. The reflection should be symmetrical in each cornea. Briefly covering one eye then the other should not alter the axis of the contra-lateral eye. Once there is suspicion of a squint, and this includes the mother's and relatives' observations, ophthalmic referral should be made. In infancy and early childhood the acuity of an eye can rapidly worsen if diplopia is present.

14

Orthopaedic disorders

Deformation and malformation occur, the commonest problem being deformations secondary to pressure during intra-uterine life. These often correct with growth, the main difficulty in management being anxious parents who need sympathetic explanation and support by the practitioner.

Congenital dislocation of the hip (C.D.H.)

In theory, this problem could be diagnosed on routine medical examination or at least before the child starts weight bearing, but in practice, this ideal has proved difficult to achieve.

The incidence of C.D.H. is approximately 1 in 600 births. There may be a family history. It is commoner in girls, first-born children and in breech presentations; this suggests both genetic and mechanical factors being implicated.

The principal method of diagnosis is the routine examination of the hips using Barlow's technique. The baby is placed supine and the legs grasped symmetrically in each hand, the middle finger on the greater trochanter and the thumb on the medial aspect of the thigh at about the junction of upper third and lower two thirds of the femur. The knees are flexed and the legs initially adducted and then gently and symmetrically abducted; this manoeuvre may result in either a click or a clunk. The points to note are:

(i) As the legs are adducted, does the joint dislocate?

(ii) As abduction is carried out, does the head of the femur return to the acetabulum? This occurs if adduction causes dislocation, or if the joint is already dislocated before adduction is attempted.

199

(iii) In the abducted position, is it possible to manipulate the head of the femur in and out over the lip of the acetabulum?

(iv) When the full position of abduction is attained, is it symmetrical for the two legs?

If the dislocation is unilateral, shortening of the leg on the affected side may be detected; the other sign described, that of asymmetry of the posterior skin folds of the upper leg, is of limited value.

The timing of the examination is important. The joint is likely to be lax in the immediate neonatal period due to the secondary effect of maternal hormones. This means that the 7 to 10 day examination is a useful time to examine for C.D.H. Manipulation of the hip joint should be performed with care, particularly soon after birth, as there is a risk of damaging the vascular supply to the head of the femur.

The hip joint which definitely dislocates must be immediately referred for orthopaedic assessment and treatment. The 'clicking joint' may be a significant pointer to dislocation, but often it is merely due to tendon movement. Sometimes, in fact, the click originates from the knee joint which is of no significance. The babies with a clicking joint must be re-examined and, if there is still doubt at six weeks, referred for specialist opinion.

Despite routine screening, some dislocated hips are still identified later. It may be that some are diagnosable and have been missed, but it also seems likely that the routine test is inadequate in picking up some unstable joints early (Fixsen, 1978, 1979). The earlier an abnormal joint is identified the easier management will be and it is important to make the diagnosis before the child starts walking. Examination of the hip joints should be part of the routine when infants are seen for developmental surveillance and also, ideally, at all consultations during the first year of life.

Once diagnosed, the condition is treated by putting the babies' legs in an abduction splint; there are a number of methods available. This treatment may be required for many months but it is surprising how mobile these infants become, in spite of being subjected to this constraint. The long term results are usually excellent particularly with early diagnosis.

Talipes equinovarus and calcaneovalgus

This is one of the commonest problems of infancy. Most degrees of talipes require minimal treatment to the infant, but often considerable explanation and reassurance to the parents. The usual deformity is talipes equinovarus where the foot is plantar flexed and inverted at the ankle. Calcaneovalgus, where there is dorsiflexion and eversion, is less common. Both conditions may be unilateral or bilateral. It is often possible to 'wrap the baby' into the intra-uterine position and so demonstrate the aetiology to the parents. Minor degrees can be easily corrected passively and the parents instructed in this manoeuvre. If there is any doubt, then early referral is important as this makes management easier. Remember that deformity of the foot may reflect abnormal pressure on the hips, and examination for dislocation of the hips is part of the assessment of talipes.

Metatarsus varus and valgus may occur; here there is simply deviation of the forefoot, which almost always resolves spontaneously. The abnormal position may very well persist or even become more marked during the crawling phase, but once upright posture and walking is achieved, the deformity gradually resolves with growth.

Abnormalities of toes, crossed or over-riding, are often inherited in a dominant fashion. Usually, they require no treatment other than the commonsense advice of ensuring well fitting shoes.

REFERENCES

Fixsen J A 1978 Diagnosis of congenital dislocation of the hip. Journal of Maternal and Child Health 3: 300–302
Fixsen J A 1979 The management of congenital dislocation of the hips in the first year of life. Journal of Maternal and Child Health 4: 300–304

15.

Disorders of the blood

Primitive red cells appear in the embryo at about three weeks. The definitive type of erythropoiesis begins at six weeks of intra-uterine life. The haemoglobin level in the fetus is constant between 25 and 36 weeks at 14·0–14·5 g/dl. During the last month of gestation, the haemoglobin rises to levels above those seen in the adult. It is important that the normal variations and the differences between infant, child and adult haematological values are fully appreciated.

The mean cord haemoglobin at term is 16·8 g/dl (range 13·5 g–21 g). The mean cell volume (M.C.V.) is also greater (104–118 fl) than in the adult (75–100 fl). In the first few hours after delivery, the haemoglobin level rises, in part due to the volume of blood received by the infant from the placental circulation. The site of sampling will alter the results, capillary heel prick values of haemoglobin being greater (by up to 5 g) than venous samples. After 24 hours the haemoglobin starts to fall, but only reaches levels lower than the cord values after two or three weeks. This fall is caused by the shorter life-span of some of the red cells, a fall in the M.C.V., and an increase in the total blood volume. Erythropoetin, a hormone which regulates erythropoiseis, is present during fetal life but falls abruptly at birth, reappearing at about six weeks of post-natal life. Marrow activity is minimal until the third month of life, so the lowest levels of haemoglobin are reached at this time, the lowest limit of normal being 9·5 g/100 ml. There is then a moderate increase, but between three months and two years, the normal range of haemoglobin is 11·5 g–12 g/dl.

There is wide variation in total white count at birth and initially, the neutrophil exceeds the lymphocyte count. The total count falls during the first week and the differential count changes to give predominantly lymphocytes, this remaining the normal differential pattern until mid-childhood. The main haemoglobin in the fetus is HbF which consists of alpha and gamma chains. At term, 85 per cent of the total haemoglobin is still HbF, the remainder being HbA. There is very little synthesis of the gamma chain after birth, and the concentration of HbF falls to around 10 to 15 per cent by four months.

The most common haematological problem during the first year is iron deficiency anaemia, followed in incidence by the haemolytic and inherited anaemias.

Iron deficiency anaemia

This may present towards the end of the first year and is more likely to occur in the preterm infant, as the iron stores are laid down in the fetus during the last trimester of pregnancy. The diet during early infancy has poor iron content until full mixed feeding is achieved.

Symptoms and signs

Pallor may be the presenting feature and non-specific symptoms, such as listlessness and irritability may occur. Pica is an important symptom of iron deficiency and may develop towards the end of the first year. Malabsorption and bleeding need to be considered as possible causes. The diagnosis is confirmed by a blood film, which will show hypochromic microcytic cells.

Management

Moderate degrees of anaemia may be treated with iron supplement (for this age group, Plesmet and Sytron are palatable preparations), as long as the response is checked. If the haemoglobin does not rise or the anaemia recurs, then referral for further investigation should be made.

Haemolytic anaemias

The causes of blood group incompatability are discussed in

Chapter 3. Congenital spherocytosis is a common inherited anaemia in the U.K. and may present in the newborn period as hyperbilirubinaemia or as an anaemia either at that stage or later during childhood. Inheritance is by a dominant gene, though penetrance may vary. There is often a family history of splenectomy or gall bladder disease. Diagnosis is made on examination of the blood film, which will show the spherocytic cells, and the red cell fragility test. Aplastic crises may occur. The ideal treatment is splenectomy but the timing of this is important in view of the possibility of increased susceptibility to infection after splenectomy in early childhood.

The other haemolytic anaemias may be associated with red cell enzyme deficiencies or abnormal haemoglobins. Those which may be seen will vary in different areas depending on the immigrant population. Glucose-6-phosphate dehydrogenase deficiency occurs in Mediterranean, Negro and north European races in different forms but all are inherited in a sex-linked fashion. Sickle-cell disease due to the abnormal haemoglobin HbS occurs in the African races, and β-thalassaemia (failure of synthesis of the β-chain) in the Mediterranean races, particularly Cypriot and Greek communities, but also in children from the Far East. The gene is also present in the British (Knox-Macaulay et al, 1973). Since the HbF in these haemoglobinopathies is of normal form, the conditions tend not to present until the second half of the first year. However, techniques have now been developed to make antenatal diagnosis possible. Severe disease occurs only in the homozygous individual, but the trait is detectable in the heterozygous by haemoglobin electrophoresis.

Haemophilia may present during infancy as a haemorrhagic problem, either from the cord or after circumcision. It is a sex-linked recessive condition. It requires diagnosis by assay of factor VIII, and treatment should always be organised via a specialist haemophiliac centre.

Leukaemia is rare in the first year. When it does present this early, the prognosis is very poor.

REFERENCE

Knox-Macaulay H H M, Weatherall D J, Clegg J B, Pembry M E 1973 Thalassaemia in the British. British Medical Journal 2: 150–155

Part III

Specific aspects of care

Part III

Specific aspects of care

16.

Immunization

'It is generally recognized that immunisation is one of the best and most effective investments which any government can make towards the health of its citizens'. (Kampala Conference Declaration 1971).

What has gone wrong in the U.K.? The 1978–79 pertussis epidemic directly resulted from a most remarkable 'trial by media' of the policies enshrined in the opening sentence of this chapter (see Fig. 16.1). Unsubstantiated medical and lay anecdotal records of a *possible* link between immunization and brain damage has undermined the policy of mass immunization against disease in this country.

Poorly informed and often frightened parents now become inordinately worried about what should be a simple decision

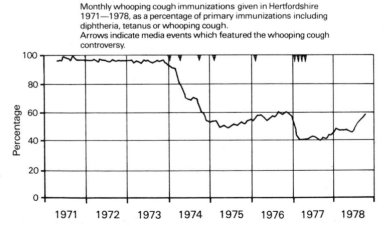

Monthly whooping cough immunizations given in Hertfordshire 1971—1978, as a percentage of primary immunizations including diphtheria, tetanus or whooping cough.
Arrows indicate media events which featured the whooping cough controversy.

Fig 16.1 Recent trends in whooping cough immunization. (*Reproduced with permission from the Health Education Council*)

207

over a safe procedure. Pathetically, it seems that it is those children most at risk, whose parents refuse immunization most often. Class IV and V parents seem to systematically refuse some, if not all, immunizations as a result of what they have heard and seen and misunderstood on the media. Because overcrowding and poverty are the lethal statistical multipliers of the risks of catching, in particular pertussis (but also, poliomelitis, diphtheria and measles), it is to many working in the field of preventive medicine something of a miracle that the summer of 1978 did not see a poliomyelitis epidemic in addition to the pertussis one.

A disaster in the Netherlands showed what the lethal effects could be when over 100 cases of poliomyelitis (one-third paralytic) occurred in members of a sect that had refused all immunizations on religious grounds.

In this country, very belatedly, a prospective study is now being directed at establishing whether a link exists between pertussis immunization and brain damage associated with its use. So far, the most careful analysis has shown no such link. In the meanwhile, years of innuendo and outright condemnation of pertussis immunization by some members of the profession have strengthened parent's resolve, albeit mistakenly, to refuse pertussis immunization and then, by association, all the immunizations offered.

However, it is reassuring to see at last the tide running so strongly the other way, with parents clammering for all immunizations as a result of splash coverage in the media of the severity of the present epidemic. The lessons for all of us have been salutory, and the profession must share the blame. Any immunization policy must have its safety record backed by *continuous* monitoring to confirm its safety. In addition, much greater attempts must be made to obtain realistic notification figures from doctors who see the diseases in the field. Any government that wishes its citizens to be protected by immunization must be responsible for the continuing monitoring of such a policy and the careful recording of side effects, to convince the public of its safety.

At this moment, the government has responded to the current pertussis epidemic by altering, yet again, the approved schedule of immunization. Until recently, the received message was that it was wise to put off immunization until children were at least six months old because of the possible neurotoxic effects of the vaccine on the immature brain. In addition, evidence was adduced that starting immunization early, created the need to give booster injections at 18 months when the current opinion was that the pertussis component was likely to again be neurotoxic.

In the haze of opinions often strongly held, it is very

Table 16.1 Notifications and deaths from five infectious diseases 1940–1974

Year	Tetanus	Diphtheria		Pertussis		Poliomyelitis			Measles	
						Non-para	Paralytic			
		N[a]	D[b]	N	D	N	N	D	N	D
1940		46281	2480	53607	678				409521	857
1941		50797	2641	173330	2383				409715	1145
1942		41404	1827	66016	799				286341	458
1943		34662	1317	96136	1114				376104	773
1944		23199	934	94044	1054				158479	243
1945		18596	722	62691	689		858	139	446796	729
1946		11986	472	92936	808		680	128	160402	204
1947		5609	244	92662	905		7776	707	393787	644
1948		3575	156	146383	748		1855	241	399606	327
1949		1881	84	102809	527		5982	657	385871	307
1950	71	962	49	157781	394	2195	5565	755	367724	221
1951	81	664	33	169441	437	1085	1529	219	616192	317
1952	63	376	32	114869	184	1163	2747	295	389502	141
1953	61	266	23	157842	243	1571	2076	338	545050	245
1954	61	173	8	105912	139	641	1319	134	146995	50
1955	43	155	12	79133	88	2619	3712	270	693803	176
1956	52	53	3	92410	95	1483	1717	137	160556	30
1957	46	37	4	85017	87	1667	3177	255	633678	94
1958	41	80	8	33400	27	575	1419	154	259308	49
1959	38	102	0	33252	25	289	739	87	539524	98
1960	32	49	5	58030	37	131	257	46	159364	31
1961	41	51	8	24469	27	169	707	79	763465	152
1962	29	16	2	8347	24	59	212	45	184895	39
1963	21	33	2	34736	36	12	39	3	601255	127
1964	28	20	0	31594	44	8	29	4	306801	73
1965	33	25	0	12945	21	36	55	3	502209	115
1966	27	20	5	19427	23	4	19	1	343642	80
1967	25	6	0	33531	17	3	16	0	440103	94
1968	22	15	1	17367	15	5	19	0	225789	47
1969	17	9	0	4866	5	1	9	0	131305	33
1970	21	22	3	16244	15	0	6	0	289893	40
1971	10	17	1	15933	23	1	5	1	126068	24
1972	13	4	0	1988	2	2	3	0	136147	29
1973	7	2	0	2437	2	1	4	0	152484	33
1974[d]	9	3	0	16230	13	1	5	0	109636	20
1975		11	1	8913	12	1	2	0	143072	16
1976		2	0	3907	3	3	10	0	55502	14
1977		2	0	17475	7	1	15	0	173361	23

[a] Number of notified cases
[b] Number of deaths
[c] Deaths due to tetanus or fatal injuries complicated by tetanus
[d] 1974 figures are uncorrected

Dates when national immunisation campaigns were started:

Tetanus	1939	(the Armed Forces)
Diphtheria	1942	
Triple vaccine	1954	Programme started; fully implemented 1957
Poliomyelitis	1956	Salk-type inactivated poliovaccine (I.P.V.)
	1961	Sabin-type oral poliovaccine (O.P.V.)
Measles vaccine	1968	

The above figures apply in the main to England and Wales. Data extracted from the Annual Reports of the Chief Medical Officer, The Department of Health and Social Security.

difficult for the individual doctor faced with worried parents to see how to start persuading them that immunization 'is a good thing'. I believe that Table 16.1 goes a long way in showing parents that immunization has an effect.

To persuade them that the vaccines are *safe* is quite another matter. Evidence from other countries is so contradictory that many now are beginning to believe that most, if not all, so-called pertussis immunization reactions are nothing of the kind. To convince parents of the *safety* of the currently used vaccines, the doctor himself needs to have the information confirming this at his finger tips.

The illogicality of some of these 'approved' contra-indications (Table 16.2) is that in the U.S.A. children with cerebral palsy are probably rightly considered at increased risk of pertussis-induced brain damage, if they should be unlucky enough to catch it, and therefore, a special effort is made to immunize such children.

Table 16.2 Contra-indications to use

Inactivated 'killed' vaccines		*Live attenuated vaccines*	
Diptheria, pertussis, tetanus, flu vaccine		Poliomyelitis, measles, BCG, rubella, smallpox	
1. *General contra-indications*			
(a)	Febrile illness	(a)	Febrile illness
(b)	Intercurrent infection	(b)	Intercurrent infection
2. *Specific contra-indications to pertussis*			
(a)	Epilepsy in mother, father or siblings	(a)	*Eczema, (BCG), (smallpox)
(b)	*Epilepsy in the child	(c)	*Immune defficiency
(c)	*Febrile convulsions	(c)	*Corticosteroid or immuno-suppressive therapy including radiotherapy
(d)	*Cerebral irritation severe enough to have needed phenobarbitone in the newborn period	(d)	Allergy to egg protein (measles, BCG in tuberculin positive patients)
(e)	Allergy to egg protein (influenza vaccine)		

*absolute contra-indication

Furthermore, in the U.K. it is considered that if a child has a reaction either generalised or local to the first dose of triple vaccine immunization should proceed with the pertussis component left out, uncritically assuming that it is the pertussis component that has caused the reaction.

Despite all the conventional precautions over the years, reaction to many vaccines have been reported. Wilson (1976) reviewed the data and isolated six main reasons why disasters have occurred:

   (i) *Normal toxicity and reactivity.* Local and general reactions occurred with early measles vaccines.

  (ii) *Faulty production.* This has caused diptheria and tetanus due to residual toxicity. Bacterial contamination has caused septicaemia, viral contamination and hepatitis. Poliomyelitis and rabies have been caused by incompletely inactivating the virus in the vaccine.

 (iii) *Non-sterile apparatus.* Tuberculous abscesses have been caused by operator contamination.

 (iv) *Allergic reactions.* Neuritis and encephalomylitis have been reportedly caused by pertussis and triple vaccines.

  (v) *Abnormal sensitivity of patient.* Smallpox vaccine has caused generalised vaccinia in immune deficiency.

 (vi) *Indirect effects.* Provoking effect: diptheria/tetanus vaccines with adjuvant are said to have caused poliomyelitis in a patient who was possibly carrying live wild virus at the time.

The total of these reactions is infinitesimal compared to the numbers immunized.

Perhaps only now with the government taking the first steps at last to follow the Danish precedent and compensating as of right all children damaged by vaccine, can we begin to see how much of a problem we have. In Denmark, after a famous actress's child developed a reaction said to be due to pertussis immunization, the Danish government agreed to compensate fully the parents of all children similarly affected. The most remarkable fact is that not one single parent has been paid compensation since.

At the moment in this country chaos reigns. Immunization programmes are beginning at three, four and six months or not at all and some areas have been actively discouraging mothers from asking for pertussis vaccine for their babies, with such a disastrous effect on the level of pertussis notifications, that a hasty turn-about has been ordered and every attempt made then to immunize children missed the first time round.

It probably *does* matter when immunization should begin. Recent evidence suggests that starting triple vaccine at three months produces only a slow rise in immunity. Delaying the start until six or seven months means that with a second injection a month later a substantial degree of protection is achieved. The third injection, done at any time convenient thereafter, merely makes protection complete. If every child's immunization schedule were to be planned on such a time scale, there would be no problem. At the present time, with older children not protected coming home with the disease and infecting their younger unimmunized siblings, the situation has been worrying.

Recently, too, there has been a change in policy towards poliomyelitis vaccine. The DHSS circulars CMO(78) 18 and CNO(78) 12 suggest that at least the mother, and both parents if possible, should receive oral live vaccine (Sabin) at the same time as the child receives it. The reason is that over the last five years, 10 out of the 31 cases of poliomyelitis recorded in this country have occurred in association with immunization, 5 cases in the parents of immunized children; all these cases were caused by either type II or type III strains found in the vaccine.

Viruses excreted by vaccinees—especially in young children—tend to revert to greater virulence, and adolescents and young adults are more liable to have paralytic poliomyelitis than babies. The actual risk is one or two per 5 000 000 doses in the U.K. This could be eliminated by using killed vaccine (Salk).

Measles immunization policy is also the subject of controversy and guilt by association. Some doctors and many parents are unconvinced of its efficiency. It is apparent that there is ignorance of the actual morbidity and mortality caused by measles. (See Table 16.1.)

The early experiments using a two-stage immunization, first with killed then with live vaccine, revealed an unsuspected adverse effect in that the vaccinees tended to develop a modified measles which caused debility to children in their teens.

The present vaccine is highly effective as long as the

attenuated virus is still alive when given. Inadequate control of temperature during storage kills the vaccine and this is probably the main reason why some children still catch measles after receiving the vaccine. Ten per cent of children develop a pyrexial illness in association with vaccination, and slightly fewer a fleeting rash five days after immunization. Protection is complete by the sixth day after immunization.

Official policy on when to immunize is probably unsafe in suggesting, as it does, that the vaccination should be carried out at 13 months. Delaying vaccination until two years ensures probable life-long immunity. Vaccination at 13 months certainly does not.

However, with such low levels of uptake, the risk of teenage measles is probably worth taking, in order to ensure temporary protection in the first five years of life. If every child were to be immunized, then two years old would be the time of choice.

Lastly, parents may still be wondering why their child should be immunized. It is important to bring to their attention the two main reasons. Firstly, to protect their child, and secondly, to prevent their child infecting others. Our recent experience in the detection of the infecting child in the recent pertussis epidemic, and advising mothers of these children of their obligations in preventing infection in others, shows how little this second reason is considered when parents make a decision on whether or not their child should be immunized.

In the U.S.A. the declared aim is to eliminate measles within three years by a vigorous programme of measles immunization. What a pity we can't follow their example.

17.

Prescribing for babies

Recently, a doctor told me how he placed his prescription pad on a table at the opposite end of his consulting room from his desk. This, he said, certainly made him think carefully about what he needed to prescribe.

Many general practitioners are becoming more self-critical of their prescribing habits and becoming concerned with effect as well as side-effect (Marsh, 1977; Taylor, 1978). Nevertheless, the large numbers of prescriptions dispensed yearly for broncho-dilators for infants under a year, tetracycline derivative syrups for children and barbiturates for adults, show that there is plenty of room for improvement in understanding the pharmacology of drugs and their effects (Cleary, 1976).

The most dangerous myth about prescribing in general is 'if you don't, the patient keeps on coming back' (Stimson, 1975). Marsh's (1977) figures and data from general practitioners who adopt a policy similar to that of Marsh of *NOT* prescribing for simple self-limiting conditions, demonstrate that low prescribing rates are not linked with high consulting rates (Howie & Hutchinson, 1978).

Stimson and Webb in '*Going to the doctor*' (1975) describe parents who are deeply concerned with the constant prescription for their children of antibiotics which patently have no effect on a simple cold and which do little else apart from causing inconvenient diarrhoea.

The prescription

Four questions need to be asked by the prescriber:
    (i) What is the drug for?

214

(ii) How much need be given?

(iii) For how long should it be given?

(iv) What are the likely effects—including side-effects?

(i) *What is the drug for?* A medicine like promethazine (Phenergan), that some say causes night sedation, is in reality only effective for this purpose in a minority of infants. It is taken as the universal panacea for infant sleeplessness but does not really seem to meet the requirements adequately. Is an antihistamine really the drug of choice for infants in need of sedation?

(ii) *How much need be given?* The convenience packs of antibiotics and the ubiquitous 5 ml. dosage seem, at first sight, to make administration easy and it hardly seems necessary to calculate the accurate dosage required by a three month old child—as 'a little bit extra can't do much harm'. But is this really a safe assumption? Sometimes nothing could be further from the truth.

(iii) *For how long should the drug be given?* Until he's better is the parent's fervent wish and fortunately perhaps, usually the reality. Half completed bottles of antibiotics kept like talismans in the family refrigerator attest to this attitude. Yet full compliance in some conditions is absolutely essential for success. Do we always stress this when prescribing? (Dunnell & Cartwright, 1972).

(iv) *What are the likely effects—including side-effects?* Apart from the expected effect, many surprises are in store for the inexperienced paediatric prescriber. Diarrhoea and rashes caused by antibiotics are probably the complications most commonly observed, but there are many others. Barbiturates, given to prevent convulsions, cause paradoxical irritability in many children. Strong codeine-containing cough linctuses, so often given in excess of the stated dosage by anxious parents, can cause dangerous respiratory depression and can predispose to more serious infection. (see Table 17.1). How often does our prescribing for babies fail to secure our objectives? Can we afford a hit-or-miss philosophy?

An up-to-date knowledge of the pharmacology of drugs used by the paediatric prescriber is essential and constant vigilance is required to prevent inappropriate or irrational prescribing. Every urge to prescribe needs to be met by as strong an urge to resist. Instead, careful explanation to the parents about the child's illness, simple instructions on care, backed up by a visit from the health visitor, will give the

Table 17.1 Recognised side effects of some commonly used drugs in the infant

---

ANTIBIOTICS

Penicillin	At 'normal' dose levels	Allergy, diarrhoea, thrush
	At excessive dosage	Haemolytic anaemia, nerve damage in i./v. doses
Tetracyclines	At 'normal' dose levels	Diarrhoea, thrush, affects bone growth and both stains and stunts tooth growth
Nitrofurantoin	At 'normal' dose levels	Affects teeth and bone growth
Gentamycin, Neomycin Kannamycin, Tobramycin	At 'normal' dose levels	Ototoxic effects not uncommon unless regular drug assay performed
Long-acting Sulphonamides	At 'normal' dose levels	Allergy, and competes for binding sites with bilirubin, displaces it into the brain predisposing kernicterns in the preterm infant
Nalidixic Acid	At 'normal' dose levels	Cause acidosis in new born and raises intracranial pressure

ANTICONVULSANTS AND SEDATIVES

Chloral hydrate	At 'normal' dose levels	Slow detoxification can cause accumulation
Barbiturates	At 'normal' dose levels	Excitation and suppression of cough
Phenytoin	At 'normal' dose levels	Nystagmus, drowsiness, ataxia sometimes irreversible

VITAMIN PREPARATIONS

Excessive quantities of some vitamins slow metabolic transformation and interfere with basic body processes.

Vitamin D	At 'high' dose levels	Hypercalcaemia
Vitamin A	At 'high' dose levels	Generalised toxicity manifesting itself as a scurvy-like condition
ASPIRIN	At 'normal' dose levels Great care should be taken to use the correct dose	Acidosis and interference with carbohydrate metabolism and blood glucose levels. Rashes, gastric irritation
	At excessive dose levels	Poisoning and death caused by metabolic acidosis and hyperpyrexia

ATROPINE and atropine-like substances	At 'normal' dose levels	Children with Down's syndrome are especially sensitive to excessive side effects but all children are more susceptible than adults
DIGITALIS	At 'normal' dose levels	Unless the greatest care is taken, it is notoriously easy to give overdoses and deaths from overdosage occur (always check the dose)
CORTICOSTEROIDS as topical preparations		Absorption through skin is greater than in adults and florid Cushing's Syndrome, caused by fluorinated corticosteroid cream or ointment—if used for eczema and nappy rash, it is not rare
PARACETAMOL	At excessive dose levels	Combined renal and hepatic damage
ANTIDEPRESSANTS	At excessive dose levels	Dysrythmias and circulatory collapse (particularly tachycardia)
ALCOHOL	Used as a vehicle in many paediatric preparations, teething medicines etc.	C.n.s depression and even addiction

parents greater confidence to manage their child's illness this time *AND* the next time he's ill.

If any prescription is necessary then it is well to answer the four questions listed above. The parents are often too shy to ask but are enormously relieved by explanations of the likely effect of the prescription, backed up, if necessary, by a piece of paper on which the doctor has written the salient points. This is important in the light of the fact that patients rarely remember more than three things told them in the course of a single consultation. It often pays to write down for them the name of the disease you have identified in their child. It adds very little time to the consultation but is enormously reassuring.

Pharmacology of drugs in the infant

There are six main factors which influence drug uptake and effectiveness in babies in the first year of life.

(i)   The toxicity of drugs is usually greater in babies than in older children and adults. The breakdown and excretion of drugs is *usually* slower (with the exception of barbiturates, when it is faster). This can cause problems as the formation of different breakdown products leads to varying side effects.

(ii) The kidneys are immature and accumulation can occur (particularly in drugs of the gentamycin group, causing ototoxicity).

(iii) The varying protein-binding capacity of the jaundiced new born baby causes unpredictable uptake and makes prescribing hazardous. The competition for binding sites between bilirubin and drug causes the concentration of the unbound drug to rise to higher levels in the tissue fluids than would be expected from the dosage given. Alternatively, if the drug competes selectively with the bilirubin for binding sites, the bilirubin can be displaced and so increases the risk of kernicterus.

(iv) The size of the baby is obviously the most important factor in drug uptake. However, babies have a higher extra- to intra-cellular fluid ratio than adults and a proportionately higher total body water content than adults, and this materially affects drug concentration in the various body compartments. Moreover, fluid retention and fluid loss occurs more readily in babies than in older children. Prescribers must bear this in mind.

(v)   The central nervous system in the new born baby, by virtue of its immaturity, is proportionately more responsive than in the older baby to some drugs. Atropine and its derivatives form a good example.

(vi) Enzyme development is incomplete in the neonate and slower conjugation and detoxification of drugs can sometimes lead to unsuspected high levels of drugs unless care is taken. It is true to say that 'it's difficult to predict (in babies) either the toxic or therapeutic effects of drugs from available adult data' (Gill et al, 1974).

To sum up; every prescription given to an infant should be judged in terms of likely outcome with the additional consideration of its effects on parent-doctor dependency.

Formulation and mode

Even when a drug is formulated for paediatric use by a manufacturer, it is important to be aware of the shortcomings of the individual drug. Short half-lives in the bottle and in the body make attention to timing essential. Do not prescribe more of a ready-mixed antibiotic than can be taken within its 'discard' time. Ensure that the mother knows what '6 hourly dosage' really means, on those occasions when such frequent dosage is really necessary in general practice. For many mothers '6 hourly' means three times a day, not 4 times in 24 hours. Most penicillins are inactivated when taken with food and only careful instructions can ensure adequate blood levels.

The size of the individual dose must be calculated to take into account not only the baby's size but also hepatic and renal capacity for conjugation and excretion. Many formulae have been used but the percentage method of dose calculation, which takes into account body surface area, the square of the cube root of weight, the extracellular volume and the metabolic rate, is probably the safest for most drugs (in adults, too) see Table 17.2.

Table 17.2 Dosage calculation system

	Average weight*		Dose as % of of adult dose	in mg/kg if adult dose = 1.0 mg/kg
	kg	lb		
Over 2 weeks	3·2	7	12	2·0
4 months	6·5	14	20	
1 year	10·0	22	25	1·5

From Catzel P 1978 Paediatric prescriber, 5th edn. Blackwell, Oxford.
*In obese children, use age, not weight, as fat does not usually affect drug metabolism

The method should *NOT* be used to calculate drugs for premature, jaundiced, very ill or starving babies, or new born babies under two weeks old.

The mode or route of the drug prescribed is also important, especially in young babies. An intravenous bolus dose, can cause transient very high blood levels, swamping metabolic processes and so allowing sustained toxic levels which can produce permanent damage.

In the vomiting, ill baby, however, the intramuscular route is the one of choice for at least the initial dose. Hospital experience shows that quite often all that is required to cure a very ill baby is to change the route of antibiotic already prescribed by the general practitioner from the oral to the intramuscular. The general practitioner could save some admissions by this small change in technique. It may be wise in small infants to give the injection in divided doses, one in the outer lateral aspect of each thigh to avoid problems like persistent bruising or nerve damage. The oral route is, however, always preferable in the less ill baby. Paediatric suspensions where the dose is given via a 1 ml dropper have obvious advantages. Spillage is less likely to occur and the smaller quantity less likely to be rejected by the baby. This is a major problem concealed by parents from doctors. Mothers are often too ashamed to admit their baby won the battle and spat out the medicine however carefully it was disguised. Happily, relatively few infants continue this practice when really ill. The spoonful of medicine can end up in many places—the dropperful normally in the right one. Mothers sometimes discover for themselves the advantages of using droppers to space out 5 ml. doses over half an hour or more.

A small repertoire of drugs is all that is required and it is then relatively easy to remember the correct dosages. A paediatric *vade mecum* is indispensible. The small book edited by Ben Wood (9th edition Lloyd Luke, Birmingham 1977) is an excellent one.

The umprescribed or misused medicine

Parents give medicine to children for many reasons; tonics, gripe water, teething jellies, vitamins, 'pain killers', nose drops and sedatives. All these can be bought without prescription from chemists. Occasionally, mothers give far more than the stated dose in desperation or even in a deliberate attempt to poison or harm.

This is especially so with sedatives and cough and catarrh treatments containing antihistamines. Particularly in a stress situation, like overcrowding, a crying baby can bring anger and occasionally violence down on its head. In conditions like this, excessive quantities of sedatives and antihistamine containing medicines are used to 'hush up' the baby. For this reason, repeated requests for prescriptions for any drug likely to have this effect, should be closely scrutinized (Austin and Parish, 1976). One and a half litres of one such preparation given by a very disturbed mother to two young children over a 10 day period, caused the author* many anxious moments until he realized what she had done and why. This is an isolated example but there is a great temptation for mothers and fathers living in impossible situations to do this and an ever watchful eye should be kept for such abuses.

Another potentially serious habit of some mothers is to use excessive quantities of nose drops 'for snuffles'. Easily obtained over the chemists' counter, their use provokes not only rebound phenomena but unpleasant and intractible bacterial secondary infection. Only careful questioning reveals the problem and weaning off the habit is difficult (see Ch. 5).

The prescription has many uses. Doctors need to be aware of them. Apart from the obvious ones they also make parents and doctors happy by preserving the mystique of 'the treatment'. Sometimes these seem to be the most important ones to an outsider (Stimson, 1975).

Yet, an explanation to the mother of a child's behaviour in self-limiting illness and advice on management without a drug prescription from the doctor, gives the average mother strength in her *own* abilities to cope and is often a far healthier solution in the long term.

Certainly, doctors who practise this approach report its success. However, success will only occur when the mother realizes that the drug prescription is not necessarily the objective of every consultation—and the doctor does too. Nothing replaces skilled diagnosis, explanation and, if necessary, frequent review—certainly not a prescription.

REFERENCES

Austin R, Parish P 1976 Prescriptions written by ancillary staff. Paediatric prescriptions. In: Prescribing in General Practice. Journal of Royal College of General Practitioners, 26 (1)
Cleary J 1976 Ibid
Dunnell K, Cartwright A 1972 Medicine takers, prescribers and hoarders. Routledge Kegan and Paul, London

*Dr G. Curtis Jenkins

Gill S E, Davis J A 1974 The pharmacology of the fetus baby and the growing child. Chapter 45 in Scientific Foundations of Paediatrics. Heinemann Medical Books, London

Howie J G R, Hutchinson K R 1978 Antibiotics and respiratory illness in general practice. Prescribing policy and work load. British Medical Journal 2; 1342

Marsh G M 1977 Curing minor illness in general practice. British Medical Journal 2, 1267–1269

Stimson G V & Webb B 1975 Going to the doctor. Routledge Kegan and Paul, London

Stimson G V 1976 Doctor patient interaction and some problems for prescribing in: Prescribing in general practice supplement No 1 Vol 26. Journal of Royal College of general practitioners

Further reading

Wood B (ed) 1977 A paediatric vade mecum, 9th edn. Lloyd Luke, Birmingham

Taylor R J 1978 Towards better prescribing. Journal Royal College of General Practitioners 28: 263–270

18.

The handicapped child

The first year of life is the period during which evidence of handicap is most likely to arise; it may be that diagnosis is possible at birth due to congenital malformation or obvious chromosomal abnormality, or diagnosis becomes apparent during the early months of life. Often in this period neurological disorders, congenital heart disease and cystic fibrosis become evident or neuro-developmental handicap for which no specific diagnosis is obtainable. All these situations will require identification of the child at risk, investigation, assessment and continuing management for the child and parents, often involving a number of different professional skills. It is with neurological handicap that this chapter is chiefly concerned, though the general observations concerning parental reactions and management are applicable to all types of handicap.

Although many parents are vaguely aware that babies are not always perfectly normal, almost invariably the abnormalities which may occur are thought of as being experienced only by someone else. There is, therefore a response which has been likened to that of the grief reaction which follows bereavement, associated with the realization by parents that their infant is not normal. A degree of mourning, for the normal child that might have been, has to be experienced before the handicapped child can begin to be accepted. Reactions include those of shock, disbelief, denial, guilt, depression and anger. If these feelings can be understood by the parents and those involved with the care of the whole family, then acceptance of the handicapped child is more likely to follow. This understanding must be assisted by practical help and support, often involving many disciplines

223

during the child's development. Parents will inevitably look ahead and this anxiety about the future must be met by much more than the dismissal phrase: 'it is too early to think about it, don't worry'. Neurological handicap may be physical, intellectual or involve the special senses, particularly vision and hearing. The presence of multiple handicap is common. Co-ordination of this care is best achieved via a district handicap team (Court, 1976) which, particularly during the child's first year, will be associated closely with the paediatric department. Full involvement of the general practitioner and health visitor in this co-ordinated approach to the care of child and family is important.

A classification of some of the more important causes of handicap is given in the following list:

Prenatal :   Malformation—First trimester e.g., genetic
                          trisomy 21, infection, rubella,
                          drugs
    Maldevelopment—Maternal illness
                          —Pre-eclampsia
                          —Placental insufficiency

Perinatal: Stress of labour—Placental insufficiency,
                          acute or chronic
    Stress of delivery—Preterm delivery
                          —Hypoxia
                          —Trauma
    Newborn complication—Respiratory distress
                          —convulsion
                          —Hypoglycaemia
                          —Hypoxia
                          —Hyperbilirubinaemia

Postnatal: Infection—Meningitis
    Injury—accidental in the home
                environment, RTA, immersion
             —non-accidental
    Epilepsy
    Degenerative disorders of nervous system

Some of these causes are avoidable and have been more fully discussed in Chapter 3.

Identification of handicap

This may be possible at birth as, for example, the infant with a myelomeningocoele or Down's syndrome. More frequently, the handicap will become apparent as the child shows developmental delay, and here lies the importance of developmental surveillance during infancy as discussed in Chapter 6. Some infants will have a history predisposing to neurological damage and these particularly need regular developmental examination; ideally, all children should be monitored. There is advantage in identifying handicap early so that the appropriate management may be started as early as possible. On the other hand, care must be taken to identify normal variations in the progression of developmental milestones. Infants with definite evidence of cerebral palsy should be referred immediately, as advice given early can both be helpful to the parents and prevent the development of abnormal posture and patterns of movement. The baby with impaired vision or hearing can be helped greatly during infancy; cataract operations can be carried out and contact lenses fitted, so aiding the development of vision. The earlier deafness is diagnosed, the better the prognosis and audiometry at three months by the paediatric audiologist can be helpful. An important problem to detect quickly is that of the child whose developmental progress is arresting or possibly regressing. Though rare, such developmental arrest may be indicative of one of the degenerative diseases of the central nervous system. Referral and diagnosis may not help that child particularly, but a definitive diagnosis may be vitally important with regard to genetic counselling, and may open the way for antenatal diagnosis in subsequent pregnancies and so prevention of similarly affected children being born.

Management

Referral for diagnosis and assessment will be necessary once a definite handicap is suspected. The continuing specific care will depend on the nature of the handicap; it is likely to be monitored by the district handicap team, where this team exists. In areas where there is as yet no definitive organisation, the paediatric department is likely to be responsible for co-ordinating care. Treatment of the individual child is only part of the problem. There is the emotional response of the parents to be considered; this includes both their immediate reaction and their many questions and misgivings regarding the future. Almost every form of handicap now has some central voluntary agency which specialises in advising and helping with problems that arise. The general practitioner should ensure that the appropriate organisation is brought to the notice of the parents, and give every assistance to them to join if that is the parents' wish. Purely practical aspects include domestic help, travelling and finance, and certainly not least the effect on and involvement of other members of the family, particularly brothers and sisters of the child. The family practitioner is in a position to see their problems as a whole and so contribute advice and help in the overall management of the handicapped child and family.

19.

Non-accidental injury

Children have been ill-treated for generations but it is only relatively recently that the problem has been assessed and studied in any depth. In this volume, our brief is for the infant. Certainly the young child is particularly vulnerable, but it must be stressed that abuse of the young is not confined to the under five years old, though this age group can less easily voice a protest; the problem occurs throughout childhood and into adolescence. Society generally, and the medical profession particularly, has a duty to recognize non-accidental injury and then to follow up and take appropriate action to protect the young.

Though child abuse was recognized in the last century, it was only in the 1940s that more precise documentation began and the present interest was stimulated by Kempe's work, (1962) reported under the title of the battered child syndrome. This emotive title had a vitally important part to play in focussing attention on the problem, but the more reserved description of non-accidental injury is now to be preferred.

Incidence of non-accidental injury is difficult to determine. There are problems of recognition and of accurate and consistent reporting. Estimates in the past decade, based on a number of localised surveys, suggest at least 3000 children under five years old in Great Britain are seriously injured in this way. The individual family practitioner may, therefore, see only one example in five years of professional life. The incidence of serious injury has shown some decline recently but the incidence of less severe cases has increased. This may be due to earlier and more efficient recognition, or a true increased incidence, or both. The problem is worldwide. It is not confined to any particular social strata but is commonest amongst the Registrar General's social classes IV and V.

Symptoms and signs

The greatest incidence is amongst children under three years old. A high degree of suspicion is often necessary to achieve early diagnosis. Detection on first encounter is important, as sometimes the next opportunity is too late for that child. The history, particularly the initial history, is fundamental. There is often a delay of some hours or even days between the alleged accident and presentation. It is also not unusual for the child to be taken direct to a casualty department, rather than the general practitioner. The history of the 'accident' may be inconsistent with the injury sustained, and there may be evidence of more than one episode of injury (e.g., bruises in different stages of resolution). The type of injury varies widely but any child with an unusual injury in the first year of life must be fully examined and this means taking all the clothes off. A detailed past and family history must be obtained. It may well be that the family that has just moved into one's practice, and about whom least is known, is the family with the child at greatest risk.

The external injuries will mainly be bruises; both the type and distribution of the lesions are important. Bruising around the face, particularly ears, eyes and lips, with rupture of the frenum may be found. They may show the characteristic feature of a slap, pinch or finger tip pressure, the latter particularly if one of the limbs has been tightly grasped. There may be marks suggesting the use of some other weapon of abuse; it is important to remember cigarette burns and scalds, the latter particularly of the buttocks. Bony injury of skull and limbs may occur. Trauma to the abdomen may rupture liver, spleen or intestine, the duodenum being particularly vulnerable. Shaking the child may cause intracranial bleeding and retinal haemorrhages. It is a matter of speculation how many children retarded for undetermined cause may, in fact, be victims of non-accidental injury. Ophthalmic examination for intraocular haemorrhage should never be omitted.

The past history and family history is frequently signifi- cant. A study at the Park Hospital, Oxford, compared the abused child in the family with a sibling, and found a number of factors which were particularly prominent in respect of the affected children. These included abnormality of pregnancy, labour or delivery, neonatal separation, other episodes of separation during the first six months, illness in the child, and maternal illness during the first year of the child's life (Lynch 1975). Other factors which have been found to be relevant are young and immature parents, premarital conception, and marital disharmony.

Ill-treatment of children is not confined to physical trauma. Emotional deprivation and deliberate poisoning occurs. The spectrum of deliberate injury of children moves towards and merges with neglect and it is important for this latter problem to be recognized, not only so that help may be given but because injury and neglect often run hand in hand.

Management

If non-accidental injury is suspected, then immediate measures should be taken to ensure the safety of the child. This can usually be best achieved by referral to the hospital paediatric department. The child can then be admitted, radiological and haematological investigations carried out and a full assessment of the situation made. The parent may even be secretly wishing for this to take place. Since 1974, the health service districts have organised procedures to assess and manage non-accidental injury and it is encumbent on all those responsible for child health to be aware of the local arrangements. Amongst the obstacles in managing this problem are those of doctor/patient relationship, confidentiality and professional rivalry. These must always take second place when the mortality and morbidity are considered.

The ideal management of this condition is prevention, but as further knowledge is still required regarding aetiology, prevention demands both medical and social measures. However, attention can be directed to the avoidance whenever possible of those factors known to be associated with increased incidence. Knowledge of these factors helps towards the identification of the family at risk; support can then be offered when it is required during critical periods. It remains to be seen how effective this approach to the problem will be. Smith (1975), in an excellent study, points out that it may be that an abnormal psychiatric state is a major cause and in such cases successful rehabilitation of the parent/child relationship will always be difficult and sometimes impossible to achieve.

Further consideration is given to some aspects of this problem in the next chapter.

REFERENCES

Kempe C H, Silverman F N, Steele B F, Droegemueller W, Silver H K 1962 The battered child syndrome. Journal of the American Medical Association 181: 17–24

Lynch M A 1975 Ill-health and child abuse. Lancet 2: 317–319

Smith S M 1975 In the battered child syndrome Butterworths, Sevenoaks

Further reading:

White F A (ed) 1975 Concerning child abuse. Papers presented by the Turnbridge Wells study group. Churchill Livingstone, Edinburgh

Kempe R S, Kempe C H 1978 Child abuse. Fontana, London

20.

Serious illness and death

The fall in infant mortality has been discussed in the Introduction and efforts for further improvement continue. However, the achievement over the last 50 years has been considerable, and this, in itself, has altered both the pattern and the expectations of Western society. One hundred years ago, it was not uncommon for more infants in a family to succumb than survive. Because of the increased survival of infants today, together with the acceptance of and advances in contraception, parents can choose with some degree of precision when to have their children. There is also little reason for them to fear that their child will not survive, so such an event is not anticipated. Families 60 years ago, both parents and siblings, would frequently experience severe illness and death amongst the newborn and infants. Today this happy lack of first-hand experience of disease and death leads to a reduced ability for society in general and doctors in particular to cope adequately when dealing with terminal illness and bereavement. Perhaps, also, the attitudes and pace of modern life and the tendency for families to be more scattered has added to this problem, as there may be less immediate family support.

Reaction to bereavement

When trying to help families who have suffered a bereavement, it is necessary to understand the usual stages of grief and their effects on the individual. The initial reaction, following a death, is one of shock, often followed by denial; there will then be a period of depression with eventually, in the healthy outcome, a re-establishment of normal emotional reactions associated with the acceptance of the loss. There may be various symptoms occurring during the mourning process; these include guilt, anger and somatic complaints. Some of the feelings may be so disturbing, particularly those affecting reality of the situation, that the parents may have anxiety about his or her own mental health.

Seventy-two per cent of childhood deaths (that is, from the first day of life until the 15th birthday) occur during the first 12 months, just over half of these during the first week. If stillbirths are included, then 80 per cent of all childhood deaths occur between the 28th week of pregnancy and the end of the first year of life. Many of these deaths, particularly the neonatal deaths, occur in hospital but of those occurring after the first month of life, the post neonatal deaths, only 50 per cent occur in hospital (Emery, 1976). However, the care and management of the bereaved family will not be the sole responsibility of the medical and nursing staff in hospital, when death occurs there. The general practitioner is usually involved, at least with the mother prior to any tragedy, and he will need to be informed immediately so that he can help with the care and recuperation of the family after the loss of an infant. The family doctor will also be in the best position to know how the parents are likely to respond to the death of their child. It is essential, therefore, that those working in hospital keep closely in touch with those involved with the family at home when a child is seriously ill or dies. Conversely, there may be a part to be played by the consultant paediatrician in helping those families who lose a child at home; sometimes these will be children who are expected to die due to congenital abnormalities or chronic illness, but more often they will be victims of the sudden infant death syndrome (cot death).

Sudden infant death syndrome

There is a group of infants in which death occurs without apparent signs or symptoms of previous ill health, nor can any known defineable cause be identified at post mortem. This accounts for approximately one in 500 childhood deaths per year in the U.K. occurring principally between six weeks and four months, usually at home but occasionally in hospital. There is considerable research into the cause, producing a number of theories as yet none proven, the likelihood being that the phenomenon has no single cause but heterogeneous factors are involved. Recent evidence focuses on central nervous system lesions (Emery, 1979).

The causes put forward for this syndrome have included suffocation, both accidental and non-accidental, overwhelming infection either respiratory or generalized, cow's milk sensitivity, apnoea related to varying ability of the infant to develop the capacity for mouth breathing and cardiac dysrhythmias. Considerable research over 20 years has been undertaken in Sheffield; perhaps one of the more important observations, with practical implications, being that the deaths are not so sudden (Emery, 1976). Retrospective histories, difficult though interpretation may be in view of the distress and guilt feelings involved, suggest that recognition of early signs of ill health in infants is not always fully appreciated by parents. There are also antenatal factors which may be relevant such as illegitimacy, early age of marriage, delayed antenatal booking, preterm delivery and poor social conditions.

The usual history is that the baby is put into the cot after taking a normal feed and is then found dead when the parent returns, perhaps at the next feed time, this often being over night. The incidence is greater during the winter months.

It is important that every attempt is made to arrive at the cause of death and referral to the coroner for post mortem examination is mandatory.

The parents will need acute and follow-up counselling and support (see below). It is extremely rare for the syndrome to occur twice in one family.

The Sheffield study has shown that in that city the incidence of this syndrome can be reduced; this being achieved by identifying families at greatest risk and increasing the home supervision by health visitors. It may be that the risk factors vary in different parts of the country, but this approach would seem to be worthy of consideration until the syndrome can be further defined. It is likely that the families at risk from this problem overlap with those at risk for non-accidental injury to children, so the effort involved may have more widespread beneficial affects.

Finally, a mention of the near-miss sudden death in which it would seem that only the fortuitous arrival of the parent at home or the nurse in the hospital ward prevents catastrophe occurring—the infant being found collapsed but responding to resuscitation. These occasions are most alarming for parents and doctor and following the incident, investigation and observation in hospital is often indicated. However, subsequent management really can be only that of reassurance. The home use of an apnoea alarm mattress has been suggested and tried in these circumstances, but the overall benefits are debatable. Inevitably the parents are going to be anxious after such an event and will require close support and supervision for some weeks.

Stillbirth

Perhaps on the fringe of this volume, but nevertheless closely concerned with neonatal care and not infrequently the care of subsequent infants, is the management of parents of a stillborn infant. In the past, the prevailing attitude has been that the stillborn infant should be whisked away from the mother, wrapped quickly in a towel, too awful to contemplate. The mourning process has been briefly mentioned; it is complex and, for some, difficult to endure and to come through successfully. There is psychiatric evidence and opinion, which can be reinforced by any practitioner taking the opportunity of talking to mothers, that grief is more easily met if the separation and loss are fully appreciated. The mother, from the early months of pregnancy, lives with the expectation of giving birth to a normal healthy child and for the pregnancy suddenly to end in a void is likely to make the mourning process more difficult or impossible. The question is immediately raised that a stillborn infant may be horrific to view, as it may be deformed. Certainly, it is not easy to present a dead infant to a mother, but it has been her living child and many mothers recognize the need to see their child and must not be denied this opportunity.

There will, of course, be some who feel unable to go through with this but it needs to be recognized that denial of the event may make the future more difficult. There is no place for dogmatism, but neither should the issue be fudged. It may very well be that the dead child can be presented to the parents in such a way as to minimise any actual malformation. It needs to be considered that the mother's imagination of her child having an appearance that is 'too awful to be seen' may produce a far more damaging affect than the reality; a reality calmly and compassionately presented and explained by experienced and understanding staff. It needs to be asked whether it is not the inhibitions and lack of training of the professional staff that makes this task so difficult, rather than the parents inability to face the situation (Bourne, 1968).

Mothers who have had stillborn infants describe feelings of failure and such feelings, together with the inevitable depression, are likely to be accentuated rather than lessened by those surrounding her refusing to face up to the event. There has been recent discussion concerning the management of parents of a stillborn infant in response to the proposal for the use of a specific leaflet but personal involvement between the professional staff and the parents is the vital aspect of this problem (Beard et al, 1978 Heward et al, 1978).

Serious illness

The management of the seriously ill neonate broadens this discussion. The paediatric department is likely to be closely and quickly involved but some problems, particularly the more serious malformations, may present immediately. The early impressions and conversations following delivery are often those most vividly remembered, so all those involved with obstetric care need to be adequately prepared for dealing with these situations when they arise. Every effort must be made to allow the parents to hold and see the infant and, if possible, to avoid too rapid removal of the child to a special nursery. If special treatment is required, then, if the medical condition of the baby allows, time must be given for as much parental contact as possible. It has become the policy of special care baby units to encourage parents to see and handle their babies, if only to the extent of holding the infant's hand whilst intensive infant care continues around them. It may also be possible to involve the parents in decisions relevant to the continuation or not of supportive care in serious illness (Benfield et al, 1978). It may be that the child needs to be transferred to another hospital and every effort must be made so that the father can accompany the child and both he and the staff keep the mother informed of progress.

Sometimes parents find it hard to visit a seriously ill newborn infant. There is an understandable fear that the baby will not survive, and so the less attached they become, the easier it will be should the infant die. Whatever the outcome, it is more likely the parents will adjust to the survival or the death of their child if they can be encouraged to maintain close contact.

If the baby dies, care of the parents and family needs to be continued until they have all satisfactorily completed their mourning. The intense grief at the moment of a child's death will prevent any specific information being received. How this time is handled will depend on the parents, the circumstances and the length of illness, the latter being relevant to anticipatory grief reaction. The factors recognized as being relevant to recovery from the loss of the child are the importance of seeing the baby after death and the funeral and burial arrangements (Lewis 1976, 1979). One of the most frequent problems is the secrecy and silence which surrounds the sudden loss of an infant. Within the maternity department, the mother may be whisked into a side-room and sedated. Perhaps this is the management which is appropriate for some, but it may be that grief can be better faced without sedatives and that, given the chance, a more open attitude towards the event may help both the bereaved and the other patients on the ward; most of those present will have some notion that a tragic event has occurred.

This abnormal suppression of the event, the 'forget it' attitude, may persist once the mother has returned home. There may be a difference in attitude towards the event between mother and father, one willing to discuss the child and the other not, or a similar reluctance to speak of the death between other members of the family. A visit to the home at this time by the general practitioner or health visitor, and follow-up over the next few weeks, may be an invaluable help to these families.

It is also the custom of paediatric departments to offer parents an appointment to come and discuss the infant's illness and death. The timing of this is difficult as it has to be when the parents are receptive to discussion and full post mortem details are available. About six weeks after the event is the time to attempt to cover all the aspects of the situation. At this visit, further appointments can be offered without a specific date but it seems that the one interview usually is sufficient. If further specific genetic counselling is required, then this will need to be arranged as a separate issue. The earlier visit of the family doctor to the parents once the mother has returned home is also important; this makes efficient communication between hospital staff and the general practitioner vital.

The seriously ill neonate, in fact any seriously ill child, gives the parents a sense of helplessness. In the newborn period, the mother has anticipated caring for a new child and if an infant becomes acutely ill needing hospital treatment, parents have to give up the immediate care of their child to others. There is no doubt that the more parents can be encouraged to help care for their children by the hospital staff, the more likely the distress they feel will be relieved. This applies especially to the child with a congenital malformation as, in this situation, opportunity for the parents to see the child and discuss the problem early and then have further informed discussions, is essential (Klaus & Kennell, 1976).

The sudden infant death syndrome (cot death) is an important cause of infant mortality where rehabilitation of the family is invariably required. The preceding discussion with regard to grief is appropriate to the terminal illness and death of any infant. The management of the child with an acute fulminating illness leading to death, or a chronic illness or handicap involves, wherever possible, an adequate explanation of the cause of death; such a discussion with the parents should mean that the majority come through the mourning period satisfactorily. When an infant dies suddenly and no such adequate medical explanation is forthcoming, the parents will need closer supervision and support, and this need for support is likely to be further reinforced once a subsequent child is born. It is important that every attempt is made to arrive at a cause of death and the attitude that a post mortem examination is likely to be too distressing should be strongly avoided. The parents will need to be interviewed early, and again later to discuss the post mortem results, also to give an opportunity for the feelings of guilt and imagined lapses of care for the child to be openly discussed.

In conclusion, it is important to emphasise that it is not only the medical personnel who have a part to play in caring for the bereaved, but also social workers, priests and voluntary organisations (such as The Foundation for the Study of Infant Deaths*), some of which have evolved from this particular need. It must be remembered that the siblings

*address: 23 St. Peter's Square, London W6 9NW

will also have a reaction to the death of a neonate or infant; this reaction will greatly depend on the age of the surviving children. The apparently superficial and recurring references to a recently deceased brother or sister by a young child may deepen the distress of the parents unless it is deliberately explained how young children normally react to death, and mention is made of the variation of this reaction with the particular age of the surviving children (Lindsay & MacCarthy 1974).

That man has an overwhelming need for the expression of grief is apparent by observations of customs and cultures throughout the world. Nearer home, who else but Shakespeare could so succinctly express this fact:

> Give sorrow words: the grief that does not speak
> Whispers, the o'erfraught heart, and bids it break.

REFERENCES

Beard R W et al 1978 Help for parents after stillbirth. British Medical Journal 1: 172–173

Benfield D G, Leib S A, Vollman J H 1978 Grief response of parents to neonatal death and parent participation in deciding care. Pediatrics 62: 171–177

Bourne S 1968 The psychological effects of stillbirth on women and their doctors. Journal of the Royal College of General Practitioners 16: 103–112.

Editorial 1977 The abhorrence of stillbirth. Lancet i 1188–1190

Emery J L 1976 Unexpected death in infancy. In: Hull D (ed) Recent advances in paediatrics No 5 Churchill Livingstone, Edinburgh

Emery J L 1979 the central nervous system and cot death. [Annotation]. Developmental Medicine and Child Neurology 21: 239–248

Heward J et al 1978 Help for parents after stillbirth. British Medical Journal 1: 649

Jolly H 1976 Family reactions to stillbirth. Proceedings of the Royal Society of Medicine 69: 835–837

Klaus M H, Kennell J H 1976 ed In: Maternal-infant bonding Mosby, St. Louis, ch 5, 6

Lewis E 1976 The management of stillbirth coping with an unreality. Lancet 2: 619–620

Lewis E 1979 Mourning by the family after a stillbirth or neonatal death. Archives of Disease in Childhood 54: 303–306

Lindsay M, MacCarthy D 1974 In: Burton L (ed) Care of the child facing death. Routledge and Kegan Paul, London, ch 16

Further reading:

Burton L (ed) 1974 Care of the child facing death. Routledge and Kegan Paul, London

Kübler-Ross E 1969 On death and dying. Macmillan Co, New York

Stephens S 1972 Death comes home. Mowbray, Oxford

Acknowledgments:

1. Updated developmental schedules are included in Knobloch H, Stevens F, Malone A: (1980) *A manual of developmental diagnosis*: the administration and interpretation of the revised Gessell and Amalinda Developmental Schedules, Harper and Rowe, Hagerstown, Md.

2. The photographs were taken by Dorothee Von Grieff.

3. We wish to thank the Developmental Paediatric research group for permission to reproduce the protocols of examination for the 7 month and 12 month old child, the descriptions of the examination and the examination proformas.

Self Assessment

A. Multiple Choice Questions

I. M. Stanley MB ChB MRCP MRCGP
Lecturer in General Practice
University of Leeds

B. Modified Essay Question

J. H. Walker MD FFCM FRCGP DPH
Professor of Family and Community Medicine
University of Newcastle upon Tyne

J. D. E. Knox MD FRCP FRCGP
Professor of General Practice
University of Dundee

A. Multiple Choice Questions

1 *Among children in England and Wales:*

A respiratory disease represents more than 50 per cent of reported illness

B deaths from respiratory disease exceed 2000/annum

C the majority of deaths from respiratory disease occur in the first year of life

D the overwhelming majority of deaths from respiratory disease occur in hospital

E deaths from measles exceeded deaths from pertussis in each of the years 1967–1977

2 *During a professional career of 40 years, a General Practitioner in the U.K. can expect to encounter in infants:*

A ten cases of congenital dislocation of the hip

B two cases of intussusception

C one case of fibrocystic disease

D five cot deaths

E five cases of epiglottitis

3 *The following terms are correctly defined:*

A perinatal mortality rate is the number of stillbirths and deaths in the first week of life per thousand total births in the same year

B post-neonatal mortality rate is the number of deaths between six weeks and one year per thousand live births in the same year

C infant mortality rate is the number of deaths in the first year of life per thousand live births in the same year

D neonatal mortality rate is the number of deaths under six weeks per thousand live births in the same year

E birth rate is the number of births (live and still) per thousand population

4   *The following conditions are more frequent in children belonging to low socio-economic groups:*

A   convulsions

B   nocturnal enuresis

C   pyloric stenosis

D   dental caries

E   strabismus

5   *Population trends in the U.K. during the period 1950–1978 show:*

A   an overall fall in population in the years 1977 and 1978

B   a fall in all age-specific birth rates between 1951 and 1971

C   a steady fall in the post-neonatal mortality rate over the last 15 years in England and Wales

D   a uniform rate of illegitimate births as a percentage of all live births

E   an average of 1.8 children per family in 1978

6   *The following fetal conditions can be detected pre-natally:*

A   sickle-cell disease

B   myelomeningocoele

C   trisomy 21

D   haemophilia

E   galactosaemia

7   *Mongolism due to trisomy 21:*

A   occurs in about one in 600 pregnancies in the U.K.

B   occurs in about one per cent of pregnancies conceived by mothers aged 40–45

C   leads to 50 per cent of mongol children being born to women aged 35 years or more

D   can be reliably predicted before conception by chromosome analysis of the mother in the majority of cases

E   is rarely the result of mutation

8   *In the ante-natal diagnosis of fetal abnormality:*

A   amniocentesis carries less risk if ultra-sound control is used

B   false positive serum alpha feto protein levels are rare

C   amniotic alpha feto protein levels decline during the last trimester

D   gestational age is not important in deciding on the significance of serum levels of alpha feto protein

E   fetal neural-tube defects are associated with a low level of serum alpha feto protein at about 16 weeks

9   *The Respiratory Distress syndrome:*

A   is a result of lack of production of surfactant

B   requires the administration of naloxone (Narcon) immediately after delivery

C   is likely to occur if the lecithin/sphingomyelin ratio in amniotic fluid prior to induction is greater than 2:1

D   is accompanied by patent ductus arteriosus in the majority of cases

E   is less likely to occur if betamethasone is given to the mother for 48 hours before delivery

10 *In resuscitation of the newborn:*

A   the larynx should be aspirated as a routine procedure

B   once respiration is established, gastric aspiration is a useful procedure

C   sternal recession in the first 10–20 minutes strongly suggests trachea-oesophageal atresia

D   a heart rate of more than 100/min is rated at 1 on the Apgar score

E   a pink body with blue extremities is rated as 1 on the Apgar score

11 *The Dubowitz assessment:*

A   is carried out 24–48 hours after delivery

B   contains two sets of criteria

C   total score cannot be related to gestational age

D   uses infant breast size as one criterion

E   scores no lanugo more highly than abundant lanugo

12 *The normal infant:*

A   should be put to the breast as soon as possible following delivery

B   should be protected from colonisation by organisms on the mother's skin

C   should be left with a cord stump of 15 cm routinely

D   needs to be bathed daily

E   will show separation of the umbilical cord about 7–10 days after delivery

13 *Breast milk:*

A   is thought to reduce atopic symptoms in the genetically susceptible, when compared with cows' milk

B   is a better source of vitamin K than artificial feeds

C   is a better source of vitamin D than artificial feeds

D   contains lactoferrin

E   is the source of large amounts of immunoglobulin

14 *In infant feeding from one week to six months of age:*

A   150 ml of fluid is required per kg per 24 hours

B   initial on-demand feeding has been shown to result in a 4-hourly regime by 10 days

C   20 minutes feeding per breast is a useful rough guide

D   breast feeding up to three months is now less commonly practised than a decade ago

E   the electrolyte load provided by artificial milks is comparable to that of breast milk

15 *The following drugs if taken by the nursing mother do not represent a hazard to the infant:*

A   diazepam (Valium)

B   tetracycline

C   cascara

D   pentazocine (Fortral)

E   chlorpromazine (Largactil)

16 *The following neonatal conditions are likely to resolve spontaneously:*

A   caput succedaneum

B   sub-conjunctival haemorrhage

C   erythema toxicum

D   milia

E   neonatal mastitis

17 *Neonatal conjunctivitis:*

A   accompanied by lid swelling should by treated by systemic chloramphenicol

B   with profuse and purulent discharge soon after birth is likely to be due to chlamydial infection

C   caused by gonococcal infection is readily confirmed in the laboratory by dry swabs

D   due to infection by chlamydia is effectively treated in most cases by one per cent chlortetracycline ointment

E   where sulphacetamide eye drops are indicated, requires these to be instilled every one or two hours for the first 24 hours of treatment

18 *In the neonate:*

A   rectal bleeding is usually the result of mucosal fissure

B   breast milk jaundice is a strong indication for discontinuing breast feeding

C   born at home with respiratory distress, transfer to hospital should by by incubator

D   absence of the usual weight drop suggest the presence of acyanotic heart disease

E   hypoglycaemia is a recognised cause of respiratory distress

19   *In relation to low-birth-weight infants:*

A   low birth weight is defined as 2.5 kg or less

B   by dysmature is meant those below the 20th centile for their gestational age

C   pre-term is defined as less than 37 weeks from the last menstrual period

D   post-term is defined as more than 40 weeks from the last menstrual period

E   by definition 10 per cent of the dysmature group are normal infants

20   *Neonatal hypoglycaemia:*

A   is less common in the dysmature infant than in the normal

B   is a complication from which the infants of diabetic mothers are especially at risk

C   leads to apnoeic episodes in an affected infant

D   may be exacerbated by excessive glucose feeding

E   is more likely if hypothermia develops

21   *Mothers discharged from hospital 48 hours after delivery:*

A   commonly believe that their infants do not respond to sensory stimulation by smiling

B   will receive two statutory visits by the health visitor in the first 10 days

C   often exhibit a disturbed sleep pattern

D   are more likely to develop puerperal depression than those who are discharged at 7–10 days

E   are less likely to continue breast feeding for one month or longer than those who are discharged at 7–10 days

22 *In the first full neonatal examination at home of the baby delivered in hospital within the last 10 days:*

A the demonstration of gaze avoidance (violation) is not usually possible

B less distress is caused to the mother if the examination takes place out of her sight

C an impression of baby's general demeanour will be useful in advising future management

D the testicles should not be in the scrotum in the normal full-term infant

E the liver edge is not normally palpable at this stage

23 *Depression occuring in the puerperium:*

A can be predicted on the basis of obstetric and gynaecological factors in the patient's previous history

B tends to produce heightened mother–child bonding

C is a symptom which in the majority of cases indicates the need for psychiatric referral

D if treated with imipramine will permit the safe continuation of breast feeding

E if treated with lithium will not permit the safe continuation of breast feeding

24 *In considering those children at risk from child abuse in the U.K.:*

A the rate of physical injury is thought to be less than the rate of emotional deprivation

B children in care are at above average risk

C physical or mental handicap in the child decreases the risk

D low-quality housing does not seem to be an important risk factor

E one-parent families exhibit an increased risk

25 *The following are recognised signs of prolonged emotional deprivation in young children:*

A   inertia

B   a tendency to play excessively

C   pica

D   lack of separation anxiety

E   warm extremities

26 *The majority of normal infants can:*

A   vocalise single vowel sounds (e.g. ah, eh, uh) at four weeks

B   hold a rattle actively at eight weeks

C   laugh aloud at 16 weeks

D   discriminate strangers at 24 weeks

E   shake a rattle at 28 weeks

27 *At 12 months routine examination of the normal child will usually reveal:*

A   the ability to walk if both hands are held

B   the ability to localise sounds accurately laterally but not vertically

C   upper incisor teeth

D   language of at least 2 words, apart from 'Mama' and 'Dada'

E   a neat pincer grasp

28 *The normal child:*

A   loses 15 per cent of birth weight during the first four days

B   regains the birth weight by 7–14 days

C   will gain weight after 14 days averaging 150–180 g (5–6 oz) per week

D   has energy requirements of 110 cal/kg/24 h

E   will treble the birth weight in six months

29 *In the assessment of hydration in infancy:*

A   a useful clinical sign is skin turgor of the abdominal wall

B   the anterior fontanelle is a reliable index of dehydration

C   clinical evidence of dehydration is not apparent until 15 per cent of body fluid is lost

D   fluid requirements are approx 120 ml/kg/24 h by the age of 12 months

E   similar changes in skin turgor are produced by tissue or fluid loss

30 *In the diagnosis of congenital heart disease:*

A   tachypnoea when feeding is an important sign

B   hepatic enlargement is rarely more than 1 or 2 cm below the costal margin in the presence of congestive failure

C   if cyanosis is present, transposition of the great vessels is the most likely diagnosis

D   short ejection-type systolic murmurs heard during the first six weeks are often innocent

E   patent ductus arteriosus may present with a murmur audible only in systole

31 *In the 'snuffly' infant:*

A nasal decongestants have no part to play in treatment

B foreign body in the nose is a recognised cause

C who is preterm, bacterial super-infection of coryza is a remote risk

D unlike the normal infant, breathing occurs preferentially through the nasal airway

E mothers should be discouraged from cleaning the nasal airway with cotton wool sticks

32 *In laryngo-tracheitis (croup):*

A symptoms are more often seen in the child over two years than in the first two years of life

B infection by respiratory viruses is the only recognised aetiology

C intercostal recession does not reflect the severity of the condition

D sedation is an important part of management

E pallor during a coughing bout suggests the need for urgent admission to hospital

33 *In the treatment of acute bronchospasm in the child under one year of age:*

A beta-stimulators are less effective than in the older child

B aminophylline suppositories may be divided to ensure the correct dose in relation to body weight

C oral fluids are an important aspect of management

D corticosteroids should not form part of home treatment in this age group

E promethazine (phenergan) is useful in the more severe attack

34 *Broncholitis:*

A   is most commonly seen between six and 12 months of age

B   is caused by infection with Haemophilus influenzae

C   is preceded by upper respiratory symptoms for 24–48 hours

D   is recognised as a cause of downward displacement of the liver edge

E   is characteristically associated with high fever

35 *In pertussis (whooping cough):*

A   neonatal infection is rare, due to the passive transfer of maternal antibodies

B   the incubation period averages 14–21 days

C   the classical whoop is not a feature of the illness in infancy

D   inhalation pneumonia is a recognised risk

E   auscultation of the lung fields, in the uncomplicated case, reveals characteristic fine crepitations

36 *Oral candidiasis:*

A   is less common in the breast-fed infant

B   is effectively treated by amphotericin B 100 mg after feeds

C   is usually asymptomatic

D   may be associated with napkin dermatitis

E   exhibits characteristic white patches which are readily detached

37 *In hypertrophic pyloric stenosis:*

A   symptoms commence in the first four weeks of life

B   projectile vomiting of bile-stained fluid is characteristic

C   the diagnosis is established by palpating the abdomen during a dextrose/water feed

D   visible small bowel peristalsis is a characteristic feature

E   there are no long-term sequelae following Ramstedt's operation

38 *Intussusception:*

A   is the most common cause of intestinal obstruction in infancy

B   affects boys twice as often as girls

C   may recur following operation

D   leads to early vomiting in the majority of cases

E   may be palpable per rectum

39 *In the management of gastro-enteritis in infancy:*

A   oral electrolyte solution (e.g. dioralyte) is essential even in the mild case

B   daily assessment of hydration is essential until normal feeding is re-established

C   diphenoxylate (Lomotil) is a useful preparation

D   antibiotics lessen the risk of subsequent lactose intolerance

E   the substitution of water for milk feeds for 24 hours will lead to marked electrolyte depletion

40 *Cystic fibrosis:*

A   once established, is characterised by loss of appetite

B   leads to symptoms only after weaning

C   is associated with an increased incidence of rectal prolapse

D   in the early stages, may exhibit only a raised respiratory rate

E   is inherited as a sex-linked recessive condition

41 *Hypothyroidism in infancy:*

A   is suggested by prolonged neontal jaundice

B   may lead to difficulty in breathing

C   often exhibits an umbilical hernia

D   characteristically exhibits thyroid enlargement

E   will be associated with raised TSH (thyroid stimulating hormone) levels

42 *Hypospadias:*

A   has an exellent long-term prognosis following surgery in the majority of cases

B   is a contra-indication to circumcision

C   is usually associated with penile curvature

D   associated with meatal stenosis requires urgent treatment

E   associated with urinary tract infection suggests associated renal malformation

43 *Urinary tract infection in infancy:*

A   should lead to radiological investigation of the urinary tract in all cases, where infection is proven

B   is usually due to Streptococcus faecalis

C   will be confirmed by pyuria of 50 pus cells per cm^3 in a girl

D   will often need to be treated without bacteriological confirmation

E   may present as a febrile convulsion

44 *Seborrhoeic dermatitis in infants:*

A   is usually present at birth

B   is associated with cradle cap

C   leads to excoriation

D   does not affect the napkin area

E   responds to topical steroids

45 *A febrile convulsion in a child under one year of age:*

A   can be effectively controlled by rectal diazepam

B   should lead to an examination of the CSF in all cases

C   is commonly the result of an upper respiratory tract infection

D   should not require surface cooling if adequate anti-convulsant medication has been administered

E   will require attention to the airway as the first priority of treatment

46 *In the diagnosis of congenital dislocation of the hip:*

A the baby is best examined seated on the mother's knee

B asymmetry of posterior skin folds is a useful sign

C the optimum time for examination is 7–10 days after birth

D clicks during hip adduction-abduction may arise in the knee

E one examination with normal findings is sufficient in the first year

47 *The following statements concerning immunisation are correct:*

A oral polio vaccine should be given to infant and mother on the same occasion

B measles vaccine produces a satisfactory immune response six days after administration

C measles vaccine at 13 months will produce life-long immunity

D triple vaccine at three months of age leads to levels of immunity comparable with those produced by triple vaccine at six months of age

E eczema is an absolute contra-indication to BCG vaccination

48 *In the diagnosis of non-accidental injury:*

A retinal haemorrhage is a recognised sign

B the highest incidence is in children over three years of age

C the average GP will see one case every five years in the U.K.

D finger-tip shaped facial bruises are a recognised sign

E delay in presentation to a doctor following injury is a characteristic feature

49 *In prescribing for infants, the following considerations are important:*

A   drugs with marked protein-binding have particular hazards for the neonate

B   immaturity of the kidneys may lead to therapeutic failure through excessive renal loss of the prescribed drug

C   hepatic enzyme systems are not fully developed

D   nitrofurantoin affects the growth of teeth

E   cutaneous absorption of corticosteroids is greater than in adults

50 *The sudden infant death without ante- or post-mortem evidence of disease:*

A   usually occurs between six weeks and four months

B   has not been recorded in a child in hospital

C   has a higher incidence in the summer months

D   is less likely to occur if 'at-risk' families are supervised by health visitors

E   shows a strong tendency to occur more than once in the same family

MCQ ANSWER KEY

Q	1	2	3	4	5	6	7	8	9	10	11
A	T	F	T	T	T	T	T	T	T	F	F
B	T	T	F	T	F	T	F	F	F	T	T
C	T	T	T	F	F	T	T	T	F	F	F
D	F	T	F	T	F	T	F	F	F	F	T
E	T	F	F	T	T	T	F	F	T	T	F

Q	12	13	14	15	16	17	18	19	20	21	22
A	T	T	T	F	T	F	T	T	F	T	F
B	F	F	T	F	T	F	F	F	T	F	F
C	F	F	F	F	T	F	T	T	T	T	T
D	F	T	F	T	T	T	T	F	T	F	T
E	T	T	T	T	T	T	T	T	T	F	F

Q	23	24	25	26	27	28	29	30	31	32	33
A	T	T	T	F	T	F	T	T	F	T	T
B	F	T	F	F	F	T	F	F	T	F	F
C	F	F	T	T	T	T	F	T	F	F	T
D	T	F	T	T	T	T	T	T	F	F	T
E	T	T	F	T	T	F	F	T	F	T	F

Q	34	35	36	37	38	39	40	41	42	43	44
A	F	F	T	F	T	F	F	T	T	T	F
B	F	F	T	F	T	T	F	T	T	F	T
C	T	T	F	F	T	F	T	T	F	F	F
D	T	T	T	F	F	F	T	F	T	F	F
E	F	F	F	T	T	F	F	T	T	T	T

Q	45	46	47	48	49	50
A	T	F	T	T	T	T
B	T	F	T	F	F	F
C	T	T	F	T	T	F
D	F	T	F	T	T	T
E	T	F	T	T	T	F

B. Modified Essay Question

This MEQ is designed to enable the reader to assess his knowledge of certain aspects of this book.

To obtain the maximum benefit from this section, the reader should answer the component questions in strict numerical order and should avoid looking at later sections before completing each step.

1   Having read this book, you are enthusiastic to put its principles of health surveillance into practice. Your three partners, however, are sincerely sceptical of the advantages to children and their parents of what they see as a time consuming activity.

Q.   *List the benefits which you believe effective health surveillance may produce.*

2 Your partners, convinced by your arguments, agree that a programme should be established in the practice, but ask you to outline the way in which it will be organised, its implications for attached and practice staff, and the record-keeping system you propose.

3 You establish a surveillance programme as a rational extension of your ante-natal routine. During one of the clinics, Mrs McFarlane attends for a follow-up. She is a 26-year-old mother whose first two pregnancies ended with intra-uterine deaths at 38 and 39 weeks, respectively. Her third pregnancy, three years ago, produced a living boy of 2000 gm at 38 weeks.

She is now 16 weeks, and is booked for hospital delivery with shared ante-natal care. On examination there are no abnormal findings; her uterus corresponds to her dates, but she is concerned that she has been asked to attend hospital for an ultrasonic scan.

She asks 'What does it entail, and why should I have to have it?'.

4 Fetal growth is monitored satisfactorily throughout pregnancy. Mrs McFarlane is induced at 39 weeks and delivers a girl weighing 2500 gm. The Apgar score is 8 at one minute, and Mrs McFarlane is given the baby to handle.

Q.1 *What does an Apgar score of 8 mean?*

Q.2 *What are the advantages of mothers handling their infants immediately after birth?*

5 Mother and baby go home on the tenth day. Breast feeding, begun in hospital, is continued.

You are called a week later, however, to find Mrs McFarlane looking worn out and complaining that Julie refuses to sleep for more than two hours at a time, and that she is particularly troublesome at night when she hardly sleeps at all.

Mrs McFarlane asks 'Is there anything wrong with her? John, my first baby, was never like this. Should I put her on the bottle? What can I do?'.

Q.   *How do you respond?*

6 Your advice is followed, and Julie's sleep pattern becomes acceptable to her parents. They are reluctant, however to have Julie immunised, particularly against pertussis.

Q. *What are the specific contra-indications to immunisation, and what advice do you give the McFarlanes?*

7 At seven months of age, Julie attends for routine examination. She appears to be quite bright but, whilst capable of sitting supported, falls over when left for even a second. Mrs McFarlane remembers that at this age her son John sat up and took much more notice of his surroundings.

Q. *How do you reply to her question 'Is she going to be backward?'.*

8 Examination one month later is reassuring, and Julie's development appears to be within normal limits.

She is now on mixed feeds and is well, apart from occasionally loose stools which Mrs McFarlane attributes to the inclusion of new items in her diet. She asks you, however, 'How would I know if the diarrhoea was becoming serious? What should I do?'.

Q.   *How do you respond?*

9 Shortly before Julie's first birthday, her parents call you urgently at 2.15 a.m. Julie had apparently been perfectly well, apart from a slight cold, when put to bed, but awoke at 2 a.m. 'desperately frightened and choking'. Julie and her parents were terrified. Over the telephone you can actually hear her stridor punctuated by a hoarse, barking cough.

Q.1 *On this limited information, what is the most likely diagnosis?*

Q.2 *What other diagnosis would you consider whilst driving to the McFarlane's home?*

Q.3 *What clinical features are you going to regard as particularly important in making your assessment and planning management?*

10 Julie is acutely ill and you take her, with her parents, to hospital immediately. Despite urgent treatment, Julie dies later that day.

Q.1 *What pattern might Mrs McFarlane's grief reaction follow?*

Q.2 *How can you, and those who work with you, help her in this situation?*

Index

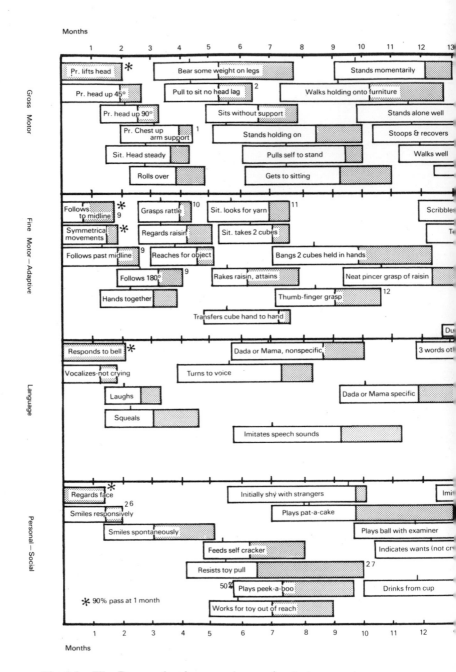

Fig 4.1 The Denver developmental screening test